When A Believer Marries A Nonbeliever

How To Grow Together In Love, Faith, And Joy

Bebe Nicholson

Priority Publishing
Alpharetta, Georgia

When A Believer Marries A Nonbeliever

Published in Alpharetta, Georgia, by Priority Publishing, Inc.

In the interests of privacy, some names have been changed.

Library of Congress Catalog Card Number: 94-12045

Nicholson, Bebe.
    When A Believer Marries A Nonbeliever / Bebe Nicholson
      p. cm.
    Includes bibliographical references.
    ISBN 0-9655127-0-3 for hardcover
    ISBN 0-9655127-9-7 for softcover

    1. Evangelistic work. 1. Nicholson, Bebe. 2. Title.

    Edited by Yvette McCann

Printed in the United States of America

This book is dedicated to my husband, Lee.

CONTENTS

"If I speak in the tongues of men and of angels, but have not love, I am only a resounding gong or a clanging cymbal. If I have the gift of prophecy and can fathom all mysteries and all knowledge, and if I have a faith that can move mountains, but have not love, I am nothing. If I give all I possess to the poor and surrender my body to the flames, but have not love, I gain nothing.

Love is patient, love is kind. It does not envy, it does not boast, it is not proud. It is not rude, it is not self-seeking, it is not easily angered, it keeps no record of wrongs. Love does not delight in evil but rejoices with the truth. It always protects, always trusts, always hopes, always perseveres."

1 Corinthians 13:1-7

ACKNOWLEDGMENTS

There are several people whose support and encouragement made this book possible. First, I want to thank my mother, Myrtle King, for teaching me the principles of Christian living, the importance of integrity, the value of perseverance, and the meaning of unconditional love. My father, John King, deserves special thanks for his confidence in me and for revealing to his children the significance of relishing life's simple pleasures.

I would also like to gratefully acknowledge the love, support, and encouragement given me by my mother-in-law and father-in-law, Gini and Lee Nicholson.

My profound thanks to Mary Lee, my friend and beloved sister. Her wisdom, insight, tremendous faith, and gentle guidance have shown me much about what a personal relationship with Jesus Christ really means.

Thanks also to Dr. Joe Bowen for his enthusiastic support of this book, and to both Dr. Bowen and Reverend David Tinsley for their spiritual guidance and friendship.

Deep appreciation goes to Yvette McCann at Rhyme Tyme Publications for her tireless assistance and expertise regarding the technicalities of book production, as well as to Dr. Edward Boudreaux, chemist and physicist, for his valuable editorial input in Part Four.

Finally, I thank God for all His blessings, especially for my three children, Blair, Lee King, and John, and for my husband, Lee. This book is also Lee's book, since he acted as advisor and editor, improving the manuscript with his suggestions, encouraging me to rewrite when necessary, and always lending me his wholehearted support. He is truly my best friend.

To The Reader

"With man this is impossible, but with God all things are possible." Matthew 19:26

Several years ago at a church education seminar, I was asked to talk about an experience that had made a difference in my life. I shared the fact that my husband, though not a Christian when we married, had invited Jesus Christ into his life eight years later. At the end of the seminar, an enthusiastic young woman made a point of introducing herself.

"You don't know what it meant to me to hear you tell about your husband becoming a Christian," she exclaimed. "You see, my husband doesn't attend church. He doesn't believe in religion. But after hearing your story, I suddenly knew there was hope that someday he can change."

This woman's words confirmed what I had already come to suspect: many Christians are married to people who either don't share their faith, are openly antagonistic to their faith, or profess to be Christians but aren't experiencing a personal relationship with Jesus Christ. The believing spouse has often employed all his or her powers of persuasion to encourage an unbelieving partner to attend church or make a profession of faith, only to have those entreaties fall on deaf ears. The resulting frustration can, at best, eliminate any possibility of attaining the spiritual oneness we all seek with our marriage partner. At worst, persistent attempts to convert an unwilling spouse can seriously damage the relationship.

God's design for marriage, as a blessing to ease both our physical and spiritual loneliness and as an environment for raising godly children, is evident in Scripture:

> "The Lord God said, "It is not good for the man to be alone. I will make a helper suitable for him" (Genesis 2:18).

> "For this reason a man will leave his father and mother and be united to his wife, and they will become one flesh" (Genesis 2:24).

> "Has not the Lord made them one? In flesh and spirit they are his. And why one? Because He was seeking godly offspring" (Malachi 2:15).

When God's purpose is not being accomplished through this most intimate and closest of all human relationships, His love cannot flow as freely as it should. Thus, the miraculous potential for oneness with another human being is not achieved. Two people, no matter how much in love, cannot become true soul mates.

In his book, *The Marriage Builder*, psychologist Larry Crabb says, "God created us in His image, personal beings unlike all other creatures and like Him in our unique capacity for relationship." This unique capacity for relationship reaches fruition when it is developed within the context of placing God first. But even among believers, true intimacy based on spiritual oneness is difficult to achieve. Our imperfect human natures are constantly erecting barriers to God's perfect plan.

To a believer married to a nonbeliever, spiritual compatibility can seem like a remote pipe dream. *This is why it is so important to realize that becoming true soul mates with your spouse is possible, even if you have very different beliefs.*

My husband, Lee, and I can attest to this. We have been able to achieve spiritual compatibility in a wonderful relationship that defies the pessimistic statistics for couples holding widely differing religious beliefs when they marry. Our relationship seems all the more remarkable when I consider that before our marriage, Lee had been a staunch agnostic who asked me to renounce my own faith. How well I remember that unhappy day 21 years ago!

The Challenge

We were separated by a kitchen counter no wider than two feet, but we might as well have been separated by an ocean as vast and cold as the Arctic. His words were widening the gulf between us, causing my heart to lurch in despair.

"We can't marry unless you believe in the same things I believe in," he said. "And I just can't believe in God without some sort of proof."

Forgotten were the hamburgers sizzling on the grill, the moonlit night outside. Here was the man I wanted to marry, yet he was telling me that unless I renounced my faith in God, we could never be serious. I wanted us to be together forever. All I had to do was say I really didn't believe in all this God business.

But Jesus' words in Matthew 10 were clear and unequivocal: "Whoever acknowledges me before men, I will also acknowledge him before my father in heaven. But whoever disowns me before men, I will disown him before my father in heaven."

With heavy heart and a dismal outlook for our future together, I said I could not deny my beliefs. I took a job in a different state, and we went our separate ways. But that wasn't the end of the story, because God had a different ending in mind. Eventually, Lee and I renewed our relationship. He did not ask me again to renounce my faith. Instead, one bright October day he asked me to marry him.

Many Christian counselors would probably have advised against this marriage. They would have pointed out that marriage is tough enough without the added problem of conflicting religious beliefs. But I was young and optimistic and in love. I said *yes,* and by doing so, began a journey that would show me the faithfulness of God's love and the significance of placing Him first in our lives.

For several years, I have wanted to share with others the route my own marriage took from religious conflict to spiritual oneness. Christianity's potential for bringing immeasurable joy and hope influenced Lee to become a believer. That joy and hope were realized when his first tentative reach toward faith became a wholehearted embrace that transformed our marriage and our lives. In looking back over the past twenty years, I am able to see God's guidance. He led us through a step-by-step process that encouraged my husband to believe, while at the same time enhancing and increasing my own faith. It has long been my goal to share this step-by-step process, in the hope that many more couples can realize the joy to be gained from placing God first.

This book is designed to present a clear, distinct course of action the believer can follow to influence an unbelieving or "unspiritual" spouse toward greater faith. Although it is God who ultimately draws us to Him, He uses us for the accomplishment of His purposes here on earth. Just as He works through missionaries who spread His message to the remotest regions of the world, He works through the believing spouse to share His message of true salvation and joy with the unbelieving partner.

Sharing Our Faith Effectively

I have divided this book into four sections, because sharing your faith effectively with an unbelieving spouse involves four major elements.

First of all, the Christian must lead by example, becoming an effective witness through actions rather than words. In *Becoming A Contagious Christian,* author Bill Hybels writes that the power, attractiveness, and potential of an authentic Christian life comes from living it authentically and boldly. The life we lead is a vital part of our witness. We reveal in our attitudes and actions that Christianity offers great joy and abundance not available through any other means. Faith in Jesus Christ makes it possible to live a happy, fulfilled, joyous life in the midst of a world too often characterized by loneliness, misery, and despair. *When we live our Christian lives with enthusiasm, others will want to tap into the secret of our continual joy.*

Part One: *Leading By Example,* shows how we can live life in such a way that we kindle in the nonbeliever a desire for what we have. By incorporating the principles outlined in this section, anyone can become a joyous, contagious Christian.

The life we lead is our most powerful testimony. In his book, *Living Proof,* Jim Peterson says, "We have seen that a person with a good testimony is one who, because his life is characterized by faith, hope, and love, is redemptive in his relationships. Wherever he goes, he sows life and hope rather than despair, conflict or death. Such a person is the most significant figure in our society. Jesus called him the salt of the earth, the light of the world, and the good seed. He is a singular exception in a disoriented world." The joyful Christian becomes that singular exception, setting an example of life and hope the nonbeliever will want to emulate.

Part Two: *Building The Marriage Relationship,*
demonstrates how to grow closer as a couple, establishing the
marriage on a foundation of love and commitment that paves
the way for greater communication. Dr. Betty Siegel, President
of Kennesaw State College in Georgia and a wonderful
inspirational speaker, said "Whether we live long or whether
we live short, it is best to live good in the company of someone
who loves us."

"Living good in the company of someone who loves us"
means building the sort of rapport that leads to a meaningful,
supportive relationship. *Building rapport is essential because
the good marriage is the best arena for bringing about
spiritual change.* When we create a marriage characterized
by faith, hope, and love, we are creating an environment
conducive to the sowing of life and hope. As we strengthen
the bonds that draw us ever closer toward spiritual oneness,
our prayers and our witnessing will be planted in the fertile
soil of a loving, intimate relationship. We will then reap all
the blessings God meant us to have when He said, "and they
will become one flesh." Effective witnessing is next to
impossible in an atmosphere of antagonism. Part Two: *Building
The Marriage Relationship,* describes how to create an
atmosphere of love in which your partner will be receptive to
your expression of faith.

Prayer's Amazing Power

As we strengthen the foundations of our marriage, it is
crucial that we continue to pray persistently and unceasingly
for our unbelieving partner. When we lift our loved ones before God in prayer, we are tapping into a tremendous and inexhaustible source of power. We are also acknowledging God's
sovereignty and bearing testimony to our own faith. Part Three:
Praying For Your Partner, examines what Scripture teaches
us about prayer.

The Bible is replete with advice on how and when to pray. There are scriptural parallels to the crisis of faith Christians suffer today when confronting the dilemma of unanswered prayer. We can discover in the Bible and in everyday life numerous examples of prayer's effectiveness.

Consider the story of a physician who could do nothing else for a terminal cancer patient. Each day, the patient was surrounded by members of his church who prayed for him. "Let them pray," the physician thought. "While it can't help a person in his condition, it can't hurt him, either."

A year later, a colleague asked the physician if he wanted to see a former patient. That person turned out to be none other than the terminal cancer patient, completely free of cancer. He had not undergone any additional treatment. Yet, a year later, after many prayers, he was a healthy man. It is no surprise that the physician became a believer in prayer!

If anyone does not believe there is remarkable power in prayer, he should consider Jesus' words in Mark 11:24: "Therefore I *tell* you, whatever you ask for in prayer, believe that you have received it, and it will be yours."

Because of prayer's astonishing power to change lives, I will reiterate here that the believer should pray for the unbelieving spouse, for their marriage, and for God's help in attaining the spiritual oneness which offers a reward of intimacy and love unequaled in any other human relationship.

Part Three: *Praying For Your Partner,* demonstrates the significance of persistent prayer and of making continuous communication with God an integral part of life. This section is about sowing those seeds of prayer in the soil you have prepared with your joyful Christian witness.

The Reason For Our Hope

There will come a time when you are called on to proclaim the reasons for your faith. It is becoming harder and harder in our increasingly secular society to witness for Christ without being able to offer a legitimate, firmly grounded and reasonable basis for our beliefs. "I believe because the Bible says it's true!" is often met with skepticism and scorn in an age of humanistic materialism. There is no longer a widespread acceptance of the Bible as God's infallible truth.

Apologetics, or the defense of faith based on reason, becomes more important in this environment. We must be able to swim against the tide of secular humanism in order to show why our faith is reasonable, logical, and applicable to the problems of everyday life. We must be able to defend our faith to the nonbeliever who has been misled into thinking that faith in Jesus Christ is somehow irrational.

Part Four: *Overcoming The Barriers To Belief,* offers information that will better prepare the Christian to explain the reasons for his hope. This section is not meant to be an extensive course in apologetics. There are many wonderful books that offer an in-depth look at why we as Christians believe in Jesus' resurrection. But an ability to deal with the most common barriers to faith is essential when the Christian is trying to overcome the unbeliever's resistance.

Faith will always be the basis for our beliefs. Jesus said, "According to your faith it will be done to you." The Apostle Paul wrote, "We live by faith, not by sight." There will never be enough "evidence" to convince the closed mind of a person determined not to believe. But we are encouraged in First Peter 3:15 to "Always be prepared to give an answer to everyone who asks you to give the reason for the hope that you have." Part Four is designed to help the believing spouse deal with those difficult questions frequently posed by skeptics: *Does the Bible conflict with science? Why would a merciful God allow bad things to happen to good people? Can the facts of the Bible be proven? Does believing in Jesus conflict with the attainment of worldly success?*

Christians do not have a faith based on nothing. We have a faith based on the most momentous event in history: the resurrection of Jesus Christ! We should not hesitate to employ evidence and logic to defend our faith.

People Do Change!

When we employ these four essential evangelizing tools: *leading by example, building the marriage relationship, praying for our partner,* and *overcoming the barriers to belief,* we are allowing God to work through us to bring about spiritual change. Peter wrote that it is possible for husbands to be won over to Christ by the actions and attitudes of their wives. No matter how resistant your spouse is to your faith, *change is possible.* This should come as no surprise, since the Bible is filled with people who underwent radical changes after being confronted with the truth.

Saul, a Pharisee from Tarsus, came face to face with the truth of Jesus Christ on the road to Damascus. This persecutor of Christians, a man who had dedicated himself to eliminating Jesus' followers, became the Apostle Paul, a missionary who spread God's plan of salvation to all mankind.

Change occurred on a grand scale in the city of Ninevah. When Jonah warned Ninevah's inhabitants to turn from their wickedness or face God's wrath, the Ninevites repented. As a result of this change, God had compassion and the city was not destroyed.

Change is possible! We see it in the Bible, and we see it in the changed lives of believers. An unbelieving spouse can learn to love the Lord. A lukewarm Christian can discover what it means to have a personal relationship with Jesus Christ. When this happens, the marriage relationship will undergo a dramatic transformation. You and your partner will grow in intimacy and love, learning to meet the deep, inherent human need for spiritual oneness.

The Benefits

The most important reason for having your spouse accept Jesus Christ is, of course, his eternal salvation. He will come to experience the fullness of life in all its abundance when he realizes the astonishing power of faith.

But there are other benefits. The most obvious is the one I have already mentioned: an improved marital relationship. Even if you have a reasonably good marriage, the change will be tremendous when both you and your partner become Christ-centered.

Sociologist Andrew Greeley discovered in a survey of married couples that those who pray together are 90 percent more likely to report higher satisfaction with their sex lives than couples who do not pray together. Spiritual compatibility is more important than physical or emotional compatibility because the spiritual transcends the physical and emotional aspects of life. If we live long enough, we will all change physically. The aging process exacts its toll. Emotionally, we will experience highs and lows, depending on our internal moods and external circumstances. But spiritual compatibility based on faith is like the rudder of a boat, navigating a steady course through life's tumultuous seas. When we are spiritually compatible, emotional and physical bonds are strengthened.

We can have an okay marriage, plodding along day after day with mundane expectations and mediocre results. But why settle for the mundane when the sublime is within our grasp? Why have an okay marriage when God means for us to have so much more?

The Framework For Happiness

Too often, in the "me first" mentality of our society, we have lost sight of the happiness to be found within the framework of placing God first. To place anything or anyone else before ourselves contradicts the pervasive present day ideal of self-centered individualism carried to its ultimate extreme. We can barely comprehend putting another person's interests above our own, let alone placing an elusive God at the center of our life.

We hear people say things like: "You can have it all. You need to find yourself. Do your own thing." We have seen the fallacy of these beliefs as we have watched social mores deteriorate. By placing ourselves first, we are losing ourselves. Jesus' words in Mark 8:36, "What good is it for a man to gain the whole world, yet forfeit his soul," ring eloquently in our pleasure-driven culture. We are "forfeiting our souls" when we place a hedonistic pursuit of pleasure above a relationship with God.

Rather than taking away from our love and concern for each other, placing God first actually enhances the same love and concern. *We do not focus on God at the expense of other people. We focus on God, and our love for others is strengthened.*

A prime example is the marriage of C.S. Lewis to Joy Helen Grisham. Lewis was a Christian apologist, scholar, philosopher and writer. Grisham, an American Jew turned Christian and the mother of two sons by a previous marriage, had been refused permission to remain in England. Seeing an opportunity to help, Lewis married her in order to prevent her inevitable deportment from the country. Their marriage, lacking love, was strictly a marriage of convenience.

Shortly after the wedding, Joy began suffering terrible aches and pains that were soon diagnosed as advanced bone cancer. As her condition deteriorated, Lewis prayed for her constantly and promised to take care of her boys. It was during this time that he realized he loved his dying wife. Lewis proposed again, and the two repeated their wedding vows at a Christian service with Joy on her deathbed.

When Joy's death drew near and doctors realized they could do no more, Lewis brought her home from the hospital. But Joy Lewis astounded everyone. Each day she gained strength. Finally, after numerous tests and X-rays, the baffled doctors announced that there were no signs of cancer spots on her bones. C.S. Lewis and his wife decided to pack a lifetime into whatever days they might have left. During Joy's three-year remission, they traveled and experienced what Lewis described as the happiest time of his life. Lewis placed God first and discovered love. Those last few years of his and Joy's life were enriched and blessed with a happiness he had not anticipated.

Two believers can become spiritual soul mates, weathering life's inevitable challenges with strength and joy born of that unique oneness which results from placing God first.

Our Own Faith Increases

Another benefit of sharing our faith is that our own faith increases. The weight lifter who bench presses every day does not diminish the size of his biceps. With exercise, his muscles increase in size and strength. It seems we can even exercise our brains. A magazine article explained how we could "jog" our brains into enhanced performance by practicing certain mental exercises, such as memorizing sequences of numbers, completing word puzzles and performing math problems in our head. People can sharpen their mental capabilities at any age by taking up a musical instrument, becoming computer literate or reading more.

In other words, by using and exercising our bodies and our minds, we keep them fine-tuned and efficient. Faith is no different. By using our faith, we keep it fine-tuned and in better working order. *When we share our faith with others, our own faith increases.*

Jesus told a parable that underscores the significance of using what we have been given. A master going on a journey entrusted five talents to one servant, two talents to another servant, and one talent to a third. The man who received five talents put his money to work immediately, doubling the amount. The servant with two talents also invested wisely, doubling his talents. But the man who received one talent, instead of using what he had been given, dug a hole in the ground and hid his talent.

Eventually, the master returned. Pleased with the two servants who had doubled his money, he put them in charge of other things and invited them to share his happiness. The man who received one talent offered a lame excuse for not making a profit. "Master, I knew you are a hard man, harvesting where you have not scattered seed, so I was afraid. I went out and hid your talent in the ground. Here it is."

In a rage, the master took this man's talent and gave it to the one who had ten talents. "For everyone who has will be given more, and he will have an abundance. Whoever does not have, even what he has will be taken away from him" (Matthew 25:14-30).

The Bible makes it plain that we are supposed to use what we have. Sharing our faith means using it, with the result being that it will stretch and grow and increase in size just like those tired, sore, newly-exercised muscles. To share our faith, we will need to delve into God's word, studying Scripture so that we can explain why we believe the way we do. We will need to spend time with God in prayer, seeking His guidance and direction. As we do these things, we will find our own faith blossoming and expanding.

Our Children Will Benefit

Finally, our children stand to benefit from an increase in Christ-centered homes. It is within the framework of marriage that we nurture godly families, training our children to serve the Lord. One parent alone can certainly rear Christian children, but it is much easier to equip our children with strong core values if two parents stand united in this effort.

There is no question that strong core values are desperately needed if we are to turn around a society that is lurching toward chaos. An article in *The Atlantic Monthly* stated that in 1990, a total of 24,932 homicides were reported. Social mayhem and crime used to be confined primarily to inner-city ghettos, but as rates of illegitimacy soar and social mores break down, the poisonous tentacles of crime will reach further and further into all classes of society. Scholars say the nation's murder rate may double, with "stranger murders" growing more and more common. Writer Adam Walinsky referred to the coming crime wave as a "long, descending night."

William Bennett and Dan Coats wrote in *The Wall Street Journal* that it is now a widely accepted fact that America's cultural breakdown will continue and worsen without the recovery of civil society. Minus the restraining influence of healthy families, churches, and neighborhoods, a society falls into chaos.

Historian and author Will Durant called the family "the nucleus of civilization."

We are at a crossroads in our country's history, with the family under severe attack. Fifty percent of all marriages end in divorce. The rate of illegitimate births is soaring, violence proliferates as children grow up in fatherless homes, sexually transmitted diseases are rampant, and a sickness of the soul is spilling into all classes and facets of society.

The problems of social decay and moral breakdown can be overcome through the strength and faith of Christ-centered, God-fearing families. We need every unbelieving spouse to become a believer and every lukewarm believer to develop a true, life-changing faith. We need parents who will instill in their children a Scripture-based value system based on God's love. We need mothers and fathers who will work together to raise brave, freedom loving, God fearing men and women. We need parents who will teach their children to love by allowing God's love to flow freely between husband and wife, parent and child. In short, we need families who will stand up and say, "But as for me and my household, we will serve the Lord" (Joshua 24:15)!

Onward

As you can see, the stakes are high and the rewards are tremendous as you and your spouse embark on this journey from religious differences to spiritual oneness. Transforming the relationship is within your grasp. You can become the joyous Christian couple you were meant to be.

You must not become discouraged if the barriers to faith seem insurmountable, or if progress, at times, seems slow. Practice the principles outlined in this book. Live your faith with enthusiasm and courage. Strengthen the foundations of your marriage. Make prayer an unceasing and indispensable part of your life. And remember: "With God all things are possible!"

"Commit your way to the Lord; trust in Him and He will do this: He will make your righteousness shine like the dawn, the justice of your cause like the noonday sun."
Psalm 37: 5,6

Part One

Leading By Example

CHAPTER ONE

Your Life is Your Witness

"...let your light shine before men, that they may see your good deeds and praise your Father in heaven." Matthew 5:16

A *Thousand Pails of Water,* by Ronald Roy, is the story of a boy named Yukio who lives in a village where people hunt whales for a living. One day as Yukio is strolling along the ocean shore, he spots a whale stranded on the beach. He watches in pity as the giant mammal, unable to escape almost certain death, thrashes its large tail helplessly.

Moved by a desire to help, Yukio hurries to the ocean's edge, fills his pail with sea water, and throws it over the whale's head. He does this again and again, even though the sun beats mercilessly on his bare back and his water pail is small next to the giant mammal. He knows he must wet every part of the whale in order to keep it alive until the tide can carry it back to sea. Fighting exhaustion, he makes numerous trips to and from the water. His back hurts. His arms ache. Still, he keeps on filling his tiny bucket and pouring water over the whale.

Finally, in spite of his efforts, Yukio collapses in the sand. He is watching the floundering whale when his grandfather lifts him gently and carries him to the shade of a nearby rock. Suddenly Yukio's attention is drawn to a cacophony of voices by the sea. He sees his father and other villagers carrying pails, buckets, and anything else that will hold water. The people, whale hunters by profession, are working together to save the stranded whale.

The Life You Lead

With his actions, Yukio sets an example that inspires a whole village. If he had elected to go door to door, explaining that he needed all the help he could get to save a stranded whale, he would probably have been laughed out of town. The derisive response might have been, "Are you nuts, kid? We happen to hunt whales, in case you hadn't noticed. A stranded one makes our job that much easier."

Yet, these whale hunters worked together to save a whale. *Why?* They did it because of one village boy's extraordinary example. Like Yukio, we must set an example that will be more compelling than all the words in the world. We must reveal our faith in the very lives we lead, remembering that this revelation will always be our most effective witness.

Many people envision witnessing for Christ as grabbing another person by the lapels and bellowing, "Have you been saved?" They recoil from this image, declaring to themselves, "I couldn't do that. I'm just not the evangelizing type."

They feel the same way about witnessing to an unbelieving spouse. "He gets irritated whenever I mention God. How in the world can I expect to convert somebody who doesn't even want to hear what I have to say?"

But as Chuck Colson points out in *Moving Beyond Belief,* Jesus calls us to *be* a witness, which implies a state of being rather than a specific activity. Colson argues, rightly, that, "The best argument for Christianity is Christians, and the best argument against Christianity is also Christians."

Mothballs and Sunday Suits

One Sunday, I sat next to a man in church who obviously did not want to be there. He refused to sing any of the hymns, although his wife belted out the songs with gusto. He appeared bored and hostile and his suit smelled like mothballs. He must not have dug that Sunday suit out of storage for a long time! I don't know what tactics his wife used to drag him to the service, but the clear impression I got was that he didn't plan on coming again.

Trying to persuade by nagging, cajoling, threatening and pleading with your spouse to attend church with you, join your Sunday school class, read the Bible or share your beliefs is tempting. You want changes right now. If you could just get him to church, you know everything would be okay. He should be willing to make the sacrifice if he loves you enough. But as tempting as this approach, born of frustration and a desire for immediate change might be, it doesn't work. It could even have the opposite effect, turning your spouse 180 degrees in the opposite direction.

The wife who demands that her husband come home from work earlier isn't bringing about the desired results because she isn't creating an atmosphere he wants to come home to. The husband who critically scrutinizes every penny his wife spends is sowing the seeds of resentment and rebellion. Similarly, the spouse who nags a reluctant partner into attending church might bring about a grudging acquiescence, but this seldom builds a lasting faith or enhances a marital relationship. *We have to persuade by example, revealing Christ in the lives we lead!*

A Solitary Old Missionary

David Livingstone traveled to Africa to convert Africans to Christianity and to end the business of selling captured Africans as slaves. When no one had heard from him in several years, the *New York Herald* sent a newspaper reporter, Henry Morton Stanley, to find him. Stanley accomplished this objective, discovering Livingstone in 1871. But the discovery led to more than a newspaper story. Henry Stanley, former atheist, became a convert.

At first, Stanley decided the solitary old missionary was crazy. He found himself wondering how Dr. Livingstone managed to live so completely by that biblical injunction to "Leave all things and follow me." Here was a man who had definitely left a lifestyle the rest of the world considered comfortable in order to carry a Christian message to the remotest regions of Africa.

But little by little, Livingstone's sympathy for others became contagious. Observing the missionary's gentleness, compassion, zeal and earnestness, Stanley's own sympathy was aroused. Eventually he was converted to Christianity, not by Dr. Livingstone's words, but by the example this great missionary set. After Livingstone's death, Stanley decided to carry on his friend's work in Africa.

We can set an example for our faith, not by loudly proclaiming the superiority of our beliefs to an unbelieving spouse, but by quietly and joyfully living our faith. Like David Livingstone, we can exhibit gentleness, compassion, earnestness, and zeal that are contagious.

Her Life Savings For A Scholarship

People who set examples of generosity, compassion, love, and kindness frequently touch us in unexpected ways. Their lives are a powerful witness, inspiring the rest of us to greater heights of kindness and generosity.

Oseola McCarty is this sort of person. She quit school to work when she was in the sixth grade. She never married or had children, but she considered her work a blessing. She lived in her old family home, took in wash for the residents of Hattiesburg, Mississippi, and spent almost nothing of the meager wages she earned. So ingrained was this thriftiness that when her Bible grew ragged from use, she bound it with tape.

Over the years, McCarty saved her money. Gradually, through the decades, dollar bills and change grew to over $150,000. Figuring this was more than she could ever use, she decided to give her money away to finance scholarships for black students at the University of Mississippi. The college has already awarded a $1000 scholarship in McCarty's name to a Hattiesburg honors student whose family did not have enough money to pay for four years of college tuition.

What does Oseola McCarty want in return for donating her life savings to a scholarship fund? She hasn't asked for a building or a statue in her honor. She just wants to attend the graduation of a student who made it through college because of her gift. Her desire is that other children have the benefit of a college education. She does not loudly proclaim the virtues of generosity. Her actions speak more eloquently than words ever could.

The Best Art Book

Like Oseola McCarty, Breattie O'Neal was a generous person. At her funeral, the minister related this story about her childhood: The oldest of nine brothers and sisters, Breattie walked to the corner store for ice-cream. Upon paying for her cone and taking the first delicious lick, she was stricken with regret. There wasn't enough money during those lean years to buy treats for everyone. Her younger siblings waited at home without ice-cream. Breattie made what must have been a wrenching decision. Clutching her prized cone, resisting the urge for another lick, she hurried home. There she was surrounded by eager siblings who took turns licking the rapidly melting ice-cream.

Breattie O'Neal, or B-B-, as we called her, was my aunt, and this story epitomized a generosity that remained with her throughout her 89 years. As the decades sped by, she gave selflessly to an ever-widening array of grandchildren, nieces, nephews and friends. My home is graced by Afghans that she made, porcelain pitchers and ginger jars that she unearthed from her attic, and a hundred other gifts that are reminders of special occasions and heartfelt remembrances.

One day my son retrieved an old-fashioned "how to draw" book from the depths of his closet. "B-B- gave me this art book," he exclaimed, examining the book happily. "It's the best art book I've got."

My aunt never demanded generosity of others. She protested when we sent her money or gifts she considered too extravagant. But with her generosity, she summoned a greater generosity from us. Like Oseola McCarty, she let her life be her witness.

With our life as our witness, we can summon a greater response from the nonbeliever than all our powerful words could elicit. As Henry Blackaby and Claude King write in *Experiencing God,* "Let the world see God at work and He will attract people to Himself. Let Christ be lifted up, not in words, but in life."

Daniel's Witness

The prophet Daniel profoundly influenced the lives of others by living his faith. A handsome, intelligent, promising young man from one of the best families in Israel, he was captured during the Babylonian invasion of Jerusalem and ordered to serve King Nebuchadnezzar. Snatched from a life of probable luxury and ease, forced into the service of a pagan king, he resolved to continue placing God first.

Daniel's first act of faith was to request permission to refuse the royal food and wine offered from the king's table. He didn't demand to be served other food. He discreetly and politely, with respect for the governing authorities, asked permission to refuse food that, according to Jewish law, had been defiled. This unusual request led an alarmed guard to protest that Daniel's health would suffer, so Daniel asked that he and the three other Israelites with him be given vegetables and water instead. When Daniel's health actually improved as a result of his special diet, he was allowed to continue eating vegetables.

Daniel served the king loyally for a number of years, rising in power and position as he became one of the king's favorites. He didn't try to convert the pagans around him with overt evangelism and exhortations. He continued to be loyal to God, steadfast in prayer, living his faith even when it conflicted with pagan laws. At the same time, he was respectful of authority and unresentful in spite of the fact that he had lost his family and former way of life.

The prophet Daniel witnessed over a period of years to King Nebuchadnezzar, interpreting the king's dreams, competently ruling the provinces that had been placed under him, but never abandoning his faith. Eventually, King

Nebuchadnezzar ended up acknowledging the sovereignty of God and admitting that God's dominion was eternal. This admission came about as a result of Daniel's obedience to God. Placing God first, Daniel set an example of faith in action.

Perhaps Daniel's greatest test of faith and greatest witness for God came during the reign of Darius. The king issued a decree that those praying to anyone other than the king would be thrown into the lion's den. Immediately after hearing about the decree, Daniel went home and, with his window open, got down on his knees and prayed. This was exactly what the king's envious administrators had been waiting for. Seeking to end Daniel's influence once and for all, they hurried off to tell the king. King Darius, agreeing that justice had to be carried out, issued an order that Daniel be thrown into the lion's den.

But God, intervening as he so often had in Daniel's life, shut the mouths of the lions. Daniel was lifted from the den and found to have no wounds because he had "trusted in his God" (Daniel 6:23). King Darius then issued a decree that everyone in the country was to fear the God of Daniel.

With his quiet and faithful witness, Daniel influenced kings. How much more effective this was, and how much more in keeping with God's will, than if he had taken up pagan ways while at the same time declaring verbally that he was a believer.

Faithfulness and obedience to God's will speak louder than words. As Herodotus said, "We are less convinced by what we hear than by what we see."

Should I Be Silent About My Beliefs?

Setting an example for Christ does not mean that you will never talk to your spouse about your beliefs. Proclaiming the gospel is a vital part of witnessing, but the time and place must be right, the soil fertile and ready for planting. You are preparing the soil with your "silent witness," getting ready for the time when your partner will want to know why you believe what you believe.

Before Lee and I met, he dated a Catholic girl who was very sincere in her faith. In his attempts to understand and perhaps accept her beliefs, Lee enrolled in classes led by Father Hadden, a parish priest. This priest must have rued the day such an argumentative man ever showed up for class, because Lee arrived with an arsenal of objections to what he considered the irrationality of believing in God. Lee had read many books by atheists outlining their objections to religious beliefs, and he was ready with these arguments. The poor priest, after answering many questions in response to Lee's demands for proof, eventually threw up his hands and said, "At some point, you just have to take something on faith!"

Lee and this young woman broke up, in part because of their irreconcilable religious differences. If I had been determined to convert Lee through debate and argument, our relationship might have ended in much the same way. I trusted in God and my instinctive knowledge that setting a joyous Christian example was the right way to open my husband's heart to an acceptance of Christ.

The Logic of Believing

Revealing your beliefs through your actions does not mean that you should ever back away from explaining your faith and standing up for your beliefs. But an adamant insistence on the truth of my beliefs over Lee's would have turned him away at this point. He did not want to believe by faith. He wanted to believe by reason. This is why he needed to see the reasonableness of Christianity in action. He needed to see Christianity's potential for bringing joy and hope into a person's life, despite the strife-filled nature of our fallen world.

It is ironic that of all the things Father Hadden said, the one thing which stuck in Lee's mind was the statement, "At some point you just have to take something on faith!" Of course that was the important thing, the very basis of Christianity. But Lee wasn't ready for the faith part. He needed to see the logic of believing. He needed to see that those who believe are happier and more fulfilled than those who don't.

Helping bring your spouse to faith in Christ through reason and logic can be, in its place, extremely important. Scripture instructs us to be prepared to answer everyone who asks us to give the reason for our beliefs. But before overcoming the barriers to belief through reason and logic, the believer must create a receptive environment in which logical arguments for faith in Christ will be considered and accepted. This receptive environment is created by the example we set, our commitment to the marriage relationship, and our prayers. Then our partner will be prepared to hear our reasons for the hope that we have. He will be ready to consider the logic of believing, because he has seen the fruits of a joyous faith.

How Do I Set An Example?

It is all well and good to say we need to set an example for Christ. But how do we set such an inspirational example that we overcome barriers to belief when, in some cases, there is resentment and hostility resulting from erroneous ideas about our faith? How can our lives "shine like stars in the universe?"

First, we need to realize that setting a Christian example does not mean we have to be perfect. If that were the case, I would have given up long ago! It is God who saves people, and God who will bring your spouse to salvation. God pursues people relentlessly, as C.S. Lewis discovered when he finally discarded his agnostic beliefs at the age of 31 to embrace Christianity.

You are God's instrument, but God touches the hearts and minds of people with His truth. If you keep this in mind, you will not worry about the times you doubt or backslide. God would not work His wonders through us imperfect humans if our every failure led to total and irrevocable defeat. He works through our failures, helping us to grow and learn from them. Our failures may even be a source of inspiration to a spouse who realizes a Christian does not have to live up to some impossible ideal of perfection.

The Importance of Integrity

What setting a Christian example *does* mean is that we are always trying, in spite of our imperfections, to live our faith with integrity. We will not always measure up, but we are forever striving to "walk the walk." Just as Daniel refused to eat food and wine that would defile, we must refuse to indulge in activities that would undermine our effectiveness as witnesses. If we make mistakes, as we inevitably will, we need to remember that Jesus is still with us and loves us. We need to acknowledge the mistakes, repent, ask for forgiveness, and get right back into the game!

The significance of living our faith with integrity is dramatically emphasized in a story told by R.C. Sproul in his book, *Objections Answered*. Sproul writes about a young Jewish boy who lived in Germany. This boy admired his father, a man who always made sure the family's life revolved around attending synagogue and practicing their faith.

When the boy was a teenager, his family was forced to move to another town in Germany which didn't have a synagogue. The life in this new community revolved around the Lutheran Church, which included all the prominent townspeople in its membership. One day the father suddenly announced to his stunned family that they were going to abandon their Jewish tradition and join the Lutheran Church. This wasn't the result of a sudden conversion on the part of the father. He explained to his bewildered family that joining the Lutheran Church would be good for business.

The son, disappointed and bitter over his father's failure to live out his true faith, left Germany and traveled to England to study. He began to develop a new world view and to write down his ideas. Eventually, he published a book which described religion as "opiate for the masses." The boy's name was Karl Marx, and he was the founder of the Communist movement.

Never underestimate the power you have to influence other people.

A friend of mine was putting up her artificial Christmas tree, which soared to a height of over 15 feet. Perched on a ladder, she lost her balance and fell, slamming her back against the hearth. Her father, who was visiting at the time, exclaimed angrily, "That tree's a piece of junk!"

When my friend returned from a visit to the doctor, her young son strode up to her and exclaimed in an exact imitation of his grandfather, "That tree's a piece of junk!" She and I both laughed over this story, but it underscores the fact that we are influencing people even when we are unaware of our influence.

Your spouse might not read the gospel, but he will observe how you act out the gospel. If you believe, erroneously, that the way to reach your spouse is to adopt the attitude of the unbeliever, then remember that the Apostle Paul did not compromise his standards, even when confronted with unbelievers or with believers who twisted the gospel to suit their own purposes. He called for the drastic action of expelling immoral members when they twisted the gospel to justify their own immorality.

Adopting the attitude of the unbeliever is never a consideration. You must act out the gospel, setting an example of faith through your actions. With his compassion and determination, Yukio persuaded a village of whale hunters to save a dying whale. With your tireless adherence to faith, you can persuade a nonbeliever to take your beliefs seriously. *Live your faith with integrity and you will have gained your partner's respect.*

Show What it Means to be a Christian

Another thing the believer must do is to show the nonbeliever that Christianity is appealing. We need to live our lives in a way that makes any other way of life pale by comparison. The effectiveness of our witness depends on whether we live the Christian life with joy and enthusiasm, or whether we live it in somber drudgery, as something to be endured.

Setting a Christian example means persevering in the faith, even when it would seem to be to our immediate advantage to do otherwise. It means exercising forgiveness and compassion, learning to be joyful Christians by tapping into the tremendous wellspring of happiness that flows from within once we have recognized God as the source of our happiness.

Setting a Christian example means being a positive role model by loving and caring for others with feeling that translates into action. It means accepting our spouse, even as we set out to influence his beliefs. In short, setting a Christian example means living by the Spirit, with the fruit of the Spirit being "love, joy, peace, patience, kindness, goodness, faithfulness, gentleness, and self-control" (Galatians 5:22-23).

As we become joyful Christians, transforming our faith from passive to active and from stagnant to vibrant, we open our marriage to the miraculous, transforming power of God. Our life becomes our most effective witness, with God's light shining through us to illuminate the glorious, life-changing power of faith.

Chapter Summary

Persuasion by example, letting your life be your witness, is the most effective way you have of leading your spouse to faith in Christ. **Faithfulness** and **obedience** to God's will speak louder than words.

Setting an example for Christ does not mean you are to be silent about your beliefs. Proclaiming the gospel is a vital part of witnessing. But the example you set will be more compelling than words. You are preparing a fertile ground in preparation for sowing the seeds of truth.

Setting a Christian example means living your faith with integrity, showing that Christianity is appealing, persevering in the faith, exercising forgiveness and compassion, and learning to be a joyful Christian. You should be a positive role model by loving and caring for others with feeling that translates into action.

CHAPTER TWO

How To Be A Joyful Christian

"The precepts of the Lord are right, giving joy to the heart. The commands of the Lord are radiant, giving light to the eyes." Psalm 19:8

The importance of being a joyful Christian hit Cindy like a sledgehammer one Sunday afternoon. She had just returned from church, and she was in a good mood. The weather was perfect, with a green world basking in the glow of a warm September sun. Church had been inspiring. What a wonderful day to be alive!

Her husband, Dan, who was not religious, had been home all morning. He greeted her good cheer with a smile, but behind the smile his look was intent. "What is it about going to church that makes you so happy?" he blurted suddenly, his smile giving way to a puzzled frown. "I wish I could be that happy."

"Come with me and find out," Cindy quipped. But beneath the casual reply, she was excited. This might be a way to persuade Dan to attend church. If he could see that her spiritual life was a source of happiness, he might want to try it out.

Cindy had the right idea. We need to show that our faith is a cause for rejoicing. Irritable Christians who give the impression that life is drudgery and church is boring are not going to inspire the nonbeliever to say, "Hey, I want some of that for myself!" If Cindy had stormed home from church irritable and critical, her husband certainly would not have said, "I wish I could be that happy!"

Chances are, the people you admire most are the cheerful people who tackle life's challenges with vigor and enthusiasm. They genuinely like people. They endure problems and setbacks, illness and hardship, tremendous obstacles and minor irritants just like everybody else. But unlike most of us, they confront these challenges with their joy and faith and optimism intact.

This isn't to say that joyful people are always happy, or that they never succumb to rage and sadness. Anger and sadness are appropriate responses to many of life's trials. Jesus himself was so moved and troubled that he wept when he saw how unhappy Mary was over the death of her brother, Lazarus. But those with a deep and abiding faith, the joyful Christians, know they need never succumb to total, endless despair. They have Jesus' promise in Matthew 28:20 to sustain them: "And surely I am with you always, to the very end of the age."

The Source of Our Joy

Christians should step boldly forward, with God's promise of eternal salvation serving as a deep wellspring of wonder and joy. But all too often, that joy seems beyond our grasp; an elusive thing that teases us with promise and abandons us at the first sign of trouble. Our failure to claim the joy available to us reminds me of the story of an old man who lived in extreme poverty. Filthy and ragged, he seldom emerged from his dingy, roach-infested apartment. After he died, an examination of his meager belongings revealed the extent of his poverty. Then someone made a startling discovery. Thousands of dollars, totaling close to a half million, were found hidden under his mattress.

Like the man in this story, too many Christians choose poverty over wealth, although wealth of spirit is within our grasp. Joy lies beyond our fingertips, unclaimed because we never fully realize that it must come from within. We continue to rely on the externals: other people, material wealth, health, and beauty to supply our happiness. We overlook the fact that happiness based on externals can be snatched away as suddenly as the first financial crisis or disappointment with our mate.

The wife whose husband is the sole source of her happiness is the wife who is discontent and angry when he shows up late for dinner. The husband who depends on his wife to meet his needs for happiness is the husband who is disillusioned as soon as his wife fails to measure up to some impossible ideal.

I read once that the most important characteristic of a marriageable person is the habit of happiness. If we want our partners to see us as joyful Christians, we must cultivate this habit of happiness. We need to live life in such a way that people observing us will say, "I want to be like that. If Christianity is that good, I want it, too!"

Jump off That Treadmill!

Unfortunately, our joy is often blocked by the habit of negative thinking. We can't seem to jump off the treadmill of negativity, no matter how hard we try. We want to have a positive attitude. We wake up in the morning saying, "I'm going to be happy today." Then those old attitudes come right back, as certain and relentless as an ocean tide. Casting them off for good and acquiring the habit of happiness that will enable us to be joyful Christians requires some determination.

Once we have jumped off the treadmill of negativity, we need to acquire the essentials of joyous living. Without them, we poke along, never fully realizing all of our potential, wondering why life seems to pass us by. With them, we discover the key to happiness, learning to unlock the door to our God-given abilities and become positive, influential Christians. When we have acquired the essentials of joyous living, our spouse will want to acquire them, too.

Self-Esteem

Positive self-esteem is one of those essential keys to becoming a joyful Christian. Having said that, I will add that I have come to dislike that term, self-esteem. It has been diluted and cheapened by our culture's embrace of a pseudo self-esteem that has nothing at all to do with a person's true self-worth.

This new "feel good" philosophy springs from the premise that not thinking highly enough of ourselves is at the root of all our problems. We are led to believe that people take drugs, indulge in promiscuity, or murder somebody because they did not grow up in an environment that nurtured their self-esteem. This deficit, according to popular thinking, can be overcome if we are just told enough times that we are special.

Our public schools now teach classes in self-esteem. My children took something called "meology," in which they were encouraged to draw pictures of themselves and write about how special they were. There is nothing wrong with this, except that it does not accomplish the objective. Children have always enjoyed crayoning pictures of themselves and being told they are special. But as soon as they are confronted with the ridicule of an insensitive classmate or their ineptness at a particular sport or any of the numerous other things that dash fragile egos, they forget "meology." The cold, cruel world of reality sets in.

As part of the public school self-esteem curriculum, Kevin was treated to a visit from "Foo Foo," a puppet who told the children how wonderful they were. "Did this make you feel special?" His mother asked later, when Kevin mentioned the puppet.

"No. It was dumb," he promptly replied. He had been awarded a certificate of self-esteem, but the instructor filling out the certificate had misspelled his name. Kevin crumpled his certificate and tossed it into the trash.

These attempts to instill a sense of self-esteem, no matter how well-intentioned, do not work because they are based on an erroneous idea of what self-esteem is all about. The failure of self-esteem programs to translate into enhanced performance became glaringly obvious when a recent study revealed that American students actually had a very high sense of self-esteem compared with students in other countries. The American students rated their scholastic abilities quite high, even though they scored much lower on standardized tests measuring academic learning and mathematical ability.

Obviously, something is wrong here. American students think highly of themselves, yet their overall academic performance compared with their peers in other industrialized countries is dismal. Teenage drug use, illegitimacy, and violence are on the rise. All this supposed self-esteem is not coming from performance. It is certainly not stemming from a firmly-integrated, well-founded system of values. It is a "feel good," self-centered substitute for self-esteem, more accurately described as inflated ego.

Real self-esteem, or an intrinsic sense of self-worth that weathers the battering of day-to-day life, is not derived from other people. Ultimately, it is not even derived from achievements. The actor is elated by applause, the politician by reelection, and the good student by an A. But what happens when the actor's next film is a flop, the politician loses an election and the A student makes an F? Failures are an inevitable fact of life. Numerous failures can often be a measure of how often a person has tried to succeed.

The secret to handling failure and criticism while retaining your inner joy is to have your self-esteem remain intact, even when your self-confidence is severely shaken. This is possible only if your self-esteem is derived from the proper source.

The Proper Source

From where should we derive our self-esteem if we can't get it from other people or our own accomplishments? The answer, of course, is God. Jesus said the very hairs on our head are numbered. We are all special and unique, made in God's image. In Psalm 139:13-14, we are told that God knew us before we were born: "For you created my inmost being; you knit me together in my mother's womb. I praise you because I am fearfully and wonderfully made."

It is vitally important that the Christian believe we are all special and unique. Just paying lip service to the idea will not do any good. Once we truly understand that we are loved by God, that He made us in his image and endowed us with a uniqueness no one else on earth possesses, we will have acquired the basis for a real and lasting self-esteem.

It took me a long time to fully realize the truth of every person's uniqueness. Through much of my childhood, I suffered from low self-esteem. I was a chubby child, without the type of outgoing personality that catapults some children automatically into the "in crowd."

I remember wanting to take ballet lessons when I was in fifth grade. Most of my classmates, skinny girls who exuded a phenomenal self-confidence, had been taking ballet for years. I felt woefully behind. But thinking I could catch up through hard work and practice, I persuaded my mother to talk with the ballet instructor. The instructor assured us that although challenging, it would not be impossible for me to catch up. Plans were made. I was to report to my first ballet class on Tuesday after school.

Now that I had convinced my mother to let me take ballet, my low self-esteem surfaced in the form of a sudden, overwhelming horror. What if I looked fat in my leotards? Instead of envisioning myself acquiring all the grace of my confident classmates, I envisioned their derision. It was too much. I backed out. I never agreed to be on the swim team or to join Girl Scouts, either. Shyness coupled with a fear of ridicule and failure prevented me from doing these things.

It was a long time before I realized a sense of self-worth based on God's love, rather than on the mercurial approbation of peers or the transient gratification of accomplishments. This realization comes gradually, as a result of growing in faith, remaining in communication with God through prayer, and delving into Scripture. Instead of feeding our egos and revolving around our own selfish desires, a sense of self-worth rooted in the knowledge of our uniqueness before God enables us to exhibit compassion and concern for others. It is not the kind of temporal self-esteem that manifests itself in the "I'm wonderful and I can have it all" jargon of our times. Instead, it gives birth to a self-confidence that frees us to support and encourage and love others. It enables us to live as joyful Christians, laying the groundwork for a life that will inspire our partner to faith.

Those who have never discovered the true source of our self-esteem will forever demand that others meet their emotional needs. This is an impossible burden to place on a spouse, who is busy trying to have his own needs met. *Developing positive self-esteem is essential to becoming a joyful Christian and to building a good marriage. Then others will not have to meet those needs which can only be met through a relationship with Jesus Christ.*

Positive Attitude

One of my good friends has moved at least 15 times in her 30 years of marriage. When she joined my church, she jumped into things immediately, accepting volunteer positions of responsibility and leadership. She organized a gourmet cooking group in her neighborhood and entertains frequently. Her smile is contagious, her laughter frequent and spontaneous. Needless to say, she has friends from many areas of the country.

I met another woman at a party recently who was also a newcomer to our area. This woman had just moved into a beautiful home near a lake and a golf course. Her husband's salary afforded her the luxury of being able to choose whether or not she wanted to stay home. Yet her face was pinched and unhappy, her mouth turned down in a perpetual frown.

She didn't seem to know many people, so I introduced myself and asked her a few polite questions. The woman complained about the weather, the prejudiced, unfriendly people in our area, the poor schools, and her inability to find enough to keep her occupied during the day. I suggested several opportunities for community involvement, but she didn't seem cheered by the prospects. As soon as I could gracefully do so, I excused myself and went in search of a more congenial conversationalist. This woman's conversation was depressing!

These two women moved to the same area. They also happened to have moved from the same state. One was happy and enthusiastic, seizing every opportunity to turn the move into a fine adventure. The other was miserable, refusing to look beyond her discontent at the smorgasbord of opportunities available. The only difference was in their attitudes. A positive attitude is essential to becoming a joyful, influential Christian. We choose our attitudes, with that choice reflected in our words, our actions, and in the reactions of those closest to us.

The Goodfinders

In his book, *Happiness is an Inside Job,* John Powell, S.J., cites a scientific study in which researchers interviewed 100 of the most contented people they could find in an effort to come up with a common denominator for happiness. At first, the search for this common denominator proved discouraging. Education and background of the participants varied widely. Some were from wealthy families, while others had been born into poverty. Some were highly educated, and others had barely finished high school. It didn't look as if these "happy" subjects had anything in common. But finally, when all the data had been fed into a computer, the scientists discovered one trait characteristic of every one of the participants. They were all *goodfinders,* a word that had to be invented to describe this trait. In other words, they all looked for and found the good in themselves, in others, and in all situations. Goodfinders are slow to criticize, searching beyond the obvious for those pearls that no one else has bothered to discover.

Jesus, the ultimate goodfinder, said "Love your God with all your heart and with all your soul and with all your mind, and love your neighbor as yourself." Loving our neighbor sometimes means looking for the kernel that lies beyond the outer husk. We need to get into the habit of ferreting out the positive instead of dwelling on the negative. I have seen women's club volunteers, PTA presidents and others who gave their time selflessly criticized by people who never gave an ounce of time to the project in question. Yet loving our neighbors as ourselves means being slow to criticize and eager to search for the good.

Being a goodfinder means finding the good in your marriage and in your spouse. Instead of dwelling on the negative aspects of being married to someone who doesn't share your faith, concentrate on the positive. Be slow to criticize and quick to praise. Do not dilute the effectiveness of your witness as a joyful Christian by making your spouse feel guilty about not attending church. Always remember the source of your joy, and being a goodfinder will come naturally.

Get Rid of That Anger

Anger can interfere with your efforts to be a joyful Christian, in addition to harming the marital relationship. Many people appear to harbor a subterranean anger which causes them to erupt at the slightest provocation. I read a newspaper story about a woman trying to make a turn onto a busy highway. An impatient man behind her leaned on his horn. The woman raised her hand in exasperation, indicating to him that she couldn't move. Interpreting her raised hand as a personal insult, the man followed her all the way to a shopping center, waited for her to park, then strode to her car. He threatened the woman, even though she tried to explain that she had merely been indicating to him that she couldn't pull out into traffic yet. The man has followed this woman since that day, leading her to swear out an assault warrant for his arrest.

We have become a society of people expecting the worst, swearing out lawsuits, hurtling along with our tempers just millimeters from exploding. How far apart this thinking is from Paul's advice to "Get rid of all bitterness, rage and anger, brawling and slander, along with every form of malice. Be kind and compassionate to one another, forgiving each other just as in Christ God forgave you" (Ephesians 4:31-32).

The believer might be frustrated by a spouse's lack of spiritual progress or openness to new ideas. In this instance, the Christian must refrain from harboring bitterness and resentment. A positive, affirming attitude cannot coexist with rage and bitterness, faultfinding and discord. We need to discard anger that would contradict our beliefs and interfere with our ability to be goodfinders. We should remember what

Proverbs 17:27 teaches us: "A man of knowledge uses words with restraint, and a man of understanding is even-tempered."

Setting Goals and Stretching Beyond our Limits

Henry David Thoreau said, "If one advances confidently in the direction of his dreams, and endeavors to live the life which he has imagined, he will meet with a success unexpected in common hours."

At some point in our lives, we have all felt the tug of dreams calling us to soar beyond the comfortable rut of mediocrity. This is the way God made us. Paul said, "We have different gifts, according to the grace given us." In other words, God has endowed us with our own unique gifts and talents, the basic tools for serving him better. A crucial aspect of being a joyful Christian is utilizing these God-given gifts and talents.

My friend Rhonda's beautiful voice has led to her successful career in music and her tremendous contribution to her church choir. Another friend, Angie, is an outstanding teacher of foreign university students. Chris is a meticulous accountant, able to help her husband with the financial aspects of his business. Rob is a dentist and Jim an architect, Marie an attorney and Phyllis a day care worker.

We are all endowed with certain gifts, but that doesn't mean those gifts fall like manna from heaven, fulfilling us without any effort on our part. God blessed us with a great reservoir of potential and a desire to tap into that potential. It is up to us to "endeavor to live the life" we have imagined. Tapping into the reservoir could mean stretching beyond our limits, employing all our persistence and determination and faith.

This is where many fall by the wayside. They settle for a reasonable amount of comfort and satisfaction, and then, like a turtle that doesn't venture too far from its shell, they refuse to budge any further. But because God has endowed us with the seeds of greatness, we experience an underlying dissatisfaction. If we have a desire for beautiful roses and never bother to plant them; if we have always wanted to play a musical instrument, yet never get around to learning how; if being a basketball coach is our dream, but the hours and apprenticeship period seem too long, we will experience a vague depression. We will have the feeling that we are not doing enough with our lives.

Fear of Failure

Sometimes it is more than complacency that causes us to settle for the rut of mediocrity. It is fear of failure. This fear of failure is evident throughout the Bible. Moses used every excuse he could think of to avoid going before Pharoah. "I'm not good enough to do anything like that," he protested.

God didn't seem to think this was a very valid argument, but Moses continued to argue. Claiming a lack of eloquence, he tried to convince God he was unable to speak well enough to talk to the Pharoah. Finally, when all his excuses failed, Moses pleaded, "O, Lord, please send somebody else to do it" (Exodus 4:13).

Gideon is another example of someone who was terrified of failure. God instructed him to deliver Israel out of the hands of the Midianites. Gideon had God's promise of faithfulness, yet he offered a variety of excuses. He was from the weakest clan. He was the most insignificant member of his family. How could God possibly want him to lead a charge against a formidable enemy? When he realized that God wasn't going to change His mind, Gideon asked for a sign, just to be sure he was really talking to God. God showed Gideon the requested sign, but Gideon developed cold feet as the time to oppose the Midianites approached. He wanted another sign. God complied with the request. This still wasn't enough for Gideon. Pleading with God not to be angry, he asked for yet another indication that God was going to do what He said. When God provided the requested sign, Gideon finally mustered enough faith to follow God's command.

Just like Moses and Gideon, we fear failure. It is this fear of failure and rejection that prevents us from stretching beyond the limits of our perceived capabilities. We could fall flat on our faces. We might look like fools. We couldn't possibly speak in public, or go back to school, or make a sales call to the president of the company, or run for public office, or be chairman of a committee, or teach Sunday School, or take guitar lessons....you get the picture. Our fears prevent us from taking that leap of faith, trying with all our might to accomplish something, to be the best that we can be.

A fear of failure might even prevent us from trying to influence our spouse to accept Jesus Christ. What if our Christian behavior turns him off? What if he decides he can't live with somebody who exhibits a strong faith that is diametrically opposed to what he believes? The *what ifs* paralyze us, blocking our access to God's transforming power.

Overcoming The Odds

Many people have overcome tremendous odds to succeed in areas that appeared to be beyond their grasp. They did not seem to have the attributes necessary for success in these fields, but managed somehow to stretch beyond their limits, attaining goals that continued to elude "more eligible" candidates. One of these people is Chris Burke, co-star of the ABC hit series, *Life Goes On.*

When Chris was diagnosed with Down's syndrome, doctors advised his parents, Frank and Marian Burke, to put their newborn son in an institution. Fortunately, the Burkes ignored this advice. Showering him with love and attention, they sought early education and therapy and encouraged Chris to have a wide range of interests. But when Chris decided he wanted to be an actor, the family tried to dissuade him. Hollywood and acting seemed like impossible dreams for almost anyone. What chance did a child with Down's syndrome have?

Chris was undaunted. He continued to pursue his interest, corresponding with people in the film industry and taking two buses across New York City to attend acting classes each week. In the book, *A Special Kind of Hero,* by Chris Burke and Jo Beth McDaniel, Chris's positive attitude and faith in himself shine through. With typical optimism, he refers to his condition as "Up syndrome" instead of Down's syndrome.

Most Likely to Succeed

The Bible is full of people who don't appear to possess the necessary credentials for their calling. I already mentioned Moses and Gideon. There was David, a shepherd boy who became king; Deborah, a woman who led Israel to victory over the Canaanites; Rahab, a prostitute who hid Israelite spies in Jericho; Peter, a fisherman who became one of Christ's twelve disciples; Esther, a Jewish girl who was chosen to be queen of Xerxes and subsequently foiled a plan to exterminate the Jews; John the Baptist, an eccentric sort who would probably have been considered a hippie during the sixties. The list goes on, because God didn't choose those voted "most likely to succeed." He chose unlikely people who would have to rely on Him for their success.

This should be encouraging to us. If a man who was slow of speech and afraid of going back into Egypt could confront the Pharoah and lead the Israelites to freedom, why can't we arm ourselves with faith and march toward that distant goal? Each step will draw us closer. By stretching our limits and proceeding on faith, we make strides toward becoming the joyful Christians God meant us to be. We will be witnesses for our faith as we proceed in faith and obedience, stretching beyond our limits because we know that "with God all things are possible."

Enjoying Simple Pleasures

One evening I watched a movie about a man who adopted a child born with multiple disabilities. Based on a true story, the movie documented this man's efforts to find out what was wrong with his son. The child, who suffered from seizures and an inability to learn, was diagnosed as retarded. Numerous tests and doctor's visits failed to turn up a reason for the retardation or a prognosis for the future. The adoptive father continued to work with the child, at the expense of his own social life and leisure time. He sought the best schools for learning-impaired children, and nurtured his son with a tremendous amount of love and attention.

When the boy was a teenager, doctors discovered a condition among some newborn infants called fetal alcohol syndrome. Women who drank heavily during pregnancy were at risk of giving birth to children with FAS. Characterized by physical and mental retardation, the symptoms of this affliction fit the adopted son perfectly. Once the father had obtained a diagnosis of FAS, he went in search of a cure, only to find that nothing could be done. The boy's future, with little hope of developmental progress, looked hopeless.

To me, the saddest aspect of this boy's life was not that he had difficulty mastering the things normal children do. It was that he was unable to appreciate the minor, day-to-day pleasures that most of us take for granted. Some developmental abnormality associated with his condition made it impossible for him to take pleasure in the dappled shadows cast by autumn leaves or the prism of colors in a rainbow. He traveled through life's brief journey, dying when he was in his early twenties, without experiencing the magnificence of a towering redwood or the thrill of watching an eagle in flight. He could observe these things without being stirred to wonder and ecstasy, because wonder and ecstasy were casualties of his affliction. Sometimes wonder and ecstasy seem to be casualties of our own affliction: a life so caught up in worrying about the future that we fail to take pleasure in the moment. I can remember spending numerous hours as a child lying on my back, gazing at the sky. During the day I watched the clouds, great cumulus mountains or feathery cirrus brush strokes. At night I was transfixed by stars piercing the velvet black of a summer sky.

It has been a long time since I spent hours watching the sky. Maybe I need to do it again. Taking pleasure in the day-to-day things, the simple pleasures that are truly gifts from God, is essential to leading a joyful life. We can set goals and strive for them until we reap the harvest of success, but if we haven't enjoyed the journey, it will be a hollow success.

Howard Hughes was a billionaire, but he was also an eccentric recluse, unable to enjoy his billions. We can pick up an issue of *People Magazine* and read about movie stars, rap stars, and sports heroes who have achieved fame and fortune at an early age. Endowed with beauty and talent and wealth, happiness still eludes them. They lead a restless, yearning life, characterized by adultery, divorce, drug abuse, and sometimes, violence and suicide. They think, wrongly, that fame and money will bring them the fulfillment they yearn for. When it doesn't, they clutch at transient physical pleasures that might bring temporary enjoyment at the expense of their emotional and spiritual well being.

I'll be Happy When...

We waste a good portion of our lives accumulating, or trying to accumulate, material things. We tell ourselves we'll be happy when we own a bigger house. We have one built, move in, but we need more furniture. We'll be happy when we get every room decorated. We finish decorating the house, and decide the car is too small for long trips. What we need is a van. We buy the van, and decide we need a boat to take full advantage of our proximity to a lake. A sailboat should do it, but sometimes there isn't any wind. A motor would be nice.

Meanwhile the kids have been accumulating, too. Their previously bare rooms are crammed with stuff. The basement storage area is jammed, too. Even the garage is so crowded that there is no room to park the cars. What we need is a bigger house.

You get the picture. We acquire and acquire, yet it's never enough. We think it will be. Just one more thing! But just like those movie stars who have everything (wouldn't we be happy if we had what they have?), we are constantly yearning for more.

Another mistake people make is believing that a change of circumstances will allow them to enjoy life. Anne Tyler's novel, *Ladder of Years,* is about a forty year old woman, Delia Grinstead, who leaves a husband and children who take her for granted. Hitching a ride to a new town, Delia finds a job and settles down to enjoy her solitude. Soon responsibilities begin to nibble away at her newfound independence. She ends up in much the same situation that she was in before, caring for a man and a child who seem more interested in meeting their own needs than in meeting hers.

Like Delia Grinstead, we can move to a new place or find a new job, but life still manages to crowd in. We bring with us all the old attitudes and problems, until the new begins to look very much like the old. If we didn't enjoy day-to-day life before, we probably won't enjoy it when we move to that new town or get that new car or reach that career goal.

My parents have always had a tremendous ability to relish life's simple pleasures. When my father was hospitalized in 1988, I wrote this in my journal:

"Daddy is too long for the hospital bed. His feet touch the boards at the end. He is hooked to wires and tubes, and there is the constant blip of a heart monitor, along with the whir and hiss of other machines. A thick, clear plastic coil snakes around his head and his hand is punctured with a needle that leads to a tube that leads to another machine.

He might have another seizure. His lungs are diseased. He cannot drive. I am just thankful he is alive. Thank you, God, for any additional days you will give me with my dad.

His face lights up for visitors. He has lived so long...82 years. I'm glad he likes the simple things: Watching his bird feeder. His garden. A basketball game. I want him to be happy. The last time I saw him before his illness, Daddy was observing a squirrel on our deck. He mentioned that squirrels and cats both have long tails, but a cat waves hers languidly and fluidly, while a squirrel's tail moves in short jerks, like the flick of a wrist. It is like Daddy to notice and marvel over things like this. I hope this ability to marvel over everyday things, plus his capacity for humor, will keep him happy, even if he is incapacitated."

As it turned out, God did grant my father additional years. He was no longer able to build wooden bird feeders in his workshop. He couldn't play golf or plant a garden. There came a time when he could not even enjoy his favorite foods. But he still enjoys a baseball game on television, a good joke, and the gentle patter of a summer rain.

My mother hung a hummingbird feeder outside the kitchen window just above the sink. We all watch these fascinating birds, quick as bumblebees and almost as small, as they perch on the feeder, allowing us a brief glimpse of ruby throat before they dart away. The simple pleasures...these abound at my parents' house, nourishing and enriching us.

If we are able to enjoy the simple pleasures, those everyday miracles that brighten our sojourn here and direct us forever toward our Creator, then we can truly be joyful Christians. The nonbeliever will respond to that inner working of the spirit which compels us to proclaim, "This is the day that the Lord has made; let us rejoice and be glad in it" (Psalm 118:24).

Chapter Summary

Christians should set an example of joyful Christian living by cultivating the habit of happiness. A Christian's joy springs from God's promise of eternal salvation. We need to live life in such a way that people observing us will say, "If Christianity is that good, I want it, too!"

The following things are essential to joyful Christian living:

Positive self-esteem derived from the knowledge that we are all special and unique, made in God's image.

A positive attitude which enables us to search out and find the good in ourselves, in others and in all situations.

A willingness to stretch beyond our limits, arming ourselves with faith and striving to become the people God wants us to be.

An ability to enjoy the day-to-day blessings that brighten our lives and direct us toward our Creator.

An unbelieving spouse is more likely to be receptive and open to the believer's faith when he realizes that Christ-centered living is a source of great joy, in spite of life's trials and tribulations. **We need to show that our faith is a cause for rejoicing.**

CHAPTER THREE

Faith In Action

"Let us not become weary in doing good,
for at the proper time we will reap a harvest
if we do not give up." Galatians 6:9

Becoming a joyful Christian is the first step toward leading by example. The second step is showing faith in action. If we exhibit perseverance when doubts and crises arise, exercise a spirit of forgiveness and compassion, and indicate a willingness to serve, we reveal a depth of commitment that serves as an example to the nonbeliever. We are not merely paying lip service to our religion. We are showing that our faith is an intrinsic and indispensable way of life.

Henry Blackaby and Claude King wrote in *Experiencing God,* "The world comes to know God when they see God's nature expressed through His activity." Your spouse will come to know God when he sees God's nature expressed through faith in action as you live your Christian beliefs.

One of the greatest examples in literature of a person who, through acting on his beliefs, has a profound impact on another person's life can be found in Victor Hugo's masterpiece, *Les Miserables.* In this epic story, Jean Valjean is convicted for a petty offense and endures nineteen years in prison. Upon release, he finds that he is an outcast, without prospects of friendship, work, food or shelter. Hungry and miserable, he meets up with a kind bishop who offers him a good meal and a clean bed for the night.

Jean Valjean, hardened by nineteen years of hard labor, repays his benefactor by stealing off in the night with the bishop's silver candlesticks. Arrested and forced back to the bishop's house, Jean Valjean despairs over returning to prison. But the bishop does an odd thing. He demands Jean Valjean's release, declaring that the silver was a gift. Then he tells the former prisoner to make use of the silver to become an honest man.

The bishop, exemplifying faith in action, exhibits a spirit of forgiveness and compassion. His depth of commitment is more of an example to the nonbeliever than any verbal profession of faith could have been. As a result of the bishop's action, Jean Valjean becomes an honest man who exerts a tremendous influence on the many lives he touches. Like ripples in a pond, the bishop's kind act produces more ripples, with far-reaching consequences that continue to spread even after the bishop's death.

Our actions, like ripples in a pond, will produce more ripples. At the proper time, we will "reap a harvest." We cannot influence the nonbeliever by professing a faith that we fail to embrace fully and exuberantly. Like the bishop, we must act on our beliefs.

Don't Be A Hypocrite

Exhibiting faith in action means that we refuse to be hypocrites, professing to believe in Christ's love but refusing to reflect that love in our own lives.

Have you ever heard people say they don't want to go to church because they think churchgoers are hypocrites? This is true in some cases and not in others, but a few hypocrites can really stand out if a critic of Christianity is looking for a target. Think of how much damage it does to the ministry when a high profile televangelist is caught in adultery. Those who profess to be Christians are claiming a higher standard of conduct than the unbelieving segment of the population. If God's word seems so insignificant that we who call ourselves Christians openly flout it, how can nonbelievers take God's word seriously? When we are away from the church environment, would other people recognize us as Christians?

A Christian teenager was caught cheating on an exam. There were repercussions, including loss of a scholarship and a zero in the course. But the biggest repercussion was the response of non-Christian teenagers. "So this is how Christians act," one of them said. "Just like the rest of us."

Christians can't act "just like the rest of them." We must resist the temptation to emulate a secular society. This doesn't mean donning a "holier than thou" attitude. It *does* mean avoiding the hypocrisy that a profession of faith without an accompanying change of heart constitutes.

Jesus came down hard on hypocrites. "Woe to you, teachers of the law and Pharisees, you hypocrites! You are like whitewashed tombs, which look beautiful on the outside but on the inside are full of dead men's bones and everything unclean. In the same way, on the outside you appear to people as righteous but on the inside you are full of hypocrisy and wickedness" (Matthew: 23: 27, 28).

We need to be weekday Christians as well as Saturday and Sunday Christians, casting aside any hypocrisy that would be a stumbling block to our partner's acceptance of our faith. If we exhibit an active, vibrant faith, we are showing the nonbeliever that our faith is an integral part of our lives, influencing everything we do. We cannot shelve faith for now and come back to it later.

One Small Baby

Dan and Kathy Blackburn did not shelve their faith and come back to it later. If they had, many lives would have been lost.

The Blackburns faced a daunting challenge. Natives of Indiana, they had opened a Christian missionary school in Haiti. It was their dream that education would break the vicious cycle of violence and poverty relegating Haitian children to a life of despair. In spite of their hard work and dedication, the Blackburns found themselves making little progress. They could not seem to scale the barriers erected by extreme poverty and a cultural climate that included voodoo worship.

Their optimism was giving way to a feeling of defeat when an elderly woman holding a tightly swaddled newborn showed up at their door. Frantically, the woman explained that she was the child's grandmother. The mother had died in a ditch giving birth. The grandmother was unable to find milk, and could do nothing for the baby. She urged Dan Blackburn to take her grandchild.

The situation appeared hopeless. The child looked near death, and the Blackburns had no facilities for taking care of a newborn. But Kathy Blackburn was overwhelmed all at once by the desperation and misery she was witnessing. The old grandmother had walked three hours with a faint thread of hope that these missionaries she had heard about would be able to help. The decision seemed suddenly simple. They would take the baby, because to do otherwise would be to tell the Haitians about God's love without actually putting that love into practice. *What good would it do to tell the old woman about God's love, and then send her away?* Kathy Blackburn wondered.

Word spread quickly about the missionaries who took in dying infants. More babies were brought to the remote village of Maissade, where the Blackburns had made their home. Throughout the next few years of political and social turmoil, Dan and Kathy Blackburn took in 28 children who lived and many others who did not live. When the political situation in Haiti reached a crisis that threatened their lives, the Blackburns were forced to flee. But they wouldn't leave the children they had reared and nurtured along with their own children. They made a daring escape with their "family," managing to get all 28 children into the United States.

Dan and Kathy Blackburn made a difference in the lives of 28 children because this missionary couple reflected Christ's love in their lives. *What good will it do for us to tell our spouse about God's love if we don't reflect that love in our own lives?* An unbelieving spouse may seem indifferent to faith in action, but like seeds awaiting the proper harvest time, the believing partner's actions are sown in faith, cultivated in love, and await the proper time, God's time, to reap a harvest.

The Importance of Perseverance

Exhibiting faith in action through doubts and crises means a believer must develop perseverance. When we persevere, we don't give up, even if years pass with no indication that our prayers have been heard. Focusing on Jesus, we refuse to grow weary and lose heart as we continue to exhibit joy and faith in the midst of a nonbeliever's doubts. We do not allow ourselves to grow frustrated and impatient with a spouse's unbelief. Instead, we continue to let our life be our witness, recognizing that the testing of our faith develops perseverance and "perseverance must finish it's work" (James 1:3,4).

The Determined Klutz

When Lee and I took our first ski trip to Colorado, he knew how to ski and I didn't. But boy, was I determined to learn! Not wanting to hold him back, I insisted that he go to the top of the mountain and ski without me. I would take a beginner's class, then ski on the "bunny slope," a small hill where lessons were held and beginners practiced.

Clunky boots attached to long, skinny skis sent my confidence plummeting. How did anyone maneuver in this getup? To make matters worse, I have a hard time following instructions. In dance class, I am the one moving in the opposite direction from everyone else. In ski class, I was the one requiring individualized instruction once everyone else had caught on. Fortunately, I had a patient instructor. I was eventually able to master the basics before moving to Part Two: *the ski lift.*

One problem with skiing is that before you can go down the mountain you have to go up. That means riding a ski lift. But the ride isn't the bad part. The bad part is getting off, because the ski lift *doesn't stop.* It keeps right on moving, and you jump off at a designated spot, skiing rapidly away so that you don't get whacked by the next lift, or the next skier.

My heart skittered wildly as we approached this designated spot. How in the world would I manage to land on these skis and glide out of the way?

I didn't. I lurched forward, face down in the snow, and this was my graceless landing for many rides to come.

Part Three: *practicing on the bunny hill,* was no better. This hill turned out to be surprisingly formidable. It was slippery and fast and steeper than I had thought. Once, unable to stop or turn, I found myself zooming toward a group of would-be skiers taking a ski lesson. "Watch out!" I cried, my voice whipped away by the velocity of my approach. I plowed into them and we tumbled like bowling pins, a tangle of novice skiers in the snow.

It was at this point that my confidence ebbed to a new low. The ski instructor glared as he untangled us, one by one. I felt tears stinging my eyes. I would give up! I couldn't do this! This wasn't my sport! Lee could ski tomorrow, and I would stay at the lodge.

But a defiant stubbornness began to kick in. I watched agile people hurtle down the hill. I wanted to hurtle down the hill, too.

"I will," I thought suddenly. "Tomorrow I will ride to the top of the mountain with Lee and ski all the way down."

And that's exactly what I did. I practiced the rest of the afternoon, a lonely, clumsy figure on that crowded bunny slope. My frequent falls left me wet and cold. My arms and legs ached with fatigue. But by the end of the day, I could hop off the ski lift and glide out of the way without falling. I could ski down the hill, even managing to execute a few turns.

The next day, Lee and I rode to the top of the mountain. We went far beyond the bunny slope that had been so formidable the day before. My apprehensiveness faded as I gazed at the most breathtaking view I had ever seen. Magnificent mountains thrust snow-covered peaks toward a vast blue sky. Hills and valleys clothed in evergreens and draped in sparkling white tumbled away as far as we could see. I would have missed all this if I had given up! Forgotten were the sting of failure and the agony of embarrassment. Perseverance meant sticking with the task until I reaped the sought after reward.

Sometimes persevering in our faith means spending a lot of time on the "bunny slopes" before we are ready for the mountains. It calls for determination and a certain stubbornness in the face of difficulties and setbacks.

Do Not Lose Heart

The Apostle Paul knew the importance of perseverance and the magnitude of the sought after reward when he spoke these words: "Therefore, since we are surrounded by such a great cloud of witnesses, let us throw off everything that hinders and the sin that so easily entangles, and let us run with perseverance the race marked out for us. Let us fix our eyes on Jesus, the author and perfecter of our faith, who for the joy set before him endured the cross, scorning its shame, and sat down at the right hand of the throne of God. Consider him who endured such opposition from sinful men, so that you will not grow weary and lose heart" (Hebrews 12:1).

Paul realized the going would get rough. The temptation to give up would be great. But he encouraged us to think about Jesus as we encountered discouragement. Then we would be able to persevere without losing heart, confident of our ultimate goal.

Forgiveness

No quality better exemplifies faith in action than forgiveness. We can talk about love and faith and Christ all we want, but if we don't exercise forgiveness, our words are as hollow and meaningless as an echo reverberating back to us from the fathomless depths of a ravine.

If the bishop had not forgiven Jean Valjean, the criminal would have gone back to prison, the bishop would have kept his candlesticks, and many lives would have remained untouched.

Without forgiveness, racism is rampant, ethnic wars continue to rage as victims become perpetrators and perpetrators become victims, reconciliation becomes a casualty of revenge, and the opportunity for love is lost. Jesus was clear on the subject of forgiveness. When Peter wanted to know how many times he should forgive his neighbor who sinned against him, Jesus replied, "I tell you, not seven times, but seventy-seven times."

In other words, we are not supposed to keep tabs on our grievances, doling out forgiveness sparingly. We are supposed to forgive over and over again, completely and without reservation. "For if you forgive men when they sin against you, your heavenly Father will also forgive you. But if you do not forgive men their sins, your Father will not forgive your sins" (Matthew 6:14,15).

When Forgiveness Is Difficult

Forgiveness is easy enough if the grievances are minor. We can "forgive and forget" when a neighbor we didn't particularly care for anyway says something negative about us. We can count to ten, then forgive the person who cuts in front of us in traffic. Forgiveness on a more personal level, when the sins against us are truly grievous, is a much more difficult thing to come by. At times we will be terribly wronged. Feelings of self-righteous anger and even hatred could be directed at the perpetrator. In these situations, it might be impossible to overcome our hostility enough to forgive without asking God to take control of our anger.

We probably feel justified in holding onto our bitterness in certain situations. The wife whose husband has left her for a younger woman, the man who discovers his wife is an alcoholic, the children whose parents have abused them mentally or physically, would certainly seem justified in refusing to forgive. They have been grievously wronged, their lives changed forever. But a lack of forgiveness that becomes a festering hatred can do more damage than the initial sin. It can darken our lives with a blanket of depression and despair. At these times, when forgiveness seems impossible, we must turn to God, asking him to remove the burden of resentment.

In Proverbs 20:22 we are told *not* to say, "I'll pay you back for this wrong!" We are told instead to "Wait on the Lord, and he will deliver you."

A lack of forgiveness has the potential to spill into all areas of life, leaving a residue of bitterness that makes it impossible for us to set an example of Christian living. True forgiveness can set us free to proceed with the work that God would have us do.

Gianna's Example

Gianna Jessen sets an example of forgiveness bound to touch and inspire the rest of us. Born with cerebral palsy, her handicaps are the result of an unsuccessful abortion. Her mother, an unwed teenager, went to an abortion clinic when she was seven months pregnant. A saline injection was supposed to cause the mother's body to expel the "fetal tissue." Instead, the quiet clinic room was filled suddenly with the thin cry of a newborn infant. A baby girl had been born alive!

Gianna, who was subsequently adopted, discovered when she was twelve that her cerebral palsy was the result of her birth mother's attempt to abort her. Instead of being bitter and angry, Gianna forgives her birth mother totally. She and her adoptive mother, Diana DePaul, have made it their mission to travel and speak on behalf of the unborn.

Forgiveness Leads to Positive Action

Revenge rather than forgiveness seems to be the order of the day in a nation racked by lawsuits for even the slightest and most unintentional of offenses. Lawsuits are so prevalent that people were amazed when Thelma Sibley chose not to sue over the death of her five-year-old daughter, Nancy.

On a cold day in January, 1994, the drawstring on Nancy's winter coat snagged in a narrow gap at the top of the spiral slide at her elementary school playground. Sibley might have sued the clothing maker or the play-ground-equipment manufacturer, but the devout Baptist chose another course of action. She began a persistent letter-writing campaign to clothing manufacturers, government agencies, news organizations and prominent individuals. This campaign eventually led the Consumer Product Safety Commission to persuade 32 clothing manufacturers to voluntarily remove drawstrings from children's clothes.

Forgiveness leads to positive action, enabling us to do the work God would have us do.

God Took His Bitterness Away

Few people will ever have as much reason as Jerry Evers to be bitter and unforgiving toward a spouse. On New Year's Day in 1980, while relatives played checkers in an adjoining room, Evers' wife drowned the couple's three daughters.

For years afterwards, Evers couldn't sleep at night. He had trouble dealing with life until, as he put it, God took his bitterness away. Finally he was able to forgive and pray for his first wife, the mother of his drowned children, although she continued to express her hatred for him. Now Evers, who remarried eight years ago and has three children with his second wife, Dorrie, considers himself blessed. He speaks to church groups about forgiveness. His message, directed at anyone who has been wronged, is based on the theme that through God, all things are possible.

Positive action in the face of tragedy or disappointment can result from forgiveness, but never from a thirst for revenge. True forgiveness is a willingness to move on in life, letting go of rigidly held grievances and ideas. It is acceptance of our past experiences without rancor and bitterness. By exercising true forgiveness, we acknowledge that other people do not control our lives.

Our willingness to forgive is a measure of our faith that God is in control, and that he can use our past experiences, no matter how negative, for His purposes.

When a nonbeliever sees the believer exercising true forgiveness, he will see faith not as a puny thing, to be easily dismissed, but rather as a power that has the ability to transcend the things of this world.

Willingness to Serve

Mother Teresa observed that we are the wire and the current is God. We have the power to let the current pass through us, use us, and produce the light of the world—Jesus.

Passive Christianity, when compassion is absent and the current of God is not passing through us, is Christianity that has lost its strength to attract new believers. It is the opposite of the active Christianity that Mother Teresa is talking about, when our joy and love of Christ translate into compassion that leads to servanthood.

We are instructed throughout the Bible to give to the needy and provide for the poor. This generosity is not the sort of government largesse we are accustomed to, distributed on an indiscriminate and impersonal basis. Rather, it is a personal involvement that would take us directly to the sufferer; the kind of involvement found in Jesus' parable of the Good Samaritan.

In the Good Samaritan parable, a man is traveling from Jerusalem to Jericho when he is attacked by robbers. Stripped of his clothes, beaten and left half dead, the man is discovered by a priest traveling along the same road. The priest crosses to the other side of the road to avoid walking too close to the man, as does a Levite who passes by later.

Eventually, a Samaritan comes down the road. Samaritans at that time were hated foreigners, despised by the Jews, who considered them half-breeds. But it is the Samaritan, rather than the religious leader or the Levite, who takes pity on the victim. He bandages the man's wounds, pouring on oil and wine. He puts the man on his own donkey, transports him to an inn and takes care of him. The next day, the Samaritan gives the innkeeper money to look after the injured man.

This is the kind of compassion that leads to action and attracts believers. Jesus said, "Whoever wants to be great among you must be your servant." *Through service to others, we manifest that outward expression of our inner beliefs which reveals to others our authenticity as Christians.*

> "He really practices what he preaches!"
> "She means what she says!"
> "His beliefs must be real. I've never seen him do a dishonest thing!"

These are the sentiments of people who see faith in action. In his book, *Heaven Can't Wait,* Robert Jeffress says the distinguishing characteristic of a Christian is not what he doesn't do, but what he does do and who he is. Most of us tend to value other people in proportion to how they can serve us. Jeffress contrasts this with how Jesus viewed people. They were not to be used, but served.

He Will Know Your Faith Is Real

A young missionary who traveled to a foreign country to preach the gospel entertained grandiose plans of spreading God's word. Her carefully laid plans came crashing down around her as she found herself being required to do more and more housework for the native family she was living with. This was hard, backbreaking labor, washing without benefit of washers and dryers, cooking without recourse to mixes and taking care of a large family of children. She had no time to preach the gospel. She was too busy being a servant to these people!

She went through a period of resentment and rebellion before accepting the fact that this might be part of God's plan. If He called her to be a servant, who was she to argue? She would wash clothes, clean house and cook until her she ached with fatigue, even if it meant not completing her missionary work.

But an interesting thing happened toward the end of her stay. The people she lived with came to view her as friend and helper instead of arrogant foreigner. Their hearts opened to her message because she had been willing to serve. It was only by becoming a servant that she was able to accomplish the missionary work that had been her initial objective.

Your unbelieving spouse will know your faith is real and vital to you when he sees the depth of your commitment to others. Serving others, not resentfully, but with joy and compassion, is the surest way of drawing others to Christ, because service is the physical expression of Christian love.

A Word of Warning

Your willingness to serve should not lead you to neglect your spouse, since this could engender a feeling of resentment toward the "religious" work that is taking so much of your time. Showing faith in action means being committed to the relationship, with time together a priority. You don't want to spend every Sunday afternoon serving soup and sandwiches to the homeless if your spouse has asked you to drive to the lake. If you always seem to prefer being around other Christians, your spouse might be left wondering if you wish you had married one.

In 1 Peter 3:1-7, Christian wives living with nonbelievers are called on to win their husbands over with their behavior. Part of this behavior is a Christ-like willingness to submit. Husbands are called to be considerate of their wives, treating them with respect. Submission and respect are reflected by a willingness to place a high priority on our love for our partner.

The admonitions in 1 Peter to submit to each other should prevent us from becoming "holier than thou" Christians who have the potential to do great damage through prideful, arrogant attitudes. We must do everything in a spirit of love. Showing faith in action does not mean being obsessed with "doing good works" at the expense of our relationship.

What faith in action does mean is that we reveal, through a spirit of humility, love and compassion, what it means to place God first in our lives. We lead by example because we show that our faith is something that enhances our ability to forgive, to exercise compassion, and to live a meaningful, purposeful life.

Everyone wants to live a meaningful, purposeful life. This is true of the nonbeliever as well as the believer. Through faith in action, the Christian shows that living a meaningful, purposeful life it is within our grasp.

Chapter Summary

By exhibiting faith in action, we reveal a depth of commitment that serves as an example to the nonbeliever. We are not merely paying lip service to our religion. We are showing that our faith is an intrinsic and indispensable way of life.

Faith in action means that we reflect Christ's love in our own lives. We develop perseverance, continuing to exhibit joy and faith in the midst of a nonbeliever's doubts.

Faith in action means that we forgive others. Our willingness to forgive is a measure of our faith that God is in control, and that He can use our past experiences, no matter how negative, for His purposes.

Faith in action involves serving others with joy and compassion. Service is the physical expression of Christian love. The unbelieving spouse will know the believer's faith is real and vital when he sees the depth of the believer's commitment to others.

Through faith in action, the Christian shows that a meaningful, purposeful life is possible when we place God first.

CHAPTER FOUR

Attitudes That Sabotage

"Each of you should look not only to your own interests, but also to the interests of others. Your attitude should be the same as that of Christ Jesus." Philippians 2:4,5

Becoming joyful Christians and exhibiting faith in action are crucial aspects of leading by example. We are showing that our faith is a source of joy and a vital part of everything we do. But there are three attitudes so poisonous to the spirit that they can sabotage our efforts and send us down a path of negative thinking. They are self-pity, self-righteousness, and envy.

Self-pity, self-righteousness, and envy will ruin our efforts to be effective examples of Christ's love if we allow them to run rampant in our lives. We lose our ability to influence our spouse, blocking the flow of God's transforming love, when we indulge in these attitudes that sabotage.

Self Pity

Self-pity stems from our erroneous expectation that life will be fair. Regardless of all the evidence to the contrary, we continue to cling naively to the notion that we will find justice at the hands of other people. The person who works the hardest should earn the most money. The honest, righteous, upstanding person should win more admiration than the rap singer who makes millions off music that celebrates violence and denigrates women. The good wife and mother should not lose her husband to a younger woman.

But let's face it. Life isn't fair, and when we are on the receiving end of what we perceive to be an injustice, we are vulnerable to self-pity.

> "I should have had that promotion. I worked harder, but there's a glass ceiling for women in the business world."

> "That policeman questioned me because I'm black. I wasn't doing anything except minding my own business. We're always harassed in such a prejudiced society."

> "My husband has a stimulating job, adult conversation and a paycheck. I'm home changing diapers, cleaning spitup off my clothes, chasing a toddler and rushing a six-year-old to the hospital for stitches. Then he has the nerve to ask why I can't fix myself up a little more before he gets home!"

> "I've always been a faithful husband and good father. I helped around the house and turned down promotions because my wife didn't want to move. And now she's left me for another man."

Life isn't fair, and we react by feeling sorry for ourselves. We nurse a destructive self-pity that prevents the fullest expression of Christian love. Depending on men instead of God for justice, we are unable to overcome the resentments that fester against life's inequities. No matter how justified we feel in our self-pity, we lose our ability to influence our spouse through joyful Christian attitudes.

Let's have a Pity Party

When I was a single newspaper reporter in my early twenties, I frequently needed to work on weekends. My friends, who only worked five days a week and earned more money than I did, lounged by the pool at our apartment on Saturdays and Sundays. They invited me to swim and sunbathe with them, but I usually had a pressing news event to cover. I enjoyed the stimulating challenge of newspaper work: covering town board meetings, writing features about interesting people, and finding a forum for my opinions on the editorial page. I didn't enjoy sunbathing, since I am one of those fair-skinned types who freckles and burns. Nevertheless, I succumbed to an occasional stab of self-pity. Why didn't I earn more if I had to work on my days off? Why couldn't I find time to lounge around the pool? I was missing out on all the fun!

My roommate at that time, Jeanie Jones, did not succumb readily to self-pity. I remember one instance in particular, when I dragged myself back to our apartment after an especially grueling week. A dozen news stories had flown at me from every direction, making it impossible to get them all written by press time.

"I'm single and don't have time to meet anyone," I complained. "In this job, there's no time for a social life, and the pay is rock-bottom."

"Then we'll have a pity party," Jeanie announced.

"A what?"

"A pity party. We'll feel very sorry for ourselves for ten minutes, but after that, time's up. We can't feel sorry for ourselves anymore."

I have thought about our "pity party" many times since that day. If we could all relegate an attitude of self-pity to ten minutes, then get on with our lives, we would be a lot better off. People who refuse to succumb to self-pity under trying and sometimes devastating circumstances reveal an impressive degree of fortitude and tenacity.

From Defeat to Victory

He seemed destined to fail at whatever he tried. He failed in business in '31. In '32, he ran for the Legislature and was defeated. His fiancee died in '35. He went back into politics and was defeated in the election of '38. He ran for Congress and was defeated in '43. He ran for Congress and was defeated in '46. He lost a race for the Senate in '55. He was defeated for Vice President in '56. He ran again for the Senate and lost in '58.

Many people would have succumbed to self-pity at this point. They would have given up. "I can't succeed at anything. This isn't for me," they might have said.

Not this man. In 1860, Abraham Lincoln was elected President of the United States.

Martin Luther King was another man who refused to give in to self-pity. His home was bombed by terrorists, he was arrested and jailed several times while protesting injustice, yet he continued to lead the nonviolent struggle against racism. At the end of one long day in his struggle for justice, he was slated to speak on the lawn of Washington Mall. Taking a slot at the end of the schedule, he let other speakers have their say first. The crowd began to dwindle as the day progressed. The other speakers concluded their remarks. Martin Luther King did not feel sorry for himself because he had agreed to speak last. He did not resent the fact that many people had already left. He stepped to the podium and delivered his great *I Have A Dream* speech.

He Chose To Look Forward

Christopher Reeve, the actor who won wide recognition for his role as Superman, was paralyzed from the neck down in a horseback riding accident. Many people wondered how this superb athlete, an actor who performed many of his own stunts, would adjust to such a tragedy. This is what Christopher Reeve said recently at an inspirational seminar: "It is my great good fortune to have wonderful friends and family. I don't want to look backwards. I want to look forward."

Reeve acknowledged the extent of his loss. But in that loss, there had been tremendous gain. The former superstar said he had acquired a deeper appreciation for friendship, love, opportunity, and for simply being alive.

Reeve decided not to give in to self-pity and despair. He chose to look forward, setting an example of optimism, courage, and hope.

The Thing We Need To Remember

When we come face to face with life's inequities, we need to remember that God is always fair. The injustices we see now will not always prevail. By casting aside self-pity, we are able to forge ahead, experiencing true joy even in the face of apparent injustice.

The believer married to a nonbeliever may be tempted to indulge in self-pity, especially when the believer sees Christian couples attending church and enjoying church functions together. This attitude is self-defeating and harmful, undermining the believer's love for and commitment to an unbelieving spouse. It will breed resentment, not only in the Christian but also in his or her spouse, who will sense the dissatisfaction expressed through self-pity.

Surrendering to self-pity because you have an unsaved partner is a refusal to recognize God's sovereignty in all matters. When you feel sorry for yourself, you are admitting that you believe God was unfair to allow your present circumstances. Being a joyful, faithful Christian means refusing to succumb to self-pity. By refusing to feel sorry for yourself, you avoid conveying the message that you think you could have done a lot better in the marriage department. You reject an attitude that can sabotage your efforts to be a joyful, effective Christian.

Self-Righteousness

For a long time, I sympathized with the self-righteous older brother in the prodigal son parable. If you remember, the younger of two sons approached his father requesting his share of the estate. The father obliged, dividing his property between his sons. The younger one left home and squandered his inheritance on prostitutes and wasteful living. After he had spent everything, he hired himself out to feed pigs that were eating better than he was. Coming to his senses, the younger brother decided to return home and beg his father for a job as a hired man.

But the father, spotting him from a distance, was so filled with love and compassion that he forgave his son everything. He wouldn't hear of his son returning as a hired man. Instead, he told his servants to plan a party. They would kill a calf and have a feast! His long-lost son was back!

Meanwhile the older son, who was toiling in the fields, found out about the celebration. He was furious. In fact, he was so upset that he refused to attend. His father pleaded with him, but the older brother said, "I've been slaving for you all these years, and you never even gave me a goat so I could celebrate with my friends. Yet you end up killing a calf for this son of yours who wasted your money."

Every time I heard this story, I felt my self-righteous anger growing right along with the older brother's. I understood his response. It wasn't fair that the younger brother could go off and have a great time, while the older brother stayed home and did what he was supposed to do, only to have a big party thrown in honor of the young scoundrel.

But the more I have studied Scripture, the more I have come to comprehend the negative impact of the older brother's resentment. *When we wrap ourselves in a cloak of self-righteousness, we are closing ourselves to the loving and forgiving spirit that is at the root of Christ's teachings.*

The younger brother sinned, repented, asked for forgiveness and was forgiven. The older brother did not recognize his sin, but it was a sin which effectively blocked love and compassion for both his father and his brother. It is difficult to feel self-righteous and compassionate at the same time. The first emotion can fester until it becomes contempt or hatred. The second emotion can stir us to love and forgiveness.

God Doesn't Make Junk

Self-righteousness is born in pride, yet what do we possess that God hasn't given us? Our intelligence, earning capacity, physical appearance, background, skills and talents are all God given, so they should not become sources of arrogance. The Bible tells us that "God opposes the proud but gives grace to the humble." This does not mean God wants us to say, "I'm awful and stupid. I can't do a thing." To denigrate ourselves is the equivalent of saying God makes junk. Humility in the biblical sense means that we recognize and give credit to God as the source of our blessings. A properly humble spirit, the spirit Christ himself exhibited when he insisted on washing the feet of his disciples, cannot coexist with a proud self-righteousness. *No one has a reason to indulge in self-righteousness.*

What If?

Once when I was thumbing through a magazine, I came across a picture of a baby. He was as cute as any other baby, with a cherubic expression defining a round, chubby face. Upon reading the caption, I discovered that this was a picture of Hitler as a child. How could this baby become a hate-filled monster, responsible for the death of millions? Yet, all heinous crimes are committed by someone who was once an infant, with the God-given potential for goodness inherent in that small body.

In reading about the lives of criminals, serial killers, rapists and murderers, I frequently discover that they grew up in loveless, abusive homes, without fathers or with drug-addicted mothers. Sometimes they have been bounced from foster home to foster home, after being severely beaten by their own parents. Fending for themselves in violent environments, without positive role models or exposure to God's word, these children have grown up to be criminals without conscience or hope. The potential that was there to start with is twisted and warped by the devastating power of evil.

Then I think of my own childhood, in a warm and loving home with parents who took me to church every Sunday. I think of the sacrifices my parents made to dress me nicely, of the numerous times they needed to exert firm but loving discipline in their effort to instill a sense of right and wrong and curb the inclinations of my stubborn, wayward human nature.

Where would I be today, I often wonder, if I had grown up in an abusive environment bereft of love and decency and knowledge of God? *"There but by the grace of God go I"* is an expression that comes to mind. It is enough to dampen those self-righteous tendencies that surface from time to time in thoughts like, "Why should I call myself a sinner? I don't do anything really bad. I deserve that more than she does."

Don't Miss The Celebration!

When we engage in self-righteousness, we are not acting in a spirit of love. The Apostle Paul said, "If I speak in the tongues of men and of angels, but have not love, I am only a resounding gong or a clanging symbol. If I have the gift of prophecy and can fathom all mysteries and all knowledge, and if I have a faith that can move mountains, but have not love, I am nothing. If I give all I possess to the poor and surrender my body to the flames, but have not love, I gain nothing" (1 Corinthians:13:1-3).

We are sabotaging our opportunity to be joyful Christians if we cling to a sense of self-righteousness until it blocks our receptivity to love and compassion. By relinquishing his self-righteousness, the older brother could have attended the celebration. He could have enjoyed the fatted calf, too.

"You are always with me, and everything I have is yours," the father told him. Let's not miss the celebration because we resent someone else's presence there!

Envy

The husband and wife were an attractive couple, intelligent and outgoing, well off financially, with many common interests. They seemed perfectly matched, so it was a surprise to everyone when they divorced.

"He just couldn't stand it that I made more money than he did, and I was moving up the corporate ladder faster," the woman said later. "He was envious of my success."

Envy wields its insidious influence until the best of relationships are destroyed. King Saul, once David's friend and mentor, became so envious that he tried to murder David.

He ended up destroying himself and his family, while David went on to become king.

The jealousy Joseph's brothers felt toward him led them to sell him into slavery. Sarah, envious of her servant, Hagar, mistreated her until Hagar ran away. The first murder sprang from Cain's envy of his brother, Able, when God accepted Able's offering but not Cain's. Jealously and envy, coveting someone else's achievements, status, possessions, appearance, or anything else we think a person has that we would like to have, is one of the biggest stumbling blocks on our road toward becoming joyful Christians.

Envy's Destructive Power

Envy's destructive power was emphasized in a newspaper article with this headline: "Jealousy called motive in Douglas murder trial." According to the article, jealousy and animosity drove a man to use an ax to kill his boss, a wealthy stable owner. This is jealousy, the powerful motivator, carried to its extreme.

Even when envy isn't carried to its extreme, it has the power to negatively impact our lives. A friend I will call Laura was devastated following her layoff from a major company. Determined not to yield to despair, she went into business for herself. After extensive training and many long hours, she began to meet with considerable success. Her dearest friend, a woman who had been her confidante and a rock of support through the bleak months of joblessness, did not rejoice over the turnaround in Laura's fortunes. Instead, to Laura's surprise and dismay, the friend was unsupportive and envious. The friendship survived but was irreparably damaged, limping along without the earlier bond of love and support.

Envy is a repudiation of the gifts God has given us. By succumbing to jealousy we are, in effect, saying "God hasn't given me enough of my own blessings and abilities. I deserve more, so I will covet yours."

Envy is also a violation of God's commandment that we love our neighbors as ourselves. We do not love those people we envy. The opposite can occur when envy crosses the threshold into hatred and rage. At this point, it is sometimes essential to turn our envy over to God, asking Him to replace a jealous and envious spirit with a spirit of true love for the object of our envy.

In Proverbs 14:30, we are told that "A heart at peace gives life to the body, but envy rots the bones." What a graphic description of envy, hidden from the world but rotting our very bones and causing decay that will make it impossible for us to be healthy and whole! The rot might remain hidden for a while, but it is bound to emerge, damaging relationships, destroying lives, and robbing us of our joy.

Relinquishing envy means accepting God's blessings without coveting the gifts bestowed on others. The bitter dregs of discontent give way to a peace that comes with the understanding that God is in control. His gifts to us will be uniquely suited to our spiritual needs.

The Resentment Barrier

Attitudes of self-pity, self-righteousness, and envy can plague the believer married to the nonbeliever, resulting in a resentment barrier that is hard to overcome. The Christian who feels sorry for himself because he is not married to a Christian woman, the self-righteous believer who feels spiritually superior to her mate, the believing spouse who is envious of her unbelieving husband's "freedom" to indulge in behavior that she considers unreligious, are all entertaining negative attitudes that lead to "resentment barriers." These barriers cause the nonbeliever to feel justified in his unbelief and the believer to feel stymied in his attempts to exhibit Christ's love through positive action.

We can only lead by example when we overcome these attitudes that sabotage. Self-pity, self-righteousness, and envy will drag us down, preventing us from becoming joyful Christians. We must avoid them, choosing instead to be made new in the attitude of our minds; to "put on the new self, created to be like God in true righteousness and holiness" (Ephesians 4:24).

Chapter Summary

There are three attitudes that can sabotage our efforts to be joyful Christians. They are **self-pity, self-righteousness** and **envy.**

The first of these, self-pity, stems from our erroneous expectation that life will be fair. When we come face to face with life's inequities, we need to remember that God is always fair. The injustices we see now will not always prevail. **By casting aside self-pity, we are able to forge ahead, experiencing true joy even in the face of apparent injustice.**

Self-righteousness is never justified. When we wrap ourselves in a cloak of self-righteousness, we are closing ourselves to the loving and forgiving spirit that is at the root of Christ's teachings. **We are sabotaging our opportunity to be joyful Christians if we cling to a sense of self-righteousness until it blocks our receptivity to love and compassion.**

Envy is a repudiation of the gifts God has given us. By succumbing to covetousness we are, in effect, saying, "God hasn't given me enough of my own blessings and abilities. I deserve more, so I will covet yours." **Envy is a violation of God's commandment that we love our neighbors as ourselves.**

These negative attitudes can form resentment barriers that cause the nonbeliever to feel justified in his unbelief and the believer to feel stymied in his attempts to exhibit Christ's love through positive action.

"Unless the Lord builds the house, its builders labor in vain." Psalm 127:1

Part Two

Building The Marriage Relationship

CHAPTER FIVE

The Key Is Commitment

"And if a woman has a husband who is not a believer and he is willing to live with her, she must not divorce him. For the unbelieving husband has been sanctified through his wife, and the unbelieving wife has been sanctified through her believing husband." 1 Corinthians 7:13,14

The first section of this book stressed the importance of joyful Christian living designed to kindle in the unbelieving spouse a desire for faith in Jesus Christ. We want our spouse to see faith in action and say, "I want that for myself!"

This second section is devoted to building the marriage relationship. The qualities we develop as joyful Christians will greatly enhance the marriage, but this section goes beyond our own attitudes, to an examination of the marriage itself and how we can strengthen it.

The good marriage, constructed on a foundation of love, respect, commitment, and enjoyment of each other's uniqueness, will move naturally toward a state of spiritual oneness. *A good marriage is important because it is within the framework of a good marriage that the believer has the best chance of influencing the nonbeliever.*

Love, respect, and enjoyment of each other's uniqueness are crucial aspects of a successful relationship. But without commitment, there can be no good marriage, no safe harbor for the fullest expression of our love. In his book, *Can Man Live Without God,* Dr. Ravi Zacharias says, "It is in the nature of love to honor its commitments; to bind itself. If we do not understand this, all we do is transfer a pathetic self-centeredness masquerading as love."

Without a firm and nonnegotiable commitment, we cannot create an arena for spiritual growth and development. Our love will degenerate into self-centeredness, which cannot masquerade as love for long. *Without commitment, the path to spiritual oneness and marital happiness will forever elude us. We will have little chance of influencing our spouse to accept Jesus Christ as Lord and Savior if we are not fully committed to the marriage.*

The Magic Vanished

In the movie, "The River Wild," the main character is married to a workaholic who refuses to make time for his family. Gail, played by actress Meryl Streep, decides the marriage is over when she is forced to vacation without her husband for the third year in a row. Explaining this decision to her mother, Gail points out that her husband is never home, not even at Christmas. His indifference to his wife and two children is making things unbelievably hard.

Gail's mother, who uses sign language to communicate with Gail's deaf father, replies, "You don't know what hard is, because you give yourself an out. You think if I gave myself an out with your father, with his orneriness and deafness, I wouldn't have taken it years ago?"

With divorce occurring in one out of every two marriages, we all know that marriage can be hard, and that many people give themselves an "out." Even those marriages that hang together sometimes do so by a thread, with two people going in separate directions. They are bound by habit, children, convenience, or religious convictions, but they are missing that spark of enchantment and love that initially brought them together. These couples probably can't say exactly when affection became irritability and thinly-veiled hostility. They only know that somewhere along the line the magic vanished. Marriage, to these couples, has become a drudgery rather than a delight. The relationship has lost its potential to foster spiritual growth.

Yet, not all marriages fit this dismal mold. Some couples manage to retain that special electricity and magnetism; that strong attraction which states so eloquently, "You are the one. Nothing will come between us."

What makes these marriages different? Why are some couples better able to weather the storms and vicissitudes of everyday life? Why do some husbands and wives continue to grow in love after ten, twenty, or thirty years? Is this a secret unique to a minute portion of the population?

Commitment: A Decision

Growing in love after many years of marriage is not a unique secret limited to the lucky few. Most of the couples who are still in love after twenty or thirty or forty years made a *decision* to love each other. Inherent in that decision was their *commitment* to the relationship. These husbands and wives seem to cherish and nurture the characteristics which initially attracted them to each other. They have learned that marriage is something you work at, but is also a significant source of pleasure and companionship. In many instances, they have chosen to put aside a natural human selfishness and place the other partner's interests first. They have often had to weather significant storms in the relationship. At these times, commitment to the marriage became more important than their own immediate happiness.

It is interesting that couples who live together before getting married have a higher statistical probability of divorcing than couples who marry without living together first. According to popular thinking, the opposite was supposed to occur. Couples who tested their compatibility beforehand were presumed to be in a better position to commit to a permanent relationship.

What is happening here? Why are couples who opt for a trial run at greater risk of divorcing? The answer seems obvious. A "living together" arrangement leaves out the one thing, commitment, which would truly bind the relationship. These couples are saying, in effect, "I'm not really sure about this yet. I want the advantages of a relationship, but I'm not ready to say, *I love you enough to spend the rest of my life with you.*" Living together doesn't test commitment, yet commitment is crucial to the success of a marriage.

What The World Offers

The world offers us no-fault divorce and the encouragement to go out and "find ourselves." Single mothers are now the accepted norm. One mother, when speaking of her and her friends' single status, said, "We've found out we can live without men!"

But this was not God's plan when He said in Genesis 2:28, "It is not good that man should be alone. I will make him a helper suitable for him." Marriage, designed to relieve mankind's fundamental loneliness, was God's blessing to us.

Commitment is indispensable in building a happy marriage and moving toward spiritual oneness. It creates an arena for spiritual growth unhindered by a demand for immediate change. When we commit to a relationship, we are saying, "I'm in this for the long haul, through good times and bad, and I won't bail out at the first signs of trouble."

There could be times when commitment is easy, requiring no effort, and times when it is a decision at odds with our pursuit of pleasure. But it is always the cornerstone of a relationship; the foundation from which all else is built.

Commitment is difficult because it requires self-discipline, a trait that contradicts our proclivity for self-indulgence. When an athlete aspires to the Olympics, he trains extensively, exercising tremendous self-discipline and foregoing many immediate pleasures that would derail him from attaining his goal. In striving toward a successful marriage, we may have to exercise tremendous self-discipline and forego some immediate pleasures that would derail us from the ultimate goal.

Commitment, like faith, can run up against the rocky patches of doubt and disillusionment. C.S. Lewis said that faith is holding onto what we once knew to be true in the belief that it will one day be true again. Commitment to the marriage is remaining in a relationship that used to be good in the belief that it will one day be good again. By adhering to our commitment through the rocky patches, we can transform the relationship.

Commitment does not mean avoiding confrontation at all costs. Good marriages are never completely devoid of conflict, since people bring into marriage, as into any relationship, ideas and beliefs that will occasionally clash. But in a good marriage, the conflict is not damaging to the marriage itself, which is strong enough to withstand the bumps and nicks of day-to-day moods, temperaments, varying opinions, and even catastrophes. The positive outweighs the negative, with couples deriving pleasure and satisfaction from the married relationship and from each other. *A good marriage can withstand conflict, but it cannot withstand lack of commitment.*

There Had To Be Something More

A man I will refer to as Joe was a successful salesman holding a lucrative job with a high tech company. He and his wife had been married twelve years and were the parents of three children between four and ten years old. There were no major problems in their lives, no financial setbacks, illnesses, or other crises. Yet Joe found himself increasingly depressed and unable to control his temper. He blew up at the slightest provocation. His wife, whose best friend was going through a divorce, decided divorce might not be such a bad thing. Divorcing would be better than living with someone who was always irritable and angry. Joe agreed. They weren't that happy, so there seemed to be little reason for staying together. Maybe a change could cure him of the depression hovering like an inescapable black cloud. Joe rationalized that the children would probably be better off in a more placid environment, away from all the arguing.

More and more, I hear about situations like this. The circumstances may differ somewhat. One woman left her husband of fifteen years because she wanted to "find herself." The couple, blessed with tremendous financial resources, lived a lavish lifestyle. They owned several vacation homes and a fleet of expensive cars, but the wife wasn't happy. She had fallen out of love. She felt there had to be something more.

Infidelity and abuse weren't problems in these cases. There were no cataclysmic incidences precipitating a divorce. There were no great trials or tribulations testing their endurance and patience to the limits. One or more of the partners simply decided they would be happier apart.

Divorce isn't limited to the young. According to the Census Bureau, 1.3 million people 65 and older are currently divorced. Thirty percent of women 50 to 54 can expect their first marriage to eventually end in divorce. In our world of happiness at all costs, commitment among married couples of all ages has taken a nosedive.

A Disposable Commodity

In marriages where the partners are "unequally yoked," the believing spouse might feel attraction toward another person who is "more spiritual." We all have the desire for a relationship with someone who shares our beliefs. The nonbeliever who does not have religious convictions which serve as a barrier to extramarital attraction might seek an alliance with someone who better "understands" him.

Even in marriages between partners who are both believers, commitment has become a disposable commodity, discarded like a worn-out coat when it interferes with personal fulfillment. As Gail's mother in *A River Wild* said, "We give ourselves an out."

No Excuse For Abuse

Let me stress here that commitment does not mean staying in a relationship when one partner is committing adultery without repentance, or when a spouse is physically and emotionally abusive. Consider what Malachi 2:13-16 says about God's reasons for making husband and wife one in flesh and spirit, and our Lord's reaction to a violation of that loving oneness:

"Another thing you do: You flood the Lord's altar with tears. You weep and wail because He no longer pays attention to your offerings or accepts them with pleasure from your hands. You ask, "Why?" It is because the Lord is acting as the witness between you and the wife of your youth, because you have broken faith with her, though she is your partner, the wife of your marriage covenant.

"Has not the Lord made them one? In flesh and spirit they are his. And why one? Because he was seeking godly offspring. So guard yourself in your spirit, and do not break faith with the wife of your youth.

"I hate divorce," says the Lord God of Israel, "and I hate a man's covering himself with violence as well as with his garment," says the Lord Almighty. "So guard yourself in spirit, and do not break faith."

Husbands are instructed to love their wives just as Christ loved the church and to love their wives as their own bodies. Colossians 3:19 states: "Husbands, love your wives and do not be harsh with them."

Physical and emotional abuse are violations of the marriage covenant. They result in loss of respect for the victimized partner and great damage to children who witness repeated abuse. An abusive partner who does not respect his mate will not respect her faith. The children of abusive relationships frequently grow up to perpetuate the cycle, repeating the sort of relationships they have experienced at home. Parents should not remain in abusive relationships when children are suffering irreparable harm. This was not God's intended plan for marriage, as a gift to ease our loneliness and as an environment for raising godly children.

Sometimes a separation is in the best interests of the abusive partner's spiritual welfare. This was true in the case of a man who had been an alcoholic for twenty years. Finally his wife, unable to change his behavior, left. Three days later, the man became a Christian. Unfortunately, after all else has failed, an abusive spouse may have to be brought to his knees before he relinquishes sinful behavior.

Paul called on church members to expel a sexually immoral and unrepentant person from the church so *the sinful nature might be destroyed and the spirit saved.* Separation from an abusive spouse should be viewed from this perspective, as a means of destroying the sinful nature. Separation should not to be used to validate divorce so the victimized partner can rationalize marrying someone better.

The victimized spouse will have to decide whether change is possible within the present circumstances, or whether adultery and abuse justify separation for the purpose of bringing about a change in the abusive partner's spiritual life. Either way, *commitment* to the relationship is a determining factor. There can be many different expressions of commitment, depending on the particular circumstances involved. One person may change as a result of a partner's continued love and unconditional support throughout infidelities and abusive behavior. Another person might have to undergo the devastating effects of a separation.

If you or your spouse has undergone a previous divorce, commitment to your present marriage relationship is no less important. You may even need to make an extra commitment to show as much love toward your spouse's children by a previous marriage as you show toward your own children. *Your love and acceptance of your spouse's children could be a powerful witness to your unbelieving spouse, who will see faith in action as you work to overcome the resentment barriers and emotional anguish sometimes characterizing children of divorce.*

Commitment to Fidelity

The woman sitting across from me was in her mid-forties. Her long, dark hair framed a still-attractive face. "I just can't help myself," she confided sadly. "I know I'm doing wrong and I'm going to hell for it, but I just can't seem to get out of this affair. I meet my lover anytime he wants."

The woman was married to a kind, devoted man. They were the parents of three children. But she found her husband boring. "We don't have anything in common. I can't even think of anything to talk to him about. He comes home and watches TV, then falls asleep in his chair. My lover makes me happy!"

I don't know what happened to this woman's marriage. I moved away, and we lost touch. But I have seen a number of marriages since then ripped apart by infidelity. There is no place in the marriage relationship for this ultimate violation of sacred vows and this shattering of the trust that binds husband and wife together.

Our society doesn't value sexual fidelity. There is not much peer pressure steering us toward morality. Temptations are everywhere and restraint is frowned upon. Businessmen entertain clients at topless bars. Lobbyists hire strippers to accompany politicians on out of town junkets. Sex scandals have dogged our country's leaders, exposing a depth of corruption that makes yesterday's escapades seem like child's play. Television is so filled with sexual innuendos and filth that it is an embarrassment to watch it with our children. Pop psychologists advocate in their best selling books that we leave our restrictive marriages and taste the wonderful fruits of freedom and sexual exploration.

The rampant spread of sexually transmitted diseases, including HIV, has not served to end the era of sexual promiscuity. In such an environment, with no cultural restrictions on infidelity, the marriage partners must be as committed to the institution of marriage as they are to each other. Commitment to fidelity has to be strong enough to withstand the selfish desire for personal fulfillment or sexual excitement outside the marriage. Once the barrier of adultery has been crossed, the damage is often irreparable. Fidelity is an essential element of commitment. A violation of this trust can rend the most carefully-wrought structure asunder.

As Proverbs 6:32 warns, "A man who commits adultery lacks judgment; whoever does so destroys himself. Blows and disgrace are his lot, and his shame will never be wiped away."

God's Plan Versus Man's

In Biblical times, when more than one mate was often sanctioned by men even though it violated God's perfect plan for marriage, there were often lasting hostilities and repercussions. The rivalry between Joseph, a child of Jacob's favorite wife, Rachel, and his brothers, the sons of Jacob's other wife, Leah, was so intense that it almost led to Joseph's murder. Instead, one of Joseph's kinder brothers prevailed and Joseph was sold into slavery.

There was considerable animosity between Abraham's wife, Sarah, and her servant, Hagar, when Hagar became pregnant with Abraham's child, even though the whole thing had been Sarah's idea. Hagar began to despise her mistress, which led to Sarah's mistreatment and eventual banishment of Hagar. Hostilities exist to this day in the Middle East between the descendants of Hagar and the descendants of Sarah.

King David suffered the consequences of marrying more than one woman when the children of his various marriages became embroiled in a cauldron of incest, rape, and murder. David's son Ammon raped his half-sister, Tamar, resulting in Ammon's murder by Tamar's full brother, Absalom. Absalom, who incited an uprising against his father, was murdered by David's men. In one of the most profound expressions of grief in all literature, David cried, "O my son Absalom! My son, my son Absalom! If only I had died, instead of you, O Absalom, my son, my son."

God allowed men and women to persist in their own ways, taking additional wives or concubines, but they were not spared the consequences.

Fidelity and *commitment* were part of God's perfect plan. Commitment is the natural starting point from which a desire to nurture the relationship takes root and grows. Without commitment, the desire is short-lived, subject to the fluctuating whims of the moment. With it, the foundation is firm. Brick by brick, step by step, we can begin the process of building toward spiritual oneness.

The Christian's commitment to an unbelieving spouse means that the Christian has made a decision to accept the unbeliever in spite of his unbelief. The believer will nurture the relationship, creating the fertile soil of openness so vital to effective witnessing. He or she will work to forge an environment of love, respect, and shared pleasure leading naturally toward a good marriage through which God's love can flow.

Now That's Commitment!

There are few times when commitment literally means holding another person's life in your hands. But to Toshika, this is the form commitment took on a fateful day in 1994. In a special feature for *Reader's Digest,* Lawrence Elliott wrote about the 1994 earthquake that devastated the city of Kobe in Japan, claiming 5502 lives. He cited many examples of love and courage during that horrifying ordeal, including Toshika's story.

The wife of 69-year-old Hanjiro Shibahara, Toshika was seldom able to leave her husband's side. That's because Hanjiro Shibahara suffered from a wasting muscular disease that had left him paralyzed and speechless, unable to breathe without the aid of an automatic respirator that pushed air into his lungs through a permanent opening in his throat. Toshiko's only relief came on weekends, when her 32-year-old daughter, Mari, visited.

Mari was visiting on that Monday night before the earthquake. Shaken awake before dawn amid shattering glass and crashing furniture, Mari heard the high-pitched whine of her father's respirator alarm. This was a signal that both the electricity and his emergency battery had been knocked out.

Dashing to her father's room, she found Toshiko already there, urging her husband to breathe. Mari searched frantically in the dark through an open closet, where she found a manual respirator that would pump air when squeezed with both hands. Hurriedly she connected the hand pump to the respirator tube and connected that to her father's trachea. Then she began squeezing the rubber sac that would enable her father to breathe.

While Mari pumped, Toshika tried calling for help, but the telephone didn't work. She located a neighbor with a cellular phone, only to discover that the hospital line was out. The terrible truth began to sink in. There was no way to call for help! As long as they were without electricity, the two women would have to keep pumping air from the hand respirator.

In the hours that followed, mother and daughter took turns squeezing the rubber sac. They forced themselves to stay awake, talking continuously to Hanjiro. They were afraid if they stopped talking that Hanjiro would fall asleep, never to wake up again.

A second day passed without electricity. By 6 p.m. the women, deadened by exhaustion, had pumped the lifesaving sac some 32,000 times. The electricity flickered on for a few hours, then failed again. The women kept pumping. Finally, at 1:30 p.m. on the third day, the electricity came back on to stay, ending an ordeal that had lasted 55 hours.

When reporters asked Toshiko what it felt like, holding her husband's life in her hands, she replied that it was just as though it had been her own life. Commitment, for richer, for poorer; in sickness and in health, for better or worse; this is the kind of commitment Toshiko understood.

Chapter Summary

Commitment is indispensable in building a happy marriage and moving toward spiritual oneness. It creates an arena for spiritual growth unhindered by a demand for immediate change. Commitment is a decision at odds with our secular emphasis on selfishness.

Commitment is no excuse for abuse. It does not mean remaining in a relationship when one partner is committing adultery without repentance, or when a spouse is physically and emotionally abusive. Sometimes a separation is in the best interests of an abusive partner's spiritual welfare.

Fidelity is an essential element of commitment. A violation of this trust can rend the most carefully-wrought structure asunder.

In Biblical times, when more than one mate was often sanctioned by men even though it violated God's perfect plan for marriage, lasting hostilities and repercussions resulted. God allows us to make choices, but we are not spared the consequences.

CHAPTER SIX

Nurturing The Relationship

"The fruit of the righteous is a tree of life, and he who wins souls is wise."
Proverbs 11:30

Cliff was beginning to meet with consistent success in his job as a sales representative. His wife was happy with her career and their children were doing well in school. Everything seemed to be going along fine. Cliff wasn't the type to say, "I love you," or to surprise his wife with a bouquet of flowers. He didn't go in for all that mushy stuff. He didn't feel like he needed to. He was a good provider. He helped out with the children when his wife went out of town on business. She was one of those levelheaded women who understood that he loved her without his having to prove it over and over again. He was glad he had married such a sensible, undemanding woman.

Then one day Cliff's wife dropped the bomb. She announced that she was leaving. She wanted a divorce as soon as possible. The relationship had withered when Cliff wasn't paying attention.

Isn't it amazing that couples who fall in love so readily seem unable to stay in love? They enter marriage with the greatest expectations, but fail to build the intimacy necessary for the survival of the relationship.

When couples are dating, they put their best foot forward. They walk hand in hand, attuned to each other, smiling radiantly or engrossed in conversation that seems to exclude the rest of the world. They marry, and something happens. She is tired and distracted from taking care of the kids. The house is a mess. He wants some quiet time after work, and she wants to talk. Their conversation is interrupted by quarreling children, or it deteriorates into an argument over finances and spending. They are caught in a whirlwind of careers and chores and demands that leaves little time or energy for anything else. Reality appears to bear out the veracity of the cliche, "There's nothing like a marriage to break up a romance."

When Love Loses Its Bloom

Sometimes love seems to have lost its bloom. I have known married people who, after examining their lives and their mates, suddenly asked themselves, "Is this all there is?" In some instances, they got out of the relationship to search for that elusive "more." Other couples who stuck it out during the doubting times discovered love was still there, submerged beneath several layers of neglect and indifference. Just as they remained faithful to their beliefs when God appeared to be silent, they remained faithful to their love when love seemed to have diminished. They knew that in due time, with proper nourishment, love would flower again, more beautiful than ever.

But how do we nurture a relationship? How do we keep the bloom from fading and the routine from turning monotonous? How do we hold onto the magic amid the competing pressures of life? These are questions most everyone asks, and these are questions this chapter seeks to address. They are important questions, because *nourishing the relationship is crucial to a good marriage. The believer has a much better chance of influencing the nonbeliever if ordinary, day-to-day interactions between husband and wife have served to bolster and enhance their love for each other.*

Three things nourish and enrich a relationship, building that crucial intimacy which acts as a buffer against the onslaught of day-to-day life. These three things, *praise, humor,* and *touch*, can lift the relationship above the realm of the ordinary, transporting it to a new level of oneness. Warmed by the glow of sincere appreciation, enhanced by the pleasure of shared laughter, and electrified by the magic of affectionate touching, few marriages can fail to become recharged. Even those partners who feel they have "fallen out of love" can recapture the magic they thought they lost. In fact, those who believe they never loved their partners can learn to love.

Nurturing With Praise

I used to ride a feisty little mare with a noticeable stubborn streak. It was hard to persuade her to do anything she didn't want to do. I could try to urge her forward using all the rider's aids at my command, or I could give her a smart rap across the rump with a crop. But if she decided she didn't want to cross a stream, or go down an unfamiliar road, or venture too far away from the barn, there was no forcing the issue. Too much persuasion, and she was inclined to get rid of her rider.

Then I made an interesting discovery. I found that this little mare was especially susceptible to praise. When I complimented her she proceeded forward, crossing the stream, going down the road or trotting happily away from the barn as if the idea had been hers all along. All I had to say was, "Good girl!" and that little horse practically leaped to do my will.

Praise can work the same magic with people. I have seen my children motivated by the praise and approval of positive teachers and coaches. Not wanting to disappoint, they strove mightily to live up to these high expectations. Negative teachers and harsh coaches, on the other hand, served to bring out the same stubbornness in my children that I witnessed in my mare. My children rebelled immediately, opting to give one-tenth the effort rather than gratify a critical instructor.

Most people, from the child on the school bus to the man in the business suit, are bombarded by criticism and negative feedback. It is enough to bash the egos of the staunchest among us. Even if a relationship is free of overt criticism, a lack of praise can cause people to feel unappreciated and unloved. The spouse who is trying to build the marriage into a safe haven for the fullest expression of human love will make praise and positive feedback an integral part of the relationship.

"Do Not Withhold Good..."

"He criticizes everything about me, even the way I cook bacon," one woman complained.

"He never says anything positive or negative. He never says anything at all, so I don't think he needs me," another woman lamented. Both women are now divorced.

In his book, *Why Marriages Succeed or Fail,* psychologist John Gottman says there are four disastrous ways of interacting that sabotage our attempts to communicate with our partner. These four things, *criticism, contempt, defensiveness* and *stonewalling,* cause husband and wife to focus more and more on negativity and tension in their marriage.

Criticism, which involves attacking someone's personality or character, tears down, fosters negativism and feeds resentment. It is the opposite of praise, which builds up, focuses on the positive and nurtures the relationship.

A group of 12-year-olds on a neighborhood tennis team exemplified the potential criticism has for negatively impacting performance. These boys got into the habit of criticizing their doubles partners during matches. If a boy missed a shot or double-faulted on a serve, he was lambasted by his partner. He inevitably retaliated by pointing out his partner's mistakes.

Needless to say, this did not improve play among these 12-year-olds. They suffered a loss of confidence. Hostilities escalated. With this much negative baggage on the tennis court, the quality of play deteriorated. Following several losses, a coach and concerned team mom found it necessary to talk with them about the value of encouraging each other. As a result of this talk, their performance improved considerably.

"Love Builds Up"

In 1 Corinthians 8:1, we are told that "love builds up." Pointing out faults never changes anyone. It only breeds resentment. Criticism leads to the defensiveness, contempt, and stonewalling or silent treatment that Dr. Gottman refers to in his book.

Praise, on the other hand, is an expression of affection. It need not be lavish or excessive. It can be something as simple as, "I like the way you're so patient with the kids," or "You brighten my day when you get home from work." It builds up, restores confidence, and gives us strength to resist the battering of day-to-day life. We need to let our partner know he is special. Tell her how important she is to you over and over again. Learning to praise will teach you to search for the best in others, which frequently results in getting the best *out* of others.

Proverbs 3:27 advises us not to withhold good from those who deserve it, when it is in our power to act. To withhold praise from our spouse is to relinquish our power to strengthen the relationship. We might want our spouse to accept and learn from "constructive criticism," but it is generally more productive to "catch" him doing something right and opt for praise, instead.

The Picnic

It was a bright, sunny day with just a hint of fall hovering like a promise in the warm September air. Arlene and Brad decided to take advantage of the weather and their free afternoon by going on a picnic. Looking pretty in her long, denim dress and straw hat, Arlene filled a picnic basket with sandwiches, fruit, and cheese. Brad loaded lounge chairs, blanket, and thermoses in the minivan. The children had been left with friends, so this would be an outing for just the two of them. Arlene thought they might even drive to the mountains and have their picnic on the crest of a hill overlooking a picturesque valley. Envisioning mountain streams and cascading waterfalls, she mentioned her idea to Brad.

"You're not dressed for mountain hiking. Why don't you change into some jeans?" Brad replied.

"I didn't say I wanted to hike," Arlene retorted, irritated because she had taken special pains with her appearance. She usually wore jeans when they took the children along on a picnic. "You never like my ideas."

"All I did was mention that you might want to change so you'd be more comfortable."

"Just forget the mountains," Arlene snapped. "We'll go somewhere closer."

"I don't know why you have to take everything I say the wrong way," Brad mumbled resentfully.

"Quit being a jerk. Let's just go."

Angry frowns replaced smiles as Arlene and Brad slammed their car doors. The afternoon, so filled with promise, lay in tattered ruins beneath the weight of their hostility. A word of praise would have salvaged their picnic.

"You look great. I like that dress," Brad could have said.

"I don't want to go hiking. I just want to talk to you," Arlene might have pointed out. She could have complimented him on remembering to bring a blanket, or missing a televised football game to spend the afternoon with her. He could have mentioned the trouble she went to pack a good lunch. But they let these opportunities for praise slide by, with the result being that well-intentioned comments turned into criticism and escalating animosity.

Emotional Nourishment

Clinical psychologist Judith Wallerstein and coauthor Sandra Blakeslee point out in their book, *The Good Marriage,* that a main task of every marriage is for partners to nurture each other, replenishing each other's emotional reserves. When this is accomplished, the partners can gather the nourishment and confidence to venture out into the world. When it is not accomplished, the man or woman feels depleted and unappreciated. Part of this emotional nourishment takes the form of praise which reveals a genuine respect for and appreciation of the husband or wife.

Partners in successful marriages are not envious of what they give to each other. They do not parcel out kindness sparingly, hoping for some immediate return on their investment, nor do they keep records, chalking up deficits if they see themselves as being more supportive than the other partner. They accept that support and encouragement are a major part of the marriage relationship, necessary to the relationship's survival.

Happily married couples seem to know instinctively what Proverbs 11:25 teaches us: "A generous man will prosper; he who refreshes others will himself be refreshed." When we are generous with our praise, our generosity will be rewarded by a decreasing amount of tension and an increasing amount of affection that enhances and strengthens the marriage bond.

If you praise your partner, your partner is more likely to praise you. I can attest to this! Lee is a great "praiser," complimenting me frequently on everything from the clothes I'm wearing to the meal I've cooked to the way I've handled a certain situation with the children. I used to be a bit stingier with praise. Compliments just didn't seem to flow naturally and freely. Even when I saw a real reason for praising him I hesitated, thinking things like, "Maybe it will just go to his head." But Lee's constant barrage of compliments and support broke down my resistance. Gradually I learned to give him the type of encouragement he gave me, and it didn't go to his head, after all. He became even more loving and supportive.

Why Is Praising Difficult?

Why does it seem so hard for some of us to praise freely; to say, "I missed you today. You look great. I like your sense of humor. You're wonderful with the children. You mean so much to me"?

Part of it could stem from *upbringing*. Children who grow up without praise find it difficult to praise others.

Part of it could be *envy*. "Her job allows her to travel to exotic places, whereas I'm always stuck here. Why should I say I missed her?"

Part of it could be *fear of rejection*. "If I tell him he looks handsome, he'll just find something to criticize about me." We need to take a leap of faith that our praise will be accepted and not be used against us. Even if it is, we should maintain this faith and persevere, keeping in mind that we are doing what Jesus would want us to do.

Part of it could be *self-centeredness*. Busy with the demands of our own lives, we simply become too engrossed to bother praising somebody we take for granted. We may never have gotten into the habit of praising people. We expect them to know their worth. Surely they understand how important they are to us. But as Jerry D. Twentier, author of *The Positive Power of Praising People,* says: our need for approval is as essential as food, air, and water!

Praise can be a powerful motivator, encouraging us to live up to positive expectations. It can foster goodwill, replacing negative thoughts with positive ones. We aren't apt to think critically of the person who has just told us how special we are. By verbalizing the good things about our spouse, we come to acknowledge and appreciate those good things more frequently. If we are searching for things to praise, we generally find them.

Nurturing With Humor

A second important aspect of nurturing the relationship is recognizing and appreciating humor in our day-to-day lives. Someone once said, "Humor is like needle and thread; deftly used it can patch up just about anything." We can patch a lot of rifts, ease a lot of tension and inject a healthy dose of fun into a relationship when we approach life with a sense of humor. Part of setting the joyous Christian example described in Part One is cultivating a sense of humor derived from the keen enjoyment of life. Humor generates cheerfulness, and "the cheerful heart has a continual feast" (Proverbs 15:15).

The Grand Adventure

In the second week of our marriage, Lee and I embarked on a grand adventure. Leaving family, friends and everything familiar, we headed from Raleigh, North Carolina, to Chicago, Illinois, where Lee was to begin a new job with IBM. We didn't have much in the way of worldly possessions. Those few things we did own were loaded onto a moving van that was scheduled to arrive in Chicago a day after our own arrival. We set off with an abundance of enthusiasm and a meager supply of overnight items designed to see us through the 18-hour drive. So Spartan was our packing that Lee brought along only one pair of shoes—the new, black wing-tips, which were the "official" shoes to be worn by IBMers back in 1977.

After a day of driving, we pulled into an economical motel that was clean but without frills; a place that was well within our carefully-crafted newlywed budget. Lee was delighted when he spotted a notice on the end table in our bedroom advertising a free shoe shine. "If you want your shoes shined free of charge, place them outside the door of your room. They will be shined and returned to you in the morning, compliments of this motel."

Lee pulled off his glossy black wing-tips, which were just beginning to show a few scuffs here and there. "Think I should do it?"

"Why not?" I shrugged. "It's free."

Carefully, Lee laid his shoes outside the door of our motel room. The next morning when he went to retrieve them, they weren't there. An hour later, they still weren't there. Lee contacted the front desk without making any headway. An indifferent girl munching a doughnut did not know anything about free shoe shines or missing wing-tips. The terrible truth began to sink in. The shoes had been stolen.

Now this could merely have been chalked up as a financial setback if it weren't for the fact that all the other shoes Lee owned were in that moving van somewhere between North Carolina and Illinois. He was forced to spend all day in his socks, which proved embarrassing when we stopped for dinner. I can remember entering a restaurant with Lee walking inches behind me, practically on my heels, trying to hide his feet.

"Just stay right in front of me, and don't move to either side," he instructed. "Maybe they won't notice that I'm only wearing socks."

The question of what he was going to wear to work Monday morning was a thornier problem. We arrived in Chicago on Sunday evening. He was to begin his new job the following day.

"We're in the big city now. No problem," Lee said confidently. "There are bound to be shoe stores open at night."

But things were not quite as cosmopolitan as we had imagined. The only store open on Sunday evening was a discount department store. Lee purchased a $10 pair of black, plastic shoes. They were not the quality of those Florsheim wing-tips he had so carefully placed outside the motel room, but, with luck, they would get him through his first day with IBM.

This could have been a miserable start to our married life. We felt gullible and naive, poor and tired. We were hundreds of miles from home. But when Lee slipped his feet into those ten dollar shoes, we were suddenly struck by the ludicrousness of it all. Here he was, going to work for a big, sophisticated company like IBM, with ten dollar shoes. We began to laugh our way right out of a melancholy mood and back into the jolly, adventurous mood we had experienced when we embarked on our journey.

Search For The Humor!

Since that second week of our marriage, Lee and I have found a lot to laugh about. *Many situations that seem daunting, challenging, or downright impossible can be diffused and placed in their proper perspective by mining those rich veins of humor so often overlooked.*

The time we had to push our broken-down van two miles to a dude ranch, where a mechanically-inclined cowboy fixed the problem; the trip to Germany, when I needed antibiotics and was forced to pantomime my symptoms to a doctor who didn't speak English; the house-hunting fiasco which resulted in Lee, the real estate agent, and me stranded on a broken dock that had separated from shore as soon as we reached its end; these incidences that make up our lives are the rich fodder for stories that can be enjoyed by the family.

Humor should never be the kind of sarcastic, derogatory humor that comes at the expense of another person. One husband always made his wife the butt of his jokes, eliciting laughter from everyone else and frowns from her. One day she got him back. With a sharp barb aimed in his direction, she was the one who drew laughs. The hapless husband, not appreciating this exhibition of wit, lapsed into sullen silence. This kind of "put down" humor is cheap and plentiful in the media today. We should be careful not to inadvertently allow it to become the standard in our family or our marriage.

Including humor in marriage doesn't mean retelling all the latest jokes. It means being able to point out and laugh at the absurdities of everyday life, finding joy and laughter in the trivial. People with a sense of humor take pleasure in life, relishing its variety and unpredictability.

Good For The Body

Humor has even been shown to have medicinal value. When editor Norman Cousins was ill with a life-threatening collagen disease, he made the discovery that watching amusing clips of the TV program *Candid Camera* and old Marx Brothers films affected his illness. Ten minutes of laughter had an anesthetic effect that gave him at least two hours of pain-free sleep. In his book, *Anatomy of an Illness,* Cousins describes how the positive emotions of joy and laughter can produce positive chemical changes in the body.

Research has shown that humor temporarily increases the concentration of immunoglobulin A, a virus-fighter in one's saliva. Laughter also releases catecholamines (hormones that quicken blood flow), reduces inflammation, stimulates alertness and boosts endorphins. With these stress-relieving benefits, it is no surprise that Solomon said a joyful heart is good medicine.

In her observation of fifty happily married couples, Dr. Judith Wallerstein found over and over again that couples cited shared laughter as one of the most important bonds between them. Humor, according to these couples, was an intimate way of relating to each other that went beyond a recounting of the latest jokes. Humor and laughter were ways of replenishing the relationship. They were a part of everyday life that allowed a pleasurable tension, a certain positive electricity, to exist between husband and wife. Humor was a way of defusing anger, restoring a wounded ego, and putting life's minor annoyances in their place.

It is virtually impossible to be angry with your mate when you're sharing a good belly laugh. Finding humor in the mundane is a way of rejoicing in God's creation and the everyday joys available to us. Couples who laugh together create a special bond which helps them traverse the rough patches of a relationship and transcend the ordinary.

Nurturing With Touch

When people think of touch as a means of building intimacy, they usually think of the sexual relationship. But nonsexual touching, the cuddling, hugging, and other physical caresses that are outward manifestations of our feelings, can do more to develop intimacy than anything else in a marriage. Husbands and wives who have trouble expressing their love for each other can make great strides toward improved intimacy by reaching out with affectionate touching. Most of us remember the thrill of holding hands in those early dating days. We would do well to try the "simple" thrills more often in marriage.

The significance of affectionate touching is apparent when we consider the negative impact of neglecting to touch. Researchers have found that babies have trouble surviving if they are not touched and cuddled in the early months of their lives. Touch deprivation causes infant depression, and in some cases, death. Attempting to counter this devastating impact, a local hospital advertised for volunteers to hold infants born with AIDS or addicted to crack/cocaine who did not have parents to perform this vital function.

I once talked to a happily married couple with children from previous marriages. Everything was going well, except that the stepfather was having difficulty hugging his new stepsons. He figured this show of affection would come in time, when he and the boys established a better rapport. Wouldn't a better rapport have been established right away if the stepfather had been able to drop his inhibitions and hug those boys?

The human need for touch begins at birth and has long been recognized as essential for both our emotional and physical well-being. Touch is a powerful force. Couples who learn to harness that power, employing touch not only as a prelude to sex, but also as a means of enhancing intimacy on a daily basis, will find that touch nurtures a relationship as nothing else can.

Touch Is A Life Saver

A woman had been sick for twelve years. She had spent all her money on doctors, to no avail. She had only gotten worse. Then she heard the miraculous stories of Jesus, and his ability to heal. Determined to see this great healer, the woman struggled through the crowd pressing around Jesus. She did not need to say anything. If she could only get close enough to touch his clothes, she knew she would be well. Edging closer, the woman managed to come up behind Jesus. Now was her chance! Reaching out, she touched his cloak.

Immediately, the woman felt strength returning to her body. She was healed!

At once, Jesus realized that power had gone out from him. "Who touched my clothes?" He asked, turning toward the crowd.

"People are crowding all around you. How could you ask who touched you?" His incredulous disciples wanted to know. But Jesus kept looking around to see who had touched him. Finally the woman came forward and fell at his feet. Trembling with fear, she told Jesus the truth.

"Daughter, your faith has healed you," Jesus replied. "Go in peace, and be freed from your suffering."

While this woman was healed through faith, the miraculous power of touch is also evident. She had only to touch Jesus' clothes, and Jesus felt the healing power flow from him. People brought their sick to Jesus, begging him to let the sick touch the edge of his cloak. Parents wanted Jesus to touch their babies. Jesus and the people who had faith in him knew the positive, healing power of touch.

The Doors Of Life

Touch literally opened the doors to life for Helen Keller. When a serious illness destroyed her sight and hearing at the age of two, she was shut off from the world, unable to communicate. Wild and unruly, she kicked and scratched and screamed, a child locked away in her own world, apparently unreachable and unteachable. Then Anne Sullivan arrived on the scene, and was able to make contact with Helen through touch. Sullivan held the child's hand under cold running water and used a manual alphabet to spell out "water."

Gradually, Helen Keller was able to connect words with objects. Within three years, she knew the alphabet and could read and write in Braille. She went on to help others, writing books and articles, starting the Helen Keller Endowment Fund, and lecturing on behalf of the blind in underdeveloped and war-ravaged countries. The play and motion picture, *The Miracle Worker,* told the story of how Anne Sullivan was able to change Helen Keller's life through the sense of touch.

Touch In Marriage

Given its tremendous potential for impacting lives, the fact that touch is a crucial tool for expressing and enhancing the love between husband and wife should come as no surprise. Exchanging pats and hugs, cuddling, or even just holding hands now and then are a necessary part of keeping the romance alive in a marriage. A spontaneous hug or kiss can speak volumes more than words. Husbands and wives should exhibit physical affection toward each other when they part for work, when they return at the end of the day, when they wake up in the morning, and when they go to bed at night.

Hindrances to nonsexual expressions of love through touch occur when touch is used exclusively as a signal for sex, when the habit of affectionate touching is broken by the presence of children, or when husbands and wives begin to take each other for granted. At these times, couples need to get back into the habit of affectionate touching.

Touching may seem awkward at first to couples who aren't used to showing affection. Love is something that needs to be practiced until touching becomes heartfelt and spontaneous. Like most things, the more we work at it, the better we are at it. If we practice those little touches that say to our spouse, "You are special. You mean something to me," the touches will begin to come naturally. And once the touches begin to come naturally, we will have succeeded in kindling the spark that keeps the electricity of romance alive between husband and wife.

Open Hearts, Open Minds

Praise, humor and touch can go a long way toward creating that oneness between believer and nonbeliever which the believing spouse is working to build. While spiritual oneness is not achieved until both partners are committed to faith in God, the closeness that develops from nurturing the relationship opens gateways to better communication. A marriage characterized by loving touches, shared laughter, and genuine appreciation is a marriage that will open the heart and mind of your partner to your interests, ideals, and beliefs.

Chapter Summary

A relationship, just like anything else, requires nurturing in order to thrive. There are three things which serve to nourish and enrich the relationship, building that crucial intimacy which acts as a buffer against the onslaught of day-to-day life. These three things, **praise, humor** and **touch,** can lift the relationship above the realm of the ordinary, transporting it to a new level of oneness.

Praise can be a powerful motivator, encouraging us to live up to positive expectations. By verbalizing the good things about our spouse, we come to acknowledge and appreciate those good things more frequently.

Finding humor in the mundane is a way of rejoicing in God's creation and the everyday joys available to us. Couples who laugh together create a special bond which helps them traverse the rough patches of a relationship and transcend the ordinary.

The human need for touch begins at birth and has long been recognized as essential for both our emotional and physical well-being. Touch is a powerful force. Couples who learn to harness that power, employing touch not only as a prelude to sex, but also as a means of enhancing intimacy on a daily basis, will find that touch nurtures a relationship as nothing else can.

CHAPTER SEVEN

Making Time for Each Other

"Do not store up for yourselves treasures on earth, where moth and rust destroy, and where thieves break in and steal. But store up for yourselves treasures in heaven, where moth and rust do not destroy, and where thieves do not break in and steal. For where your treasure is, there your heart will be also." Matthew 6:19-21

Paul Pearsall writes in *The Ten Laws of Lasting Love* that if we hope to find love, we must first find time for loving. It takes time to develop a personal relationship, learning to share interests and concerns, objectives, goals, and innermost thoughts. But it is only through sharing these things that we become best friends and soul mates, moving away from loneliness and toward loving closeness. The bonds of togetherness are built through shared experiences that turn into shared memories. Time together is time for considering family goals and problems, relating dreams and aspirations, and discovering our partner's utmost concerns. Time together also creates the necessary environment for humor, spontaneity, and playfulness. It is essential that we create this environment if we are to build the marriage into a relationship conducive to spiritual growth and the sharing of our faith.

But finding time for loving isn't always easy. How well I remember those days after the birth of our first child, when Lee and I made vain attempts to schedule time alone. Our children were all born with radar. Some primeval instinct clued them in whenever we sat down to dinner, started a conversation, or struggled to fit in those increasingly rare moments of intimacy. Shrill infant wails, signaling to all the world that baby felt abandoned and rejected, punctured the romantic mood as completely as a thumbtack in a balloon. One time, completely frustrated at the impossibility of finding time alone, I shrieked, "They know how to make sure there aren't any siblings!"

A Matter Of Priorities

Finding time for loving isn't always easy, but it is worth the effort, since time together is a necessary prerequisite for nurturing the relationship. One husband and wife I know have a standing date for Saturday night, stretching their budget to hire a sitter. While Lee and I haven't structured our time together around a regular Saturday date, we have always managed to carve a niche of time to be alone, infant protests notwithstanding. Sometimes it's over coffee on Saturday morning. Other times, it's after dinner. Now that our children are older finding time alone is easier, but we still have to fit time together around work schedules, travel, children's sports activities, and volunteer work.

We realized early, when children, work, and life's multitude of other demands pulled us in a hundred different directions, that shared time was a haven, replenishing and renewing our love. It was a place for reaffirming our importance to each other and for reacquainting ourselves with each other's uniqueness. It was an opportunity to remind ourselves of why we fell in love in the first place.

The Bible makes provisions for husbands and wives to spend time alone: "If a man has recently married, he must not be sent to war or have any other duty laid on him. For one year he is to be free to stay home and bring happiness to the wife he has married" (Deuteronomy 24:5).

The Apostle Paul said, "Don't we have the right to take a believing wife along with us, as do the other apostles and the Lord's brothers and Cephas?"

If the Bible emphasizes the importance of spending time together, surely we can do no less! We can make time for loving, thus learning to love better. We can create an arena that allows us the room to lead by example. We can recognize that our marriage is a treasure, worthy of claiming our heart and our time.

Individualism Versus Togetherness

Time together doesn't mean relinquishing individual pursuits. Lee plays tennis and I don't. I used to ride horses and he didn't. Individual interests can provide couples with more to bring back to each other. We are enriched by hobbies and friendships that broaden our horizons and provide us with additional insights and skills. But too often in our culture, the pursuit of individual interests has turned into a search for "self-realization." When this happens at the expense of family life and togetherness, with disregard for the other's interests and goals, it has degenerated into self-centeredness. There has to be a balance between individualism and togetherness. One should enhance the other, so that togetherness affirms individuality and individuality lends meaning to togetherness.

A certain couple appeared extremely happy and independent. They almost always took separate vacations. She spent most of her free time with friends, and he put in a lot of overtime at work. They never seemed to argue or disagree. They just went their separate ways, finding fulfillment in different areas. Others envied their free-wheeling lifestyle. It just went to show, some people reasoned, that you didn't have to spend much time together to have a good relationship.

One day this couple surprised everyone by announcing their impending divorce. They didn't have anything in common. They couldn't talk to each other anymore. Their search for personal fulfillment had not enhanced the relationship, because they had not balanced the search with an equal commitment to each other.

Out Of Sight, Out Of Mind

More and more, time together is a casualty of our frenetic pace and our value system that places relationships low on the totem pole of personal priorities. A recent newspaper article talked about spousal rebellion, or the refusal of wives to continue relocating with high-powered, executive husbands who had moved frequently in their climb up the corporate ladder. The husbands were described as workaholics who were not home during the week anyway, leading their wives to wonder why they should bother relocating for a weekend relationship. The article pointed out that such arrangements could lead to an "out of sight out of mind mentality," which in turn could lead to divorce.

The trappings of modern life, supposed to free us for greater leisure, can adversely affect our time together. Fax machines and computers, voice mail and e-mail, all draw our attention away from the people we love. But spending time together is an essential part of nurturing the relationship. Without it, there is no platform for praise, touch and humor; no opportunity to set an example of faith that will influence the nonbeliever. If the pace has become too frantic, or if we have simply gotten out of the habit of spending time with our spouse, we need to slow down and shift priorities. We need to make time for *talking, listening,* and *enjoying activities together.*

Time For Talking

By talking, we reveal our secret thoughts and desires, allowing our partner to become a part of those dreams. We share day-to-day occurrences, humorous incidences, feelings and aspirations. We open the doors to communication, building bridges toward a greater friendship with our spouse.

We shouldn't use special time together to air a host of pent-up grievances. Our "date" isn't the time to say, "I'm sick and tired of your never helping out around the house. You expect me to do it all." We should not plan a candlelight dinner and seize it as an opportunity to launch into a tirade against our partner's insensitivity.

Sometimes husbands and wives spend so little time together that when they do finally wind up scheduling a "date," they can't find anything to talk about. They have gotten out of the habit of conversation. When I was a teenager, a boy I liked invited me to an event in a different town. I panicked at the thought of finding something to talk about for thirty miles of driving. Would we lapse into dreaded silence, letting the whole date go by with scarcely a word between us? Deciding to take preemptive action against this possibility, I wrote down a list of conversational topics on a scrap of paper and slipped it into my purse. Whenever conversation lagged, I stole a glance at that scrap of paper, searching for a new topic. I don't know what my date thought of these furtive glances into my purse, but I do know that we did not spend the whole date in awkward silence.

I'm not suggesting that you prepare a list of conversational possibilities and stow them away in your purse, but it might not be bad idea to think of several things you've been wanting to talk about. Maybe you have run across a newspaper article that fanned the flames of smoldering political opinion. Lee and I love talking politics and current events. Or maybe a recent novel made a point that impressed you. Your job, an incident with the children, or some new volunteer endeavor could have yielded an interesting story you've been meaning to tell. Make a mental, if not a written note of these things, at least until you get back into the habit of conversing with your spouse. Once you have regained the lost art of communication, you may find there is so much to talk about that you want to skip that movie and extend the dinner conversation a little longer.

Time For Listening

Somebody once said, "If you are not a charming conversationalist, you may still be a big hit as a charmed listener." Listening, really tuning into what another person says and responding appropriately, is actually more important than talking in developing good conversational skills. Listening to your spouse indicates a genuine interest in his career, hobbies, and point of view. We are recognizing our partner's abilities and accomplishments when we tune in attentively and respond positively. If our partner indicates a desire to talk, we should turn off the TV or the laptop computer, take the phone off the hook, or do whatever else it takes to communicate our desire to be an attentive listener.

What if you are married to someone who finds it difficult to talk about his feelings? This is especially true of men, who have been culturally conditioned to suppress their emotions and are generally not as verbal as women. An understanding spouse can learn to draw her mate out without getting angry at his reluctance to share feelings. *If we understand that silence does not always indicate hostility or unwillingness to communicate, but is rather a reflection of his different perspective on the role of conversation in a marriage, we are better equipped to bridge the communication gap.*

Ask A Question, Share A Story

I discovered that it was virtually impossible to persuade my children to talk about their school day by asking them directly about it. A "How was your day?" approach was usually met with a mumbled, "fine." But if I greeted them by sharing something about my day, maybe an interesting or humorous incident, they usually wanted to relate an experience of their own. Specific questions, such as, "Was Mrs. Jones in a better mood today?" or "Did you play basketball again in P.E.?" always worked better than general ones.

These same methods can be used with an uncommunicative spouse. Share an amusing incident of your own, or ask specific questions in an area you know your spouse is especially interested in. And be sure to tune in to the answer. If you communicate a genuine interest in knowing your spouse better, the two of you will experience growing delight in one another.

Do not interrupt your spouse or finish his sentences for him when he is in the middle of telling a story. Some people, feeling they know their partner well enough to recognize what is coming next, decide to finish the story themselves. This is a surefire way to irritate. Interrupting is like saying, "I can tell it better than you can," or "You've got it all wrong. Just let me interject my perception of the way things happened."

Be a good listener. Learn to pick up on your partner's body language. Ask questions. Show interest. Repeat things your partner has said to show that you've been following the conversation. Don't say, "I'm sick and tired of you always talking about your job." Most people want to talk about something they spend eight or ten hours a day doing. Show appreciation and respect for your partner's opinions and pursuits.

All Solution, No Sympathy

Be careful about dishing out advice, whether it's asked for or not. In a recent *Cathy* cartoon, Cathy bemoaned the fact that men always offer solutions when you want sympathy. Although people often do want and need solutions, there are also times when they just desire sympathy and understanding. The business executive who spends all day making tough decisions and handling problems that require instant solutions has a hard time abandoning this role at home. But his wife, frustrated from eight hours of changing diapers, taking temperatures, mopping floors, and cleaning clothes, doesn't generally want or expect her husband to present her with a time management plan for dealing with crises. She wants a sympathetic ear. Sometimes a simple, understanding, "I know what you're going through. It must be tough. I don't see how you handle it," is all that's required.

Be a cheerleader for your spouse, encouraging and supportive. If your spouse's new job doesn't appear to be going as well as he had hoped, don't say, "I told you so. You never should have quit the old one." Criticism, faultfinding, and second guessing are certain to send conversation escalating into an argument or to cut it off completely.

Conversation should be an open, enjoyable, and natural part of the relationship, setting the stage for sharing our faith. Then our spouse will not view a revelation of our deepest and most cherished beliefs as an attempt to convert or evangelize. He will see it, instead, as the natural sharing of innermost thoughts and ideas inherent in a relationship characterized by lively, loving and heartfelt communication.

Sharing Activities

In *The Joy Luck Club* by Amy Tan, Waverly Jong has met the man she wants to marry. He possesses many of the qualities she likes in a man, but she has put off introducing him to her mother because she is afraid her mother will point out the boyfriend's undesirable characteristics. When her mother highlights these negative qualities, Waverly fears she will begin to see her boyfriend in a different light. Her mother's criticisms will cause her own estimation of him to drop.

Like Waverly Jong, we ascribe glowing qualities to the people we care about. During courtship and the honeymoon period, we view our lover in a positive light. But as time passes we tend to overlook, take for granted, or forget those very characteristics that drew us to our mate. What Waverly feared most happens. The initial allure is lost. We begin to view each other in a different, less flattering light. We are together during illness, first thing in the morning, when baby is up at 1 a.m. and when we've just finished cleaning the toilet. It's hard to think of romance when we haven't brushed our teeth and the dog couldn't wait to go out. Mystery and intrigue don't jive with budget planning or a child's suspension from school.

This is why doing things together is important. Enjoying shared activities can help us see each other in roles other than the traditional husband/wife, father/mother roles. We are thrust into new roles that highlight athletic ability, mental acumen, appreciation of the arts, or any number of talents and interests that have lain dormant beneath a blanket of sameness and routine. Shared activities enable us to rediscover that interesting person we married. Carol rediscovered her husband's unique sense of humor when they attended a party together. Realizing how much other people enjoyed his humor, she was able to see him in a whole new light. She was reminded of the times during their courtship when she had admired his gregariousness. Because of her renewed appreciation of him, he became more attentive to her.

Carol's discovery that doing things as a couple could strengthen the relationship was not an isolated revelation. A newspaper article on divorce highlighted the importance of sharing activities with your mate. When husbands were asked why they divorced their wives, one of the most common answers was, "My wife wouldn't do anything with me."

Give It A Try

I never cared for sailing, but when Lee invited me on a sailboat cruise, I decided to give it a try. What a wonderful discovery, to find out that sailing didn't necessarily mean hours of boredom in the blistering sun. An evening sail without telephone interruptions or children's demands is a great stimulant to thoughtful conversation. And there is the added benefit of watching a fiery October sunset from the romantic serenity of a lake.

I didn't think I would like snorkeling, either. The fins and mask were awkward appendages that took some getting used to. But this was a sport my husband loved, so I tightened my foggy mask and plunged in. I've never regretted that plunge! We have snorkeled many times since then, in the Virgin Islands, Hawaiian Islands, and Bahamas, reveling in the wonders of God's marvelous creation. There is nothing more beautiful than a coral reef surrounded by a rainbow assortment of fish and the slow, graceful glide of a sea turtle through an aquamarine sea.

At some point, when the children have gone off to college or a spouse has retired, couples will find themselves in different roles, with more time to spend together. Those couples who haven't shared hobbies and interests might discover that without the diversions of children and careers, they have little in common. On the other hand, this can be a wonderful "get reacquainted" time for couples who have remained close.

A marriage should be fun. Have candlelight dinners, do chores together, laugh, talk, and fill the relationship with spontaneity, joy, and a spirit of adventure. Ruth Stafford Peale said, "Fun is where you make it." We can introduce fun into the relationship by making time for each other. In doing this, we are building the rapport which opens doors to improved communication. Ideas and beliefs flow as naturally as water between couples who have grown accustomed to nurturing each other through shared activities.

One thing the believer could do is encourage the unbelieving spouse to participate in some volunteer endeavor that brings the couple into contact with Christian friends. The spouse who will not attend church might agree to work on a Habitat for Humanity house or deliver food to a local charity.

We move toward spiritual oneness as we grow in our enjoyment of each other. The believing spouse, by saying to his or her partner, "time with you is more valuable than the time I could spend doing other things," is strengthening the foundation of the relationship.

Spending time together, we diminish communication barriers and overcome the resentments inherent in a distant, uncommunicative marriage. We continue to lay the groundwork which will lead to the sharing of our faith.

Balancing Work, Church And Family

The song, *Cat's in the Cradle,* by Harry Chapin, is a poignant testimonial to the time lost when a father is too busy to participate in his child's growing up years. The song's lyrics point to a father missing each successive stage of his son's development because he is always too busy working to pause and watch his son grow up. When the child learns to walk, there are planes to catch and bills to pay. When the son turns ten and wants to play ball, his father's response is "No. Not today." Finally, when the father retires and has some extra time on his hands, the son is too busy.

The song highlights a sad truth. Many of us are simply too busy to enjoy the true treasures in our life: those relationships which are a blessing from God. Parent/child and husband/wife relationships are unique and valuable, offering us an opportunity to love in way that will help us better understand God's love for us. *How can we experience God's love, a love so powerful that it led to Jesus' death on the cross, if we cannot experience human love in its most intimate, most wonderful, and most sacrificial form?*

But as the song says, there are bills to pay. Today it often takes two incomes to pay those bills. There are also volunteer activities at school and in church, a house to clean, a lawn to mow, and a myriad other things to be accomplished in those 24 hours allotted to each and every one of us. How can husbands and wives make time to share candlelight dinners when they can't even find time to fold last week's laundry and pay yesterday's light bill?

The answer is that love requires a sacrifice. We will not make time to do everything. Consequently, it is absolutely essential that we learn to balance work, church, family, and everything else competing for this most valuable of our resources. Maybe we will have to settle for less money if we want fewer business trips or fewer hours at the office. We might have to say no to a promotion, a position on the church finance committee or a request that we volunteer once a week in the school media center.

Promotions, volunteer work, and clean houses are good things, but making time for loving is so much better. Harry Chapin's wife asked him one day to slow down and spend more time with their children. He promised her that he would, at the end of a busy summer. Tragically, Harry Chapin was killed in a car accident that summer.

Make time for each other *now* a top priority. Nurture and enrich your marriage. Share your life and your God-given ability to love with your family. Cast aside the distractions, the excuses, the ambitions, and the trappings of modern life that would deter you from this goal. If you don't make time for loving, you may find that your other, worthier goals, are in the end, hollow and meaningless.

Chapter Summary

Spending time together is an essential part of nurturing the relationship. Without it, there is no platform for praise, touch and humor, no opportunity to set an example of faith that will influence the nonbeliever.

We must make time for **talking, listening, and sharing activities.** By talking, we reveal our secret thoughts and desires, allowing our partner to become a part of those dreams. We share day-to-day occurrences, humorous incidences, feelings, and aspirations. We open the doors to communication, building bridges toward a greater friendship with our spouse.

Listening to our spouse indicates a genuine interest in his or her career, hobbies, and point of view. We are recognizing our partner's abilities and accomplishments when we tune in attentively and respond positively.

Enjoying shared activities can help us see each other in roles other than the traditional husband/wife, father/mother roles. **We move toward spiritual oneness as we grow in our enjoyment of each other.**

CHAPTER EIGHT

Conflict Without Crisis

"A gentle answer turns away wrath, but a harsh word stirs up anger." Proverbs 15:1

He is a Democrat whose favorite president was Roosevelt. She is a Ronald Reagan Republican who wouldn't think of voting Democrat. He was brought up Episcopalian and attends the same Episcopal Church every Sunday. She grew up Baptist but decided she liked the Church of Christ. Since there wasn't a Church of Christ in their small town, she started her own, holding services in a vacant pre-Civil War house on Main Street. Their children alternated between the two churches, sitting one Sunday in the staid, hushed pews of the Episcopal Church, the following Sunday on folding chairs in one refurbished room of the old house. He is easygoing, content to take life as it comes. He owned some rental property that he wanted to sell because of the costs involved in renovations. She assumed ownership of the property, renovated it, and rents it profitably.

Can these two possibly stay married with such radically different personalities? You bet they can. They are my parents, and they have been married almost fifty years.

Two people don't have to be carbon copies of each other to get along. That's a good thing, since nobody on earth is a carbon copy of another person. God made us in his image, but he also made each of us unique, with likes and dislikes, opinions and preferences influenced by our genes, our environment, and our experiences. This uniqueness makes life interesting, and it makes conflict in marriage inevitable. We bring to a relationship our own agendas, expectations, mood swings, and the "emotional baggage" that goes along with being imperfect humans. Add to the relationship a couple of children, financial decisions, religious differences, and the stress of everyday life, and you have a recipe for confrontation.

One thing we can be certain of is that we will have conflict in our marriage. *It isn't the presence of conflict in a marriage that will determine the success or failure of the marriage. It is how the two people in a relationship handle that conflict.*

Secular Versus Biblical Advice

Advice from the secular world is abundant. In the absence of an eternal perspective, pursuit of worldly success and pleasure is paramount. We are encouraged to embrace a success that fosters envy, the accumulation of material wealth, and getting ahead at all costs. The self becomes supreme, with relationships becoming secondary. From this perspective, any course of action that facilitates success, or leads to greater personal fulfillment and happiness, is advisable over (and with little thought given to) the course of action that leads to strengthening and/or maintaining the structure of the family unit. Conflict resolution is less important than having our own way when settling differences isn't directly related to our primary goal of self-fulfillment.

This is diametrically opposed to the Christian point of view. Jesus said, "Blessed are the peacemakers, for they will be called sons of God," and "If someone strikes you on one cheek, turn to him the other also. If someone takes your cloak, do not stop him from taking your tunic."

How do we reconcile "turning the other cheek" with looking out for Number One? *We don't.* We work to resolve conflict in our marriage and in every other aspect of our life, because we are exhorted as Christians to be peacemakers. The biggest burden for conflict resolution could lie with the believing spouse, although this is not always the case. Too many Christians have abandoned the role of peacemaker to don the secular mantle of self-fulfillment.

When conflict resolution *does* seem to rest inordinately in the hands of the believer, Christians can take heart from Proverbs 21:21: "He who pursues righteousness and love finds life, prosperity and honor." As believers, we need to understand that by accepting the greater burden for peacemaking, we are pursuing righteousness. We are setting an example of faith in action and striving to create an arena for spiritual change within the marriage.

Rocky Start? There Is Still Hope!

During the first year of our marriage, Lee must have thought he had married a wildcat. For one thing, there was my temper. I wasn't setting such a good example for Christianity in those days! I tended to hold things in until I reached the boiling point. Then watch out. The kettle was about to boil. Like a volcanic eruption, all the pent-up fury of my anger would explode, decimating anything in its path. I also had a tendency to storm off during an argument. This was an immature reaction and lethal to any constructive resolution of differences, but I did it anyway. What did I care? I wasn't focused on settling our differences. I was focused on having things my way.

When something was bothering Lee, he would settle in for a good spell of silence and brooding. I took it personally.

"What's wrong?" I would say, gathering my defenses for a rebuttal.

"Nothing."

"Is something bothering you?"

"No."

"Have I done something?"

"No. It isn't you."

This drove me crazy. *I'll give him the silent treatment, too,* I would think. So I'd stop talking, and he would say, "What's wrong with you?"

"Nothing."

"Something bothering you?"

"No."

"Have I done something?"

"No. It isn't you."

As you can imagine, this got us nowhere. Fortunately, we outgrew (for the most part) these immature and destructive ways of not settling our differences. Marriage was a new adventure. We had to take another person's feelings into consideration, and grow up a little. It was rocky going for a while, but humor helped a lot. So did listening. When we really learned to listen to each other, we found out that the reasons for our arguments were usually miscommunication or wrong interpretations. I discovered that Lee's silences had nothing to do with me. He was usually bothered by something at work. He figured out that my temper tantrums did not always revolve around the issue at hand. Instead, they sprang from a series of incidences that had built up over time.

We also learned that it was terribly lonely when we weren't getting along. We were in Chicago with no relatives or friends. There was no one to turn to or confide in. (This could have been an advantage, since it is a mistake for one partner to air grievances about the other to a parent or a friend. Sympathetic feedback can fan the flames of discontent and convince us of the righteousness of our position.)

Not All Bad

Conflict isn't all bad. It can be potentially useful if it spurs us into recognizing our partner's needs and shows us which part of our relationship needs attention. When we learn to handle conflict constructively, we learn to appreciate another person's point of view. The forgiveness and reconciliation inherent in conflict resolution are instrumental in Christian spiritual development. If all conflict were suppressed in the name of peace at any cost, issues would never get resolved. One partner, always deferring to the other's judgment, would feel the smoldering flames of resentment.

Learning to resolve conflict constructively is essential if we want to avoid the hostilities that flare and resentments that fester when we are approaching issues from opposite ends of the spectrum. We can handle conflict without crisis if we retain respect for each other, refuse to indulge in the silent treatment or fight over nonissues, learn how to compromise, stick with the issues at hand, remain open to another person's point of view, and remember to treat each other with courtesy and kindness. Practicing and mastering these attitudes will ensure that conflict never tears apart the fabric of our marriage.

Let's Work It Out

According to an article in *Time* magazine, secular and church-based programs that help couples learn how to handle conflict have become big business. Over the past 15 years, the number of couples seeking professional counseling to help resolve marital differences has risen from 1.2 million in 1980 to more than 4.6 million annually. Along with an increase in two-income couples has come an increase in conflict over division of household responsibilities. When there was only one wage-earner in the family, there was little discussion about moving the whole family to a new town if an opportunity for a promotion came along. Now, with two wage earners, this becomes a decision that involves two careers.

Potential areas of conflict are many and varied. A simple solution is to opt out when the going gets rough, so it is encouraging that more couples are seeking professional counseling to deal with marital differences. This reveals a desire to stay together and "tough it out." A strong desire to make the marriage work is a necessary prerequisite for any serious conflict resolution. *It is only when the desire for a successful marriage takes precedence over our own solitary wishes that we will be able to work wholeheartedly toward marital oneness.* Marital oneness does not always mean agreeing on issues, but it *does* mean being able to disagree without splitting into separate war zones.

Retain Respect

Respecting the other person, refusing to attack the other's most vulnerable area, and viewing the other person with kindness and love, even in the heat of battle, are crucial if we are to avoid a downward spiral of negativity. We must learn to see our partner in a positive light, even when the fires of disagreement are raging. We must stick with the issue being discussed instead of attacking the other personally. We need to refrain from arguing in front of others or discussing our spouse in a negative light with other people. We need to let positive thoughts replace negative ones.

Forego The Silent Treatment

When one person retreats into silence, he/she is showing a disregard for the other person's point of view. Very few things a partner can do will "get the goat" of a spouse as effectively as the silent treatment. Sometimes a husband or wife withdraws into silence to avoid the unpleasantness of an escalating argument. Avoidance only postpones the battle, since the hot coals of resentment have not been doused by the necessary reconciliation. Grievances are still there, ready to erupt at the next provocation.

Withdrawal gets you nowhere, unless you are merely taking an opportunity to control your temper and collect your thoughts. The "silent treatment" includes storming off during an argument, since both leaving the scene and greeting any discussion with stony silence are refusals to face up to and deal with an area of conflict. Nothing is resolved and resentment is given fertile ground to grow. Although retreating into silence is better than hurtful, irretrievable words and raging hostilities, extending the olive branch of peace shows commitment to the relationship.

Don't Fight Over Nonissues

"It drives me crazy when he squeezes the toothpaste from the middle of the tube," Janet complained. "I've mentioned it a dozen times, but he doesn't listen."

This is a nonissue. Janet can resolve it by buying her own tube of toothpaste. Arguing over things that aren't important dilutes the significance of real issues. When genuine areas of concern arise, couples who are used to digging their heels in over nonissues are less likely to take a serious, thoughtful approach to conflict resolution. If one or both partners have been badgered and nagged over minor irritations and personality traits that can be overlooked, they are not going to be inclined to consider the other's point of view, to compromise, or to deal with conflict in any other effective way.

Steer clear of the nonissues. Don't nag about things that aren't important. If your husband isn't handy around the house and you want the kitchen cabinets painted, learn to do it yourself, hire someone else to do it, or forget it. Save your disagreements for important things.

Compromise

Be willing to compromise if the issue is not something near and dear to your heart. One partner should not have to do all the compromising, but both partners will have to give in sometimes.

Mike and Cynthia had different ideas about what they desired in a house. Mike wanted a place in the country on several acres of land. He had always longed to get away from it all, have a small garden and a couple of big dogs. Cynthia wanted to live in a suburb with sidewalks, convenient shopping, and proximity to schools. These were clashing desires without a solution in sight. With neither wanting what the other one wanted, what were they going to do?

They discussed the problem day and night. Mike tried to sell Cynthia on a country home. Cynthia attempted unsuccessfully to persuade Mike to settle in the suburbs. Finally Cynthia said, "I'm willing to live in the country at some point in our future, but right now, I'm afraid to be so isolated with you traveling so much. I wouldn't feel safe that far from civilization unless you had a job that allowed you to be home every night." Cynthia went on to explain that driving the children to and from after school activities would be a chore and there would be no neighborhood children around for them to play with if the family opted for a country home.

Mike, realizing that Cynthia would be the one spending most of the time in the house and that she would be put to great inconvenience if they moved to the country while the children were still young, agreed to compromise. They would live in the suburbs for now, while the kids were growing up and he was traveling. He wouldn't have much time for a garden, anyway. Later, when the children were teenagers or when he neared retirement, they would buy a country home.

This was a big issue to compromise on, but Mike realized that Cynthia would not be happy in a country home at this point in time. He, on the other hand, could be happy in the suburbs knowing that at some point they would move. It was not a forever situation. Once Mike took Cynthia's reasons for wanting to live in the suburbs into consideration, compromise was easy.

Be Open To Another Point Of View

In learning to manage conflict and work together as a team, we must learn to see things from the other person's perspective. Although we will not always agree with that perspective, being able to understand and appreciate our partner's point of view can go far toward diffusing volatile emotions. Consider the following argument. In this first scenario, the husband refuses to see his wife's side:

Wife: "I don't see why you have to play basketball when you've just been out of town three nights in a row. You never stay home, you never see the kids. You just don't care."

Husband: "How can you expect me to stay home when you nag all the time? You play tennis on Thursday nights, but you don't want me to do anything except work. Basketball happens to be my way of relaxing. Getting up at 4 a.m. to catch a plane, going on a trip when everybody's on your back about not meeting quota...it's not my idea of fun."

Wife: "And I guess your idea of fun isn't staying home with me and the kids."

As hostilities mount, husband and wife show no signs of reconciliation. The husband can either storm off to the basketball court or stay home, feeling coerced into that decision. The wife has not been completely fair in her arguing. She has taken one issue—her husband's decision to play basketball—and transformed it into an indication that he doesn't care about his family. If either husband or wife had validated the other's point of view, anger could have been diffused enough to at least attempt a compromise that did not leave one or both partners feeling like losers. The husband might have said, "I understand how you must feel, alone with the kids so much. This is a bad time in my career, since I'm under quota but we still have all these expenses to meet. I'm hoping that when sales pick up, I can ease up on the travel. In the meantime, I'll try to make sure you and the kids are my first priority."

The wife's response could have been, "I understand that you want to do something for fun after all the business travel you've had to do lately, but the kids and I miss you. We love you and like having you around."

Although neither one of these conversations offers a solution, they open the door to compromise. Husband and wife are making an attempt to see things from the other's perspective.

Stick With The Issues

Conflicts that arise from suppressed resentments having nothing to do with the problem at hand are the conflicts most likely to escalate into full-blown battles. When arguments are spurred by underlying agendas that go beyond the issues, partners tend to bring up old grudges and to attack the other person instead of that person's stand on an issue.

James addressed the cause of conflict in James 4:1: "What causes fights and quarrels among you? Don't they come from your desires that battle within you?" In other words, conflict occurs as a result of our own internal battles, rather than as a result of irreconcilable differences between us.

When a wife fights with her husband over his extensive business travel or Tuesday night basketball at the gym, she might really be fighting with him over her feeling of being neglected and unloved. When a husband argues with his wife over the amount of money she spends, the real fight might be over his attempts to assert control. In arguments that involve power struggles, couples often resort to nagging, threats, and shouting to gain the upper hand. But in reality, nothing is gained. Even if one partner does give in to the other's demands, it's a grudging acquiescence that is grounds for resentment.

We are instructed in Ephesians 4:31 to "get rid of all bitterness, rage and anger, brawling and slander, along with every form of malice." This means concentrating on correcting our own emotions and reactions instead of changing the other person. Once we correct our own emotions, conflict will not stem from suppressed resentments having nothing to do with the issues.

Courtesy And Kindness

Sticking with the issues is one way of exhibiting common courtesy and kindness, which brings us to another important characteristic of conflict resolution. We shouldn't neglect courtesy and kindness toward our mate, any more than we would neglect it toward our business associates, friends, and acquaintances. Nor should common courtesy be dependent on the other person's reaction.

I have told my children this many times. They have been taught to hold doors open for people entering a building behind them. Sometimes this gesture is met with a polite "thank you." But occasionally, their manners are either unacknowledged or met with a huffy glare from someone who doesn't appreciate having a door held open. When this occurs, and my children express a desire to slam the next door in someone's face, I hasten to assure them that we do not allow other's reactions to determine our behavior. We persist in being courteous because it is the right thing to do, regardless of how that courtesy is interpreted by those who don't know better.

Showing courtesy and kindness means we listen respectfully to our partner's point of view. An argument never escalates into hurtful words and verbal threats. We don't hurl insults, criticize, sulk, whine, shout, or refuse to speak. We follow Paul's advice to "Live together in harmony, live together in love, as though you had only one mind and one spirit between you. Never act from motives of personal vanity, but in humility, think more of one another than you do of yourselves."

Religious Conflict

When a believer marries a nonbeliever, religious differences add one more possibility to the vast arena of potential sources for conflict. I will reiterate here what I said earlier in this book: *The believer should lead by example rather than attempting to force the nonbeliever into an acceptance of the believer's faith.*

In conflict resolution, the believer will carry the burden of employing biblical principles, since the nonbeliever might be either unacquainted with biblical principles or unwilling to apply them. Although a knowledge of biblical principles places the greater burden of conflict resolution on the believing spouse, he or she should keep in mind the ultimate goal: sharing faith in Jesus Christ. This goal should provide the motivation for consistently utilizing the conflict resolution techniques mentioned in this chapter.

Resolving differences while growing in love and oneness is essential to building the marriage relationship. Once couples can resolve conflict with their love intact and the foundation of their relationship unscathed, the doors to true communication have been opened. Once the doors of communication are open, an honest discussion of faith can take place.

Chapter Summary

It isn't the presence of conflict in a marriage that will determine the success or failure of the marriage. It is how two people in a relationship handle that conflict.

Conflict can be potentially useful if it spurs us into recognizing our partner's needs and shows us which part of the relationship requires attention.

When we learn to handle conflict constructively, we learn to appreciate another person's point of view. We can handle conflict without crisis when we:

*Retain respect for each other.
*Refuse to indulge in the silent treatment.
*Refuse to fight over nonissues.
*Stick with the issues at hand.
*Remain open to another's point of view.
*Exhibit a willingness to compromise.
*Treat each other with courtesy and kindness.

Once couples can resolve conflict with their love intact and the foundation of their relationship unscathed, the doors to true communication have been opened. When the doors of communication are open, an honest discussion of faith can take place.

CHAPTER NINE

Unconditional Love

"And now these three remain: Faith, hope and love. But the greatest of these is love."
1 Corinthians 13

Talmage and Thelma were looking forward to Talmage's retirement. He sold his furniture store, netting a nice income. They planned on spending a lot of time at their beach house—a small, comfortable cottage on the shores of the Neuse River in North Carolina. They shared many happy memories of summers at the cottage. Their three children had loved to swim, ski, and feed the geese that took up summer residence along the Neuse. Brothers, sisters, nieces, and nephews had filled the cottage to overflowing with laughter and love that spanned the years, weaving a pattern of joy and contentment into the fabric of their lives.

Their children were married now, living in different states with families of their own. Many of the nieces and nephews had also moved away. Trips to the beach would not be the same bustling, chaotic vacations they had once been. That was okay. Talmage and Thelma were happy the years had not dimmed their love for each other. He still liked to say, "I married the prettiest girl in town." They relished the prospect of quiet evenings on a screened-in porch, a gentle saltwater breeze stirring the night air.

But life, with characteristic unpredictability, took an abrupt departure from their carefully laid plans. Thelma suffered a major stroke. The doctors were not hopeful. As Thelma lay in a coma, Talmage prayed with all his heart that she would live. He promised to care for her no matter what. He wanted her back, even if it meant that she would no longer be as healthy and whole as she had been; even if it meant his retirement would not be the same idyllic one he had planned.

Although Thelma lived, she emerged from the coma unable to speak clearly, walk, or even feed herself. When she was able to leave the hospital, Talmage brought her home. There, for the next ten years until her death, he devoted himself to her care. He obtained a special bed with side rails, bought a wheel chair, and equipped the house with wheel chair ramps. He purchased a speaker phone so Thelma could listen to his conversations with their children and other callers. On nice days, he draped an Afghan over her lap and strolled her up and down the sidewalk in front of their house.

As Thelma's arms and legs wasted away, Talmage fed and clothed her. He moved her from bed to wheel chair and back again, encouraging her with his unceasing love and cheerfulness. She could not speak clearly, but he learned to understand what she said and what she meant.

He lost weight, becoming a shadow of the robust man he once had been. His physical and mental health deteriorated from long years devoted solely to her welfare. Quietly, he sold the beach cottage. Yet he didn't complain. He didn't rail against this torturous twist of fate. He continued to care for her and to love her unconditionally.

When Love Is Difficult

It is easy to love in the first bloom of romance, when she is the "prettiest girl in town," and he is the dashing athlete. We are intoxicated with love and the idea of heaven on earth. But what happens when real life intervenes? What if one partner becomes a whiner and a nag, forever complaining about the other's shortcomings? What if we find ourselves married to an alcoholic who loses job, friends, and self-respect? What if illness takes a devastating toll, physically or mentally changing our mate forever? It might not be so easy to love then, when the object of our affection seems totally different from the person we thought we married. Love becomes a choice at odds with our human tendency to care about those who meet our own needs. This is where unconditional love comes in. Loving unconditionally means loving persistently and inexhaustibly, even if there is no response.

Let God Help

To love another when love is unreturned or unrewarded is virtually impossible if we depend on our mate to meet all our needs for happiness and fulfillment. Once our mate stops meeting those needs, the flow of love dries up. But it is possible to love unconditionally when our needs are met in Christ. Psychologist Larry Crabb emphasizes this in his book, *The Marriage Builder*. He states that when our needs are met in Christ, we are free to regard marriage as an opportunity to help another human become fully aware of God's love and purpose. Dr. Crabb urges us to adopt a ministry mindset, which involves a determined, continuous willingness to minister to our spouse. It requires an awareness of our partner's needs, as well as a conviction that we are God's chosen instrument to meet those needs.

Dr. Crabb points out that true acceptance requires a willingness to give of ourselves in a way that leaves us open to painful rejection. Forgiveness requires that we continue to be guided by Christian love in our words, actions, and responses, even if our partner's actions hurt and provoke us. We regard our partner's actions as separate from our own personal response.

This type of unconditional love is sometimes referred to as *agape* love, or the unconditional love that God bestows on us. Everyone wants this love, which is complete and permanent, unselfish and transforming.

Carol Kent in her book, *Secret Longings Of The Heart,* says, "Our deepest sense of significance always comes when a valued person conveys unequivocally that we are uniquely and distinctly important, personally acceptable, approved of, and profoundly wanted." We can choose to love this way if we ask God's help and maintain our ministry mindset. But it must be a deliberate choice, even though that choice will often conflict with our emotions.

"She Meant Everything To Us"

The popular television talk show, *Oprah,* aired a program featuring people who had awakened from life-threatening comas. One 38-year-old woman who suffered a heart attack on the day of her mother's funeral spent several days in a coma that resulted in severe brain damage. Upon emerging from unconsciousness, the woman was unable to remember her husband and four children, to recall day-to-day events, or to take care of herself.

Her husband, who had assumed the responsibility of caring for their four children and his incapacitated wife, told of how the family posted signs throughout the house to remind his wife of the things she needed to remember. The children's names and ages were on these "reminder" signs. Throughout the interview, the husband held his wife's hand. Several times, when she appeared to be overcome by the tragedy of her situation, he wiped her tears away with a kleenex.

She could not remember from one day to the next that her mother had died. She could no longer love and care for her children and husband. Her illness had aged and debilitated her to such an extent that she no longer resembled the attractive, vibrant and loving woman captured on the family's home videos. Yet, her husband wiped her tears and held her hand and assumed responsibility for her care.

At one point Oprah Winfrey, the show's host, mentioned this husband's loyalty and solicitude toward his wife. His simple reply was: *She meant everything to us. She was the center of our family.*

On the same day this show aired, a big news story about the breakup of a famous couple was splashed all over the front pages. Healthy and rich, with all the pleasures of life at their fingertips, husband and wife were separating in bitterness and hostility, their marriage characterized by adultery, their lawyers haggling over who should get what when the divorce was finalized.

How difficult it is to love unconditionally and unselfishly in a world that values the selfish pursuit of pleasure above all else! Yet, this is how God loves us, so much that "He gave his one and only Son, that whosoever believes in him shall not perish but have eternal life" (John 3:16). We should be prepared to love unselfishly, through better or worse. With God's help, this kind of love is possible.

How To Love Unconditionally

In his book, *Secret Choices*, Dr. Ed Wheat says we can love the agape way by choosing with our will to love unconditionally and permanently, asking God to enable us to love with His love. We must develop a knowledge of our partner's needs and how to meet them, always doing the best for the object of our love. This includes giving our partner the assurance that he/she is totally accepted and permanently loved.

If we love our partner unconditionally, our love will not diminish if he gains twenty pounds. Love will not disappear if physical disability replaces good health and fitness. Unconditional love is of the spirit, not of the flesh. It is a deep acceptance that goes beyond surface issues.

Unconditional love is essential when one partner is attempting to restore a broken relationship without the cooperation of the other partner. But just how much should we forgive? How far does the Bible tell us we need to go in order to mend a relationship? God commanded Hosea to take his wife back, loving her as God loved Israel, even though she was an adulteress and a prostitute.

Dealing with Betrayal

When a husband or wife makes the decision to love a spouse unconditionally, with acceptance and forgiveness, there is often a sense of betrayal that must be overcome. We feel that the object of our love has betrayed us if our love isn't returned and our efforts are unrewarded. We all experience betrayal, usually early in our lives, and the experience makes us cynical and distrustful.

My great nephew had his first bitter taste of betrayal at the tender age of three. He was playing outside with several older neighborhood children. Being at that precarious stage of potty training when play is more important than heeding nature's call, he had to be talked into a trip to the bathroom. But he didn't leave until a promise had been extracted from his new playmates to await his return. They promised freely, assuring Dillon that he could come right back out and join them again. Dillon accompanied his grandmother to the bathroom. Minutes later, he returned to the front yard. Imagine his dismay when he found the yard deserted, his new friends gone.

Betrayal begins early and continues into adulthood, manifesting itself in different ways. The embezzler betrays the company he works for. A parent who is abusive betrays the trust of an innocent child. An unfaithful spouse betrays his or her partner. In subtler ways, a spouse betrays a partner by failing to be supportive, by undermining the other's confidence, or by something as seemingly innocuous as failing to show up on time for a child's recital. While "betrayal" is a strong word to use for these "lesser" offenses, the victimized partner experiences the anguish of broken promises and ambiguous loyalty.

Betrayal is a fact of life because it is part of our imperfect human nature. When it comes, as it inevitably will, we can figure out how to deal with it by looking at how Jesus handled betrayal. On the night he was betrayed, Jesus responded to Judas by saying, "Friend, do what you came to do." Even though he knew all along that Judas was unfaithful, the one who would betray him, Jesus continued to treat Judas as if he were faithful.

This concept of dealing with betrayal before we can love unconditionally goes back to forgiveness. Jesus forgave sinners. Gianna Jessen, severely handicapped as a result of her mother's unsuccessful abortion attempt, forgave her mother. The prophet Hosea forgave his wife, Gomer. Forgiveness is necessary to agape love, because clinging to resentment diminishes our capacity to love. If dealing with betrayal through forgiveness seems difficult, we need to remember this: *The agape idea of love in marriage operates under the premise that marriage is designed more for giving than for taking.* Rather than being a confining idea that relegates us to a prison of self-sacrifice and misery, agape love is a freeing idea because we are living in obedience to

God's will. Dependent on Christ to meet our needs, we are freed from a dependency on human response.

Understanding Leads To Forgiveness

Understanding the reasons for another person's behavior can go a long way toward allowing a forgiving spirit to enter our heart. Let me emphasize here that loving unconditionally does not mean condoning obnoxious behavior or allowing ourselves to be used as a doormat. The spouse who takes a social drink with his alcoholic partner and keeps the liquor cabinet full is not helping the alcoholic recover. The woman who accepts a husband's infidelity over and over again earns his contempt. Hosea did not bring Gomer back into his house to watch complacently while she continued her prostitution. He brought her back in forgiveness and love, by God's command, to change her behavior.

We need to remember that *forgiveness does not mean subjecting the family to an unhealthy or abusive environment.* Infidelity can bring significant risks of disease, emotional and psychological distress, and broken family relationships. Do not try to ignore these things or handle them alone. Take your problems to God in prayer, and to a Christian counselor who can offer clearheaded, biblically based guidance. Unconditional love could mean confronting a spouse with his or her behavior, assuring the partner of unconditional love, but requesting a change of behavior for the benefit of both partners.

Unconditional Love Takes Risks

In his book, *If Christ Were Your Counselor,* Dr. Chris Thurman says agape love attempts to foster growth. This is what differentiates it from romantic love and sexual desire for another person as he or she is now. Romantic love is not concerned with what the person might become. Agape love, on the other hand, is characterized by concern for the beloved's growth and well-being. A person's actions will be influenced by what is good for the other person, even if that course of action requires a "tough love" approach that involves confrontation and request for a change in behavior.

We should be willing to communicate and reinforce certain standards of behavior with positive feedback rather than nagging. The "catch someone doing something right and praise it" approach is more effective than the "you never do anything right" plan of attack. A positive approach exemplifies unconditional love in action, with our concern being for the other person's personal growth and happiness.

Agape love requires us to take risks. A father chose to let his son spend the night in jail for some juvenile delinquency, rather than bailing him out. This was an agonizing and wrenching choice for the father, but he felt he could best show his love for his son by teaching him to accept the consequences for his actions.

There are many areas that require tough decisions. When is allowing your child to suffer the consequences of wrong actions a good thing, and when is bailing him out the better choice? If your best friend is cheating on her income taxes, do you mention it or overlook it? If your spouse is having an affair, do you leave him or stay? Choices will have to made on an individual basis, keeping in mind which course of action is most likely to be for the ultimate good of the other, in accordance with God's will. Ask yourself: "What would Jesus want me to do?"

The Rewards

So far, we've dealt with agape love as the unconditional love of another person when that love is unrewarded or unreturned. But when agape love is put into action, it usually elicits a positive response by breaking down the other person's barriers to loving. Marriages have been renewed and revitalized because one partner chose to love when the situation did not seem to warrant love.

A woman was on the brink of divorcing her alcoholic husband. Who could blame her! Drinking had destroyed his ambition and his ability to care about his family. He made everyone miserable. But this woman chose instead to love her husband, with the result being that this man and their marriage were transformed.

There is a beautiful fairy tale about the transforming power of love. In *The Velveteen Rabbit,* by Margery Williams, a little boy receives a splendid velveteen rabbit for Christmas. He plays with it for a while, but soon the toy rabbit is forgotten amidst the excitement of opening other presents. For a long time, the rabbit is neglected. It feels very insignificant and commonplace among the other toys, which are more expensive and very superior. Those toys often pretend they are real, even though they aren't. One day Rabbit asks the wise old Skin Horse, who has lived longer in the nursery than any of the other toys, what is meant by real.

"Real isn't how you are made," explains the Skin Horse. "It's a thing that happens to you. When a child loves you for a long, long time, not just to play with, but really loves you, then you become real." The Skin Horse goes on to explain that real doesn't happen all at once. Sometimes it takes a long time, and can be quite painful. The Rabbit sighs, knowing it could take a long time for him to become real.

One day, as the boy is going to bed, he can't find the China dog he always sleeps with. Nana, who is in charge of the nursery, grabs Rabbit from the toy chest and thrusts him toward the boy. "Here, sleep with your old Bunny!"

That night, and for many nights after, the Velveteen Rabbit sleeps in the boy's bed. The boy talks to him and hugs him tightly. They play wonderful games together and tell secrets in whispers. One day when the boy asks for his bunny, Nana says, "You must have your old bunny? Fancy all that fuss for a toy!"

"Give me my bunny," the boy replies. "He isn't a toy! He's real!"

Suddenly the Velveteen Rabbit realizes the magic has happened to him. He has been transformed by the boy's love and devotion. This revelation makes Rabbit almost too happy to sleep. Even Nana notices the look of wisdom and beauty that has come into his button eyes.

Yes, people can be transformed by the power of unconditional love. We are following God's command to love others as we love ourselves when we choose to love the agape way. Our blessing could be that we will find ourselves on the receiving end of that agape love. In the meantime, "Let us not grow weary in doing good, for in due season we shall reap if we do not lose heart" (Galatians 6:9).

The Believer's Love For The Unbeliever

Choosing to love the agape way might not be an easy choice. Unconditional love is difficult in a society that values self-fulfillment over sacrifice and unselfishness. It would certainly be easier for a man to abandon his invalid wife and seek comfort in the arms of a woman who could return his love. People would have considered the prophet Hosea justified had he elected to have his wife stoned to death for prostitution. But the Christian's choice is frequently at odds with society.

It is possible to love unconditionally when our needs are met through faith in Christ rather than through the approval, acceptance, and affection of others. The Christian who loves an unbelieving spouse unconditionally accepts him without resentment. The believer rejoices in a spouse's spiritual growth without becoming impatient if change does not seem to come rapidly enough. By loving unconditionally, we allow our partner the room to grow spiritually in God's time. Our love, freed from a dependency on circumstances, is not subject to the whims of the moment.

Love for our partner grows as we nurture the relationship, refusing to allow conflict to fan the flames of discontent. Unconditional love sets the stage for building our marriage into a vessel capable of containing God's love. We learn to see our partner, not as the primary source of our pleasure and comfort, but as a spiritual child of God. As this happens, we are truly leading by example. We are exhibiting the sort of love that "always trusts, always hopes, always perseveres."

Chapter Summary

To love another when love is unreturned or unrewarded is virtually impossible if we depend on our mate to meet all our needs for happiness and fulfillment. Once our mate stops meeting those needs, the flow of love dries up. But it is possible to love unconditionally when our needs are met in Christ. This type of unconditional love is sometimes referred to as *agape* love, or the unconditional love that God bestows on us.

Agape love is characterized by concern for the beloved's growth and well-being. A person's actions will be influenced by what is good for the other person. When agape love is put into action, it usually elicits a positive response by breaking down the other person's barriers to loving.

The Christian who loves unconditionally accepts the unbeliever without resentment. He or she rejoices in a spouse's spiritual growth without becoming impatient if change does not seem to come rapidly enough. By loving unconditionally, a Christian allows the unbelieving partner room to grow spiritually in God's time.

"I lift up my eyes to the hills; where does my help come from? My help comes from the Lord, the Maker of heaven and earth." Psalm 121: 1,2

Part Three

Praying For
Your Partner

CHAPTER TEN

The Importance Of Prayer

*"And pray in the Spirit on all occasions
with all kinds of prayers and requests."
Ephesians 6:18*

The first two sections of this book dealt with
preparing a fertile ground for our Christian
witness. Leading by example, we exhibit the joy
inherent in a life characterized by faith, hope, and love.
Building the marriage relationship, we create an atmosphere
of love in which our partner will be receptive to our expression
of faith. But the soil we have prepared by strengthening our
marriage and our own spiritual life in Christ will only yield a
harvest if we plant our prayers. *Praying is one of the most
effective things the believer can do for the nonbeliever.*

God's Wonderful Gift

My daughter, Blair, spends a lot of time at the stable where she boards her two horses. She was there one cloudless day in early spring when the grass had started to green, yellow wildflowers speckled the fields, and birds sang noisily as they tended their first crop of hatchlings. Finishing her barnyard chores, Blair noticed a baby sparrow that had fallen from its nest. The bird, too young to fly, hopped awkwardly along the dirt driveway between stables. Suddenly, to Blair's horror, a tractor chugged noisily toward the driveway. There was no time to alert the driver. Unaware of the tiny life in his path, he drove the tractor directly over the bird.

Blair watched in agony, and then relief, as the sparrow emerged unscathed, having somehow escaped the tractor's tires. But her relief was short-lived. One of several barn dogs populating the stable rushed to complete what the tractor had not done. The dog, whose name was Lambchop, grabbed the unfortunate bird in his jaws. Blair reacted quickly, dashing toward the dog.

"Drop that bird, Lambchop!" She commanded, seizing the dog's neck. Lambchop dutifully complied. He dropped the bird, which had not even suffered a tooth mark.

Blair transported the bird home in a shoe box. It escaped in the family room and, somehow or other, got up the chimney. When she managed to retrieve it, the bird was blackened with soot. I was not home, and neither was Blair's dad, so she made the decision herself to bathe the soot-blackened bird. Not wanting it to catch a chill after its first-ever bath in a laundry room washtub, she dried it with a blow dryer.

By the time I got home, the bird was lost in Blair's room. We searched for an hour before locating it behind her bed. Blair moved the bird to our screened porch, but it didn't have a comfortable place to sleep. We were mulling over a solution to this dilemma when I had an idea. Why not claim an abandoned nest from the bushes beside the house? This could serve as our sparrow's "home away from home." Collecting the nest, we moved it to the porch. The bird would not get into bed by itself, so I placed it gently in the nest, where it spent the night, tiny head tucked under tiny wing. The following day, we were unable to persuade the sparrow to eat. It obviously had not learned to peck at seeds or insects. We solved this problem by rubbing peanut butter over its beak. Within hours, our bird had learned to perch on our fingers and peck the peanut butter. The next logical step was eating seeds and crumbs from the floor, which our bird mastered with alacrity.

Each day the sparrow made more progress toward learning to fly. Blair helped it along by tossing it gently in the air, encouraging it to flutter toward the porch screen. Landings were rough at first, with many bumps and tumbles. But the bird rapidly perfected both its flying and its landings.

There came a day when it would no longer perch on our fingers or eat the peanut butter we offered. It fluttered frantically higher, trying to escape us as we visited it on the porch. Obviously the little bird was wild again, not recognizing us as its saviors and benefactors.

Half regretfully, we decided the time had come to free our little guest. Blair managed with some difficulty to capture the bird. Carrying it to the deck, she tossed it skyward. The sparrow had learned its lessons well. It flew gracefully to the top of a tall pine, where it landed with perfect precision. Then it flew even further, fluttering out of sight beyond the boundaries of our yard.

In some ways, God's relationship to us resembles my family's relationship to the sparrow. He protects us, rescuing us from dangers we don't see. He takes care of our needs, even when we are not aware of His presence. Yet God has given us something wonderful that Blair and I were unable to give the sparrow. He has given us the ability to perceive Him and to communicate with Him through prayer.

If I could have communicated to the little bird that Blair was its rescuer and we only wanted what was good for it, I would have. But all we could do was take care of the sparrow until it was ready for freedom. The fact that God has allowed us to perceive Him, to discover His words to us through reading the Bible, and to communicate our most heartfelt needs and desires and praise to Him, is a miraculous and wonderful thing. *Once we pray, we tap into the amazing flow of God's love. And once we tap into the flow of God's love, amazing things happen. God's love changes people and relationships. Our marriage can be transformed when we lift the relationship before God, asking Him to work in our hearts, and in the hearts of those we love.*

God Hears Our Prayers

I have seen God's power too often to doubt His continued presence in my life. I have experienced His response to prayer too often to doubt the efficacy of heartfelt praying. Both the Old and New Testaments bear witness to the importance of prayer.

"What other nation is so great as to have their gods near them the way the Lord our God is near us whenever we pray to him," we read in Deuteronomy 4:7.

David said in Psalm 6:9, "The Lord has heard my cry for mercy; the Lord accepts my prayer."

Jesus was in constant communion with the Father. He urged persistence in prayer and gave assurance that God answers prayer. On occasion, he sought escape from the crowds in order to pray.

God might not always answer our prayers in the ways we want, but He hears and accepts our prayers. He has given us the marvelous blessing of speech. When we use it for His glory, we are drawing on the power He has made available to us.

Throughout history, God has intervened in response to prayers. "Call to me and I will answer you and tell you great and unsearchable things you did not know," He told the prophet Jeremiah. He will intervene in response to our prayers, too.

God Is Not Passive

When we lift our spouse before God in prayer, we are tapping into the same amazing and inexhaustible source of power that enabled a shepherd boy with a slingshot to conquer a ten-foot giant. God was not a passive God then, and He is not a passive God now.

Before Lee and I were married, I prayed, "Lord, make Lee a believer." It seemed an impossible request. Lee's logic appeared unassailable, his demands for proof insurmountable. How could I prove that God existed? What could I say to counter the claims of agnosticism? But God can conquer the insurmountable. "Call to me, and I will answer you," He has said. When we pray, we are calling to Him, opening the channels through which His love can flow. We are accepting His gift to us, an ability to transcend earthly limitations by depending on God's limitless strength and power.

"Lord, make Lee a believer," I prayed. Eight years later, Lee accepted Jesus Christ.

The Purpose Of Prayer

Prayer has been in the limelight lately. Since prayer in public schools was deemed a violation of church and state and banned by our Supreme Court justices, critics of that decision have attempted to restore prayer to the schools. Schools in Georgia recently began observing a silent time at the beginning of each day to allow students an opportunity to reflect or to pray silently if they choose. The American Civil

Liberties Union challenged this, contending that it was a covert way of trying to introduce prayer back into the schools.

A *Wall Street Journal* article noted the emergence of workplace ministries created to give business people an opportunity to pray together. Members of these organizations said the need for this type of ministry had become greater in an age of job insecurity and indifference on the part of corporations.

There is now a National Day of Prayer when people gather in town halls across the country to pray for our country, its leaders, and the world. Many high school students join hands around their school flag pole once a year to pray before the school day begins.

Is Prayer Making A Comeback?

Are we witnessing a sudden resurgence of prayer? Are we just beginning to recognize its significance in our daily lives? Actually, prayer has been an integral part of this country's history. The early Pilgrims poured out their prayers to God. George Washington's *Book of Common Prayer* contained prayers and petitions for governors and local magistrates. Thomas Jefferson and Patrick Henry drafted a National Day of Prayer and Fasting Resolution. In his 1863 Proclamation, Abraham Lincoln said, "...we have become too proud to pray to the God that made us." Our Pledge of Allegiance to the Flag states that we are "one nation under God."   The list could go on and on, so woven is prayer into the fabric of our history.

It is only in this century that a public expression of faith in schools and on other public property came to be viewed as a violation of church and state. The Ten Commandments were snatched from courthouse walls, teachers in some schools were instructed not to say "Merry Christmas," and nativity scenes were yanked from public holiday displays. Maybe it is this overreaction in the other direction that has spurred the move toward "moments of silence" and company group prayer meetings. Or maybe, with so many of our country's social problems unaffected by secular solutions, people are turning more and more to God for answers.

But although prayer is said to be making a comeback, it has always been an integral and indispensable part of the believer's life. Why is this true, if God is omniscient? Why should we need to pray for our unbelieving spouse if God already knows our thoughts and what we are about to ask for? Why can't we tap into the flow of God's love without praying?

Why Pray?

Rosalind Rinker wrote in her book, *Prayer, Conversing With God,* that prayer's real purpose is to put God at the center of our attention. Prayer enables us to focus on God. The shackles that keep us earthbound, weighted by our burdens, are loosened. Our faith increases because we are, during the moment of prayer, breaking free of the earthly focus that tugs our thoughts into doubt and disarray.

We have all heard the familiar cliche, "What you think is what you are." Unless we are thinking about God, directing our attention toward God through prayer, we cannot hope to become more Christlike. When our minds are always directed toward the things of this world, we become more like this world, caught up in its concerns and problems. By praying, we overcome this tendency to be caught up in the "things of this world." Our focus, drawn back to Christ, becomes more spiritual. We are better able to lead by example and to build the marriage relationship if we allow the spiritual side of our being to transcend the earthbound focus of our flesh. Prayer brings us into touch with our spirituality.

The Apostle Paul wrote that prayer provides us with peace of mind. "Do not be anxious about anything, but in everything by prayer and petition, with thanksgiving, present your requests to God. And the peace of God, which passes all understanding, will be yours through Christ Jesus." What a wonderful thing, to be promised peace of mind!

A Source Of Power

Howard Chandler Christy, the artist, discovered the power of prayer. Nearly blind at the age of 41, he prayed that God would restore his sight. God did, and Christy was able to paint without his glasses.

When King Hezekiah became ill and was at the point of death, the prophet Isaiah told him the Lord had revealed that he would not recover. Hezekiah "turned his face to the wall" and began to pray. God heard Hezekiah's prayer and added fifteen years to his life.

From biblical times until the present, the power of prayer is made evident over and over again, undiminished by the march of time. The late Dr. Norman Vincent Peale once said there is no problem, defeat, or difficulty that cannot be overcome through prayer. He described prayer as a "deep, fundamental, powerful relationship of the individual to God, whereby his whole mind and heart become changed and he receives power from God."

If prayer is so powerful, and such a wonderful gift from God, why don't we utilize it more often? Why do we muddle along, anxious and dissatisfied, weighed down by our burdens?

"I Just Don't Feel Like God Cares"

A talk show host of a Christian radio show received a call from a listener who was distraught over her failure to receive answers to her prayers. "I pray and pray all the time, and none of my prayers are answered. I just don't feel like God cares," she said.

Another person called this same radio station and said, "I try and try to be a good Christian, but I don't feel God's presence in my life."

We all feel, at times, like these callers. Longing for God to touch our hearts and fill us with awareness of His presence, we are disappointed by what we interpret as God's silence. As believers, we want to be able to say to our unbelieving partners, "I feel God's presence in my life all the time, and you will too, if you open your heart to Him!" Yet, even David, anointed by God to be king of Israel, did not feel God's presence all the time. At one point he cried out, "My God, my God, why have you forsaken me? Why are you so far from saving me, so far from the words of my groaning? Oh, my God, I cry out by day, but you do not answer, by night, and am not silent" (Psalm 22: 1-3). Jesus' own words from the cross in the last hour of his crucifixion were, "My God, my God, why have you forsaken me?"

We know that God's silence did not last forever in David's life. David wrote in Psalm 40: 1-3: "I waited patiently for the Lord; He turned to me and heard my cry. He lifted me out of the slimy pit, out of the mud and mire; He set my feet on a rock and gave me a firm place to stand. He put a new song in my mouth, a hymn of praise to our God."

"Okay, Lord, I'm Listening Now"

God's silence does not last forever in our lives, either. A woman who had fallen and broken her hip told me that initially, her prayers appeared to go unanswered. "Why are you letting me go through so much pain, Lord?" she cried in anguish as she lay in a hospital bed. "I have too much to do to be laid up like this. Why did you let this happen?" Again and again she prayed, only to experience what she perceived to be God's silence.

One day, following successful hip replacement surgery, she was in bed at home when a voice spoke to her, saying, "You were not listening to my answer."

This startled woman practically bolted out of bed. "Okay, Lord, I'm listening now," she finally managed to say.

"You have a whole new hip," was the answer she received when she was ready to listen.

Barriers To Effective Prayer

The faithful Christian knows God's silence does not last forever. Prayers are answered in God's time according to His will. But there are stumbling blocks to effective prayer, erected by our own misunderstandings and misconceptions, which make us blind to prayer's true power. We pray for something and we don't get what we want. We interpret God's silence as indifference. We don't know how to pray effectively, and so our prayers become mumbled words of habit instead of heartfelt communication with God. We block the channels of communication with doubt and fear, resentment and lack of forgiveness.

The believer praying for an unbelieving partner grows discouraged when instant results aren't forthcoming. He might begin to question God, with the result being that his prayer life diminishes. Misunderstandings about prayer produce barriers to effective praying. Then we say, like the woman on the radio, "I try and try to be a good Christian, but I just don't feel God's presence in my life."

Fortunately, these barriers can be overcome. We can learn to pray effectively by studying what Scripture has to teach us about prayer. Instead of resembling the sparrow that fluttered away, we can be true children of God, proclaiming as the psalmist did in Psalm 98: "The Lord has made his salvation known and revealed his righteousness to the nations."

The next chapters in this section are about prayer. Once we learn to pray with faith, perseverance, thankfulness, and an understanding of the things which hinder prayer, we can pray for our unbelieving partners, knowing that God hears. Planting our prayers in the fertile ground we have prepared with our joyful Christian witness, we can tap into the awesome, life-changing power of prayer.

Chapter Summary

Praying is one of the most effective things the believer can do for the nonbeliever.

Prayer enables us to focus on God. Our **faith increases** because we are, during the moment of prayer, breaking free of the earthly focus that tugs our thoughts into doubt and disarray.

When we lift our spouse before God in prayer, we are tapping into an **amazing and inexhaustible source of power.**

Once we learn to pray with **faith, perseverance, thankfulness,** and an **understanding of the things which hinder prayer,** we can pray for our nonbelieving partners, knowing that God hears us.

CHAPTER ELEVEN

Making Time To Pray

"For this reason I kneel before the Father, from whom his whole family in heaven and on earth derives its name. I pray that out of his glorious riches he may strengthen you with power through his Spirit in your inner being, so that Christ may dwell in your hearts through faith." Ephesians 3:14-17

A few years ago, my Sunday School class discussed prayer. "I always fall asleep right after I start praying at night," one man confessed. "I wake up in the morning to realize I never completed my prayers." Several of us agreed that this was our experience, too. We drifted to sleep, our prayers trailing off into comfortable oblivion after the first few mumbled words or thoughts.

There is nothing wrong with praying ourselves to sleep at night, especially since prayer can lead to a serenity that encourages a good night's rest. But if this is the only time we approach God in prayer, then our communication with God is the equivalent of trying to carry on a serious conversation with our spouse in the movie theatre. We might whisper for him or her to pass the popcorn, but we save meaningful discussions until later. Our attention at that moment is directed toward the movie screen. We wouldn't dream of bringing up current finances or deciding whether our sixteen-year-old should have her own car when we are in those hushed, darkened rows. We save conversation until later, when we can focus on each other and the issue at hand.

In the same way, we need to schedule time for prayer when we can focus on God and the issues we are bringing before Him. This might seem to be an elementary concept, but many people who pay lip service to a belief in prayer simply do not set aside the time to pray. They say to themselves, "I'm going to pray for this person or that situation," without ever actually getting around to a serious, heartfelt conversation with God. We must do more than make a decision to pray. We must set aside time, away from life's myriad distractions, to communicate with our Creator. If we are to pray for the unbeliever, we must strengthen our faith and acknowledge God's sovereignty through prayer.

Keeping The Relationship Alive

When I moved to a different city, several friends from my former town kept in touch through letters and phone calls. I reciprocated, and the friendships continued in spite of the new distance between us. Other friendships fell by the wayside because of negligence on my part or theirs. There was little or no correspondence as we proceeded with our busy lives.

One woman I know complained that she initiated all the contacts with a long-distance friend. The friend always seemed glad to hear from her, yet never bothered to initiate any contact on her own. "I like her, but she doesn't seem to care if we're still friends. It's always me doing the calling and writing, or wanting to get together," this woman said. "I don't know whether or not we'll remain friends."

In the same way, our relationship with God flourishes if it is nurtured through prayer. If neglected, it fades, like those long-ago friendships that we valued once, then allowed to wither. God wants to reach out and touch our hearts, drawing us to Him just like my friend wanted to draw her long-distance friend closer. If we continually spurn God's offers to be with us and fill our very lives with His presence, we will never attain the closeness to Him that He offers.

Jesus emphasized over and over again the importance of finding time to pray. It was a priority in his own life, even when the demands of his followers made finding time alone a challenge. We see his need for the spiritual renewal that prayer offered in Matthew 14:22. After healing the sick and feeding five thousand people, Jesus dismissed the crowds surging around him. He sent his disciples ahead in a boat and he retired to a mountainside to pray. As important as ministering to his followers was, Jesus knew that communication with the Father was vital. As important as the demands on our time seem to be, continuous communication with God through prayer is vital. We must keep the relationship alive if we expect Christ to "dwell in our hearts through faith."

Praying Alone

Jesus taught us to pray alone, in privacy, away from distraction and away from the temptation to take pride in our prayers as a sign of our righteousness or eloquence:

"And when you pray, do not be like the hypocrites, for they love to pray standing in the synagogues and on the street corners to be seen by men. But when you pray, go into your room, close the door and pray to your Father, who is unseen. Then your father, who sees what is done in secret, will reward you" (Matthew 6:5,6). This passage points to the essence of prayer, which is a direct communication between the pray-er and God. Taking time from our busy schedules to pray every day should become a habit as ingrained as taking time to eat and rest.

When he was staying at the home of Simon and Andrew, Jesus rose while it was still dark and sought out a solitary place for praying. Even then, in the dark of early morning, it was difficult for him to be alone. Simon and his companions, no doubt alarmed at their guest's absence, embarked on an immediate search. Upon finding Jesus, they exclaimed, "Everyone is looking for you!"

In his book, *The Life God Blesses,* Gordon MacDonald talks about ten days he spent hiking alone in the Swiss Alps. During that time of virtual aloneness and enforced quietness, he discovered what he called soul-talk, or genuine prayer that was possible only away from the numerous distractions of everyday life. This authentic prayer, or talk of the soul, was prolonged prayer and worship that was entirely different from the meaningless prayer that results from merely going through the motions. Silence, or a minimum number of distractions, and time to prepare the soul for heavenly intimacy, were necessary prerequisites for this kind of prayer.

We don't have to hike alone in the Swiss Alps to engage in the sort of soul-talk Gordon MacDonald was describing. But we do need to remove ourselves as much as possible from all the distractions clamoring for our attention. Some people seek time alone with God, as Jesus did, in the quiet hours before dawn. Others find the necessary stillness and solitude at night, or on a walk, or during a young child's afternoon nap. But regardless of where we find it, uninterrupted solitude is a vital condition for taking our thoughts, fears, praise, pleas and questions to our Father, who "sees what is done in secret" and rewards us.

Listening for God's Answers

One aspect of praying alone is listening for God's answers. God speaks to us through the stillness of solitude in response to our prayers. He calls on us to search, listen, and at times, wait patiently. He has given us direct access to His Word through the Bible, so when we use part of our prayer time to read Scripture, we are opening communication channels.

A few years ago, my youngest child had to undergo minor surgery. Although the prognosis was good, there was a very remote possibility of cancer. A couple of nights before the scheduled operation, a tidal wave of fear and doubt overwhelmed me, obliterating my determination to be brave and optimistic. I plunged to the lowest depths of despair and worry, certain that this surgery was not going to go well. I prayed and prayed, but God seemed distant and remote. My fears were amplified by what I read in our medical book, a comprehensive guide to symptoms, diseases, and possible complications.

Finally I discarded that dismal medical book and picked up a Bible, opening it at random. The words in Mark 4:40 seemed to leap out at me: "Why are you so afraid? Do you still have no faith?" Was God talking directly to me, reprimanding me for letting my fears block my faith? The passage made me feel better, and I was able to snatch a few hours of sleep before getting the children off to school.

The next morning, filled with routine chores and errands, slid by. I nibbled a sandwich for lunch, then decided to lie down for a few minutes. My *Daily Bible,* a Bible of 365 daily readings, was in the bookcase beside my bed. Remembering how the previous night's Bible reading had soothed me enough to induce a few hours of sleep, I reached for the Daily Bible. Once again, I was opening a book at random, and once again,

Jesus' words jolted me like an electric current. "Why are you so afraid? Do you still have no faith?"

I don't know why I was so surprised. There have been many instances when I have opened a Bible to passages that spoke directly to a particular problem or situation I faced.

Prisoners of war, locked away from the outside world for years, have retained their sanity and hope by reciting memorized Bible verses over and over again. The Bible is God's way of reaching us, of touching those still, quiet places in our heart.

Dr. Norman Vincent Peale said when we pray and know the Bible, we become conditioned with a "spiritual upthrust." The Bible offers a workable formula for life, with real answers to real questions. If we are unable to hear God's answers, maybe we aren't listening and searching for them.

Group Prayers

While praying alone should be our primary means of communicating with God, praying with others is also an important part of effective prayer. Jesus stressed the value of group prayer when he said, "Again, I tell you that if two of you on earth agree about anything you ask for, it will be done for you by my Father in heaven. For where two or three come together in my name, there am I with them" (Matthew 18: 19-20).

Praying with others allows an entire group to focus attention on a single issue. It also makes us aware of others who share common concerns.

Several years ago when I was attending a group prayer meeting, one distraught woman sought the group's prayers for her husband, who was not a believer. By this time, Lee had accepted Jesus Christ and was attending the prayer meeting with me. We were, in fact, hosting a mission couple from out of town; something we would not have considered a few years earlier. I was able to offer this woman the encouragement of my own experience.

Believers have recognized the importance of group prayers since the earliest days of Christianity, when prayer meetings preceded the birth of the church. Following the ascension of Jesus into heaven, the apostles returned to Jerusalem, where they joined Jesus' brothers and several women in prayer.

An example of the tremendous power of group prayer occurred on the day of Pentecost. A small band of believers had gathered together when the Holy Spirit came upon them in a dramatic way. A sound like the blowing of a violent wind filled the house. Tongues of fire separated and rested on each of them. Suddenly the believers were able to teach the gospel to people in their own languages.

We are told in Acts 2:42 that the believers devoted themselves not only to teaching and fellowship, but also to prayer. Throughout the New Testament, prayer is central to the rapidly growing church. Followers sought contact with God through their worship together, receiving God's empowerment.

Prayer groups are still effective today, 2,000 years later. Evelyn Christenson, author of *What Happens When Women Pray,* related this incident in a book called *Unleashing the Power of Prayer:* She was standing in an autograph line when a Nigerian woman told her of a prayer group several women had started. At the time of the group's inception, not one of the husbands was a believer. The women prayed by name for each of their husbands, and eventually every single husband came to know Jesus Christ. The author went on to say that a few minutes later, a lady from England came by. This woman said she and some of her friends had initiated a prayer group, but not one of their husbands knew Jesus as Lord and Savior.

"Will our husbands find Jesus?" the woman wanted to know. In answer, Evelyn Christenson called the lady from Nigeria back. She put the English woman's question to this other believer. What were the chances that a group of husbands would come to know Jesus? The Nigerian woman's response, stemming from her own experience, was that when sisters pray, brothers get saved. Group prayers are important! Make time to pray with other believers. Remember that when we come together in Christ's name, he has promised to be with us.

How Do I Pray?

"If you turn Lee into a Christian, I'll never doubt you again," I prayed, offering God a bargain. If He led my husband to Christ, I would never again succumb to those nagging doubts that attacked my faith from time to time. I realize now that this was the wrong way to pray. We don't need to bargain with God. For one thing, keeping our end of the bargain could be a formidable task.

Consider the story of Jephthah, the warrior. When he was advancing against the armies of the Ammonites, he made a rash bargain with the Lord. "If you give the Ammonites into my hands, whatever comes out of my house to meet me when I return home in triumph will be the Lord's, and I will offer it as a burnt sacrifice."

Jephthah fought the Ammonites and won, devastating twenty towns in the process. He returned home in triumph, only to have his exuberance turn into agony. The first thing to meet him was his own daughter, an only child, dancing happily to the sound of tambourines. When this fierce warrior saw his beloved daughter and remembered his vow to God, he tore his clothes and cried. "Oh, daughter. You've made me miserable. Now I've made a vow to the Lord that I can't break!"

"My father," the daughter replied. "You've given your word to the Lord. You must keep it" (Judges 11:30-40).

God has a tendency to call us on our bargains. A woman recovering from breast cancer made a bargain with God during the worst stages of her illness. "If you'll help me recover from this, I'll play the piano in church whenever I'm asked," the woman promised.

This Baptist woman had only been home from the hospital three days when she received a call from a Catholic priest. "We need you to play the piano for us in church this Sunday," the priest said.

"But I've only been home from the hospital three days! I haven't even gotten out of bed!" the woman exclaimed.

"You're the only person available to play," the priest responded, refusing to take no for an answer.

The woman decided then and there that she had better live up to her end of the bargain. She made it to church that Sunday and played the piano beautifully.

We don't have to bargain with God. He tells us to simply ask for what we want: "Ask and it will be given to you; seek and you will find; knock and the door will be opened to you" (Matthew 7:7).

What Should I Ask For?

Many Christians have different ideas about what is or is not an appropriate request to God. Some believers feel that it is only proper to trouble God with significant concerns. "I only pray about major things, such as the safety of my children or the world situation," one Christian said. Other Christians pray for the weather to be sunny during a church picnic or for guidance in buying the right furniture for their house. Which is the correct approach to prayer? Are we being trivial when we pray for the sun to shine on our planned event? Or are we exhibiting a lack of faith in the presence, power and omniscience of God when we limit our prayers to the major things, lest we bother a busy God who must have more important things on his mind than the trivialities of our day-to-day existence?

I admit I have gone through both the "don't bother God with little things" stage and the "pray about everything" stage. When I was a fledgling young Christian with little real knowledge of the Bible, I was in the "pray about everything" phase. I remember beginning my first job as a newspaper reporter and panicking on my way to a scheduled interview with a woman who was going to be the source of my first feature article. I realized halfway to this woman's house that I had a writing tablet but no pencil. What reporter worth her salt would arrive at an interview without a pencil? I would look incompetent, approaching this woman with no means of recording what she said. I prayed for God to provide me with a pencil, and when I glanced around the car, a pencil was on the seat beside me. I was sure it had not been there before. I had searched wildly and frantically, ransacking that car.

Just when the relief of seeing that pencil was about to settle my nerves, my heart began to pound another alarm. Somewhere along this winding country road, I had gotten lost. What was I going to do? Car phones were unheard of back then. There were no service stations with pay phones in this sparsely populated area. I dreaded the thought of returning to the newspaper office and explaining to the publisher who had hired me just a week earlier that I was unable to complete my first real assignment. I didn't know if I had gone too far, or not far enough, or even if I was on the right road. Envisioning my career as a newspaper reporter ruined by incompetence and stupidity, I prayed again. "Lord, let me find that house." And there it was in front of me, the driveway with the woman's name emblazoned on a mailbox. I breathed a sigh of relief, a prayer of thanks, and wrote a feature story that was well-received by my boss.

Several years later, I entered the "don't bother God with little things" phase. I had experienced a growing concern about the many tragedies and dire events occurring around the world. Floods, earthquakes, and devastating wars seemed to shrink my paltry concerns into insignificance. What right did I have to pray about trivial concerns when thousands of people were being murdered in the name of "ethnic cleansing?" How could I bring my feeble concerns to God when pictures of starving children, their skeletal bodies ravaged by famine and disease, stared at me from the pages of magazines?

My reasoning went something like this: God has given me a certain amount of intelligence. I need to use it to remember pencils, directions, and other things that I am able to remember or accomplish on my own. I should save my prayers for truly essential things.

But something about this approach did not seem quite right, either. God had answered so many of my "trivial" prayers that it must not have been wrong to pray them. By limiting the substance of my prayers to big things, was I actually expressing doubt that there could be a God powerful and omniscient enough to concern himself with our day-to-day concerns? I did not want my prayers to exhibit a lack of faith in an omnipotent God, nor did I want to pray for things that seemed trivial and meaningless. I looked to Scripture for answers, and this is what I found:

> "Do not be anxious about anything, but in every-thing, by prayer and petition, with thanksgiving, present your requests to God. And the peace of God, which transcends all understanding, will guard your hearts and minds in Christ Jesus" (Philippians 4:6,7).

In other words, we should bring all our concerns to God. Whether or not He responds in the way we want Him to, we will experience great peace of mind through the process of praying.

Another passage reinforces this contention that we should pray at all times, in all circumstances:

"Is any one of you in trouble? He should pray. Is anyone happy? Let him sing songs of praise. Is any one of you sick? He should call the elders of the church to pray over him and anoint him with oil in the name of the Lord. And the prayer offered in faith will make the sick person well; the Lord will raise him up. If he has sinned, he will be forgiven. Therefore confess your sins to each other and pray for each other so that you may be healed. The prayer of a righteous man is powerful and effective" (James 5:13-16).

In Ephesians 6:17-18, we are exhorted to "Take the helmet of salvation and the sword of the Spirit, which is the word of God. And pray in the Spirit on all occasions with all kinds of prayers and requests. With this in mind, be alert and always keep on praying for all the saints."

Pray Without Ceasing

Scripture indicates that prayer should be unceasing communication with God, not for the fulfillment of all our selfish desires, as if God were a Santa Claus ready to grant our every wish, but as an expression of our faith, for the purpose of strengthening that faith. To bring only trivial things to God, and then to remove ourselves from His presence until time for our next request, is not the kind of faith-strengthening communication God desires. When we bring everything to Him in a context of faith, love and praise, we include both the trivial and the profound, the temporal and the eternal.

Praying unceasingly does not mean that we drop everything and check into a monastery. It means that prayer has become such an integral part of every day that even when we are not kneeling in prayer we are aware of God's presence. The habit of prayer begins in and is nurtured by solitude.

Gradually, as the habit is cultivated, life itself becomes prayer. God is always there, leading, guiding and directing us.

The believer should continue praying for the unbelieving spouse, even if years go by with no apparent results. We need to pray alone, in prayer groups, without ceasing, not with bargains and time limits, but with the knowledge that God hears and responds. The purpose of prayer, to put God at the center of our thoughts and establish a relationship with Him, is accomplished only if we make time to pray.

Chapter Summary

Our relationship with God flourishes if it is nurtured through prayer. Taking time from our busy schedules to pray every day should become a habit as ingrained as taking time to eat and rest.

Scripture indicates that prayer should be unceasing communication with God, not for the fulfillment of all our selfish desires, but as an expression of our faith, for the purpose of strengthening that faith.

The believer should continue praying for an unbelieving spouse, even if years go by with no apparent results. **We need to pray alone, in prayer groups, without ceasing, not with bargains and time limits, but with the knowledge that God hears and responds. The purpose of prayer, to put God at the center of our thoughts and establish a relationship with Him, is accomplished only if we make time to pray.**

CHAPTER TWELVE

Praying With Perseverance

"You need to persevere so that when you have done the will of God, you will receive what He has promised." Hebrews 10:36

Saint Augustine was not always a Christian. As a young man, he sought worldly success and was attracted to several non-Christian movements. Possibly he was influenced by his father, an avowed pagan. But Augustine's mother, Monica, was not only a Christian. She was an extremely persistent Christian. She prayed unceasingly for her husband, Patricius, and for her wayward son. She entered into the men's discussions, quoting Scripture clearly and concisely. In the midst of long, abstract arguments among Augustine and his peers, she brought up the subject of Christianity.

Monica followed her son to Milan when, at the age of 30, Augustine was named professor of rhetoric for the imperial court at Milan. She tried to arrange a good society marriage for Augustine, influencing him to give up his mistress. Through all this, she continued to pray.

Though Monica had to wait, her prayers were eventually rewarded in a way she probably never dreamed. Her husband accepted Christianity and was baptized on his deathbed. In 386 A.D., her son accepted Christianity and was baptized the following year. Saint Augustine went on to become one of the greatest leaders of the early Christian church.

Praying with perseverance, unceasingly and without giving up, means hanging tough through the doubting times, persisting in the face of what appears to be God's silence, and realizing that it is always too soon to quit. Monica did not give up on her husband or her son. She refused to lose faith when her husband persisted in his paganism and her son argued vehemently against her religious beliefs. She was a determined woman, out to win salvation for the ones she loved.

In his book, *When God Doesn't Make Sense,* Dr. James Dobson tells the story of his paternal grandmother, Juanita Dobson, a deeply-committed Christian. Her unbelieving husband was a moral, decent man who saw no reason for a personal relationship with Jesus Christ. He did not mind his wife going to church, but he resented any efforts to drag him there. Realizing that persuasion by nagging was futile, Dr. Dobson's grandmother began a prayer campaign on her husband's behalf. She fasted for his salvation regularly, although her prayers didn't appear to be netting any results. Then, when Juanita Dobson's husband was 69 years old, a series of strokes partially paralyzed this powerful, healthy man. Fearing death, he made an ironic request. Would his wife pray for him? Dr. Dobson's grandmother had waited more than 40 years for that request! She began to call on heaven again, and her husband accepted a relationship with Jesus Christ there on his sickbed.

Augustine's mother and Juanita Dobson both recognized the importance of persistent prayer. Jesus emphasized the significance of praying without giving up when he told his disciples the parable of the persistent widow. This widow kept coming before a stubborn judge who didn't fear God or care too much about people, either. For a long time, the judge refused to grant the woman a fair hearing. She didn't give up. She kept coming back to that judge again and again, until he finally decided he had better see that she received justice, before she wore him out with her persistence.

Jesus said that God, who is a lot more concerned about fairness than the unjust judge, will listen to those who pray persistently. "And will not God bring about justice for his chosen ones, who cry out to him day and night? Will he keep putting them off" (Luke 18:7)?

Why Persist?

Why would God want us to persist, when He knows what we need even before we ask Him? "And when you pray, do not keep on babbling like the pagans, for they think they will be heard because of their many words. Do not be like them, for your Father knows what you need before you ask Him" (Matthew 6:7,8). Why continue to pray for your spouse if you have already petitioned God once?

There are several things persistence in prayer accomplishes. The first of these is that it teaches us to pray without ceasing. If all our prayers were granted the first time around, without any perseverance or continued prayer on our part, we wouldn't learn much about how to pray. We would take our requests to God without need of faith, praise, or the sort of continued awareness of God's presence which persistence in prayer brings. We would be like the child who climbs on Santa's knee, presents the requisite wish list, anticipates the gifts to come, then forgets Santa until next Christmas when it is time to prepare a wish list again.

This is not the kind of interaction our Lord desires. He wants a personal relationship with our worship, our praise, our faith, and our love expressed through our actions and our prayers. This sort of persistent prayer is for our own good, helping us maintain that spiritual fervor which enables us to worship and serve God. As Paul wrote in his letter to Romans: "Be joyful in hope, patient in affliction, faithful in prayer."

Frank Laubach, author of *Prayer: The Mightiest Force In The World,* advocated using fractions of moments in order to keep praying all day long. It was his firm conviction that we truly could change the world by constant prayer. Sometimes he would even "shoot" prayers at a stranger on a bus or a train. At other times, he would simply whisper the word "Jesus" when he thought of our President or another country's leader.

James said, "As you know, we consider blessed those who have persevered. You have heard of Job's perseverance and have seen what the Lord finally brought about. The Lord is full of compassion and mercy" (James 5:11).

Through persistent prayer, we learn to bring all things, not just our latest wish list, before God. We learn to cling to faith, even in those dark days when our prayers appear to go unheard and unanswered. We exhibit our faith that God will act, in His own time and in accordance with His own will.

Persistent Prayer Leads To Action

If all prayers were answered immediately, there would be no need for the kind of perseverance that leads to spiritual growth and development. We would not need to couple prayer with positive, constructive action. Leading others to faith, attaining goals, making correct decisions, and fulfilling our deepest emotional, spiritual, and material desires would be a simple matter of prayer. We could dispense with the persistent, consistent, and frequently difficult actions necessary to the attainment of our goals. In other words, we could dispense with the very things which are character building, which set a positive example of faith in action, and which enable us to utilize the unique, God-given gifts each of us has been blessed with.

Monica did not curtail her activities in order to pray. She prayed unceasingly while she followed her son to Milan and talked to his friends about Christianity.

Frank Laubach coupled prayer with positive, constructive action. He traveled to country after country in order to teach millions of illiterates to read. When people learned to read, Laubach reasoned, they could open a Bible and study God's word for themselves. They could learn how to help themselves up to a better standard of living.

A Prayer and a Song

Reader's Digest published a story in its December, 1995 issue about Allyson Moring, a choral teacher at Bishop England High School. When Allyson was hospitalized with a massive systemic infection, a doctor took her husband, Danny, aside and told him there was little chance his 36-year-old wife would survive the night.

Rushing home, Danny woke their nine-year-old daughter, Elizabeth. Elizabeth asked if her Mommy was going to die. Yes, it was possible, Danny admitted. But he added that they were going to pray and pray as they had never prayed before. Then father and daughter prayed together, Elizabeth's young voice begging God to make her mother well.

As Allyson's condition continued to deteriorate, her swollen body kept alive by a respirator, Danny Moring coupled prayer with action. He was standing at his wife's bedside when two of her colleague's from school came to the intensive care unit with an audio cassette from Allyson's students. The exuberant voices of boys and girls singing Christmas carols filled the room as Danny inserted the tape and turned on the small player. Praying for God to let Allyson hear the music, Danny was astonished to see her eyelids twitch, and to feel a firm squeeze from her hand.

Through those long days of Allyson's illness, Danny played the tape over and over. The students in her choral group, determined not to let their teacher down, prayed for Mrs. Moring and carried on with the Bishop England Christmas concert that their teacher had been preparing them for. Slowly, amazingly, Allyson Moring's systems began to stabilize. Against all odds, she began to recover.

No one could say exactly why she got well, or when the turning point came, but the key fact to Allyson Moring was that her days and nights of unconsciousness were filled with the beautiful music and voices she loved. Danny, Elizabeth, and the Bishop England choral students had prayed. But they had also acted, filling those long hours with music, standing vigil at her bedside, and refusing to give up hope. Persistent prayer coupled with positive, constructive action is a powerful force!

Prayer And Spiritual Growth

While I prayed persistently for Lee's conversion, I learned the importance of setting an example of joyful Christian living. I came to understand the significance of building a good marriage relationship and of being well-acquainted with God's word and my reasons for believing. These things were more valuable to my spiritual growth than immediate answers to prayer would have been.

Prayer is a crucial part of our relationship with God. Positive, constructive action coupled with prayer is essential for our own spiritual growth.

Persistent Prayer Leads to Patience

Missionary E. Stanley Jones said he had adopted this as his life's motto: "When life kicks you, let it kick you forward!" When our prayers aren't answered right away, we are supposed to proceed forward in faith and obedience, recognizing that God's time frame is often different from our own. This continued obedience to God in the face of apparently unanswered prayers is one of the difficult aspects of the Christian faith. We want results, and we want them now! We aren't thinking in terms of eternity. We are thinking in terms of results-oriented prayer that nets immediate gratification. We aren't letting life "kick us forward" if we fail to persevere in the face of apparently unanswered prayer.

The Moravian Missionary

A Moravian missionary died shortly after his arrival in Africa. His ministry was considered a failure, since he had managed to convert only one woman. Some time after his death, a group of men ran across a copy of the Bible he had left behind. Their curiosity aroused, they met with the one woman he had converted. To their surprise, they discovered many additional converts who had studied God's word. A hundred years after his death, the Moravian's mission counted more than 13,000 converts. Though men initially considered the missionary's ministry a failure, God demonstrated that He had a different plan.

Men probably considered Jesus' ministry a failure when he died on the cross. Most of his disciples had fled. Rulers who witnessed the crucifixion sneered as Jesus approached death. Soldiers mocked him. Jesus' followers must have experienced some doubt at this point. Why didn't Jesus save himself? That would surely prove to all those rulers and soldiers and unbelievers the he was the son of God! Was his ministry going to end like this, with an ignoble death on the cross, his murderers apparently having prevailed?

Of course his murderers did not prevail. Jesus rose from the dead three days later. Christianity has persisted through the ages in spite of tremendous persecution and attempts in every century to obliterate the Christian faith. But in those three days of darkness, before Jesus rose again, it must have been hard for that devastated band of believers to cling to their faith.

Jesus could have come down from the cross. He could have hurled lightning bolts into the midst of the scoffers as they cast lots for his clothes. The immediate result might have been the conversion of a few startled, frightened witnesses. But Scripture would not have been fulfilled. Those of us who have become believers without being present as eye witnesses would have found it harder to believe in the ultimate triumph of life over death without the wonderful story of Christ's own resurrection.

Jesus' disciples had to wait three long, dark days before emerging from their despair into the glorious light of knowledge revealed to them. God's time frame is different from ours. When we persist in prayer in spite of those days of darkness, we are exhibiting the faith and obedience essential to the Christian faith.

By Praying, We Pray Better

Lee spent years researching reasons for believing or disbelieving. As a result, when he became a believer he was able to offer a valid basis for belief that would appeal to the staunchest cynic. He has become a senior high Sunday School teacher, with one of his goals being to pass along to his students a reasonable argument for faith. As his students graduate and prepare to face the cynicism and secularism prevalent in many college environments, it is Lee's hope that they will be ready to confront and overcome the inevitable attacks on their faith.

If my prayers had been answered immediately and Lee had become a believer before our marriage, he might not have been prepared to deal with the numerous questions posed by high school students struggling for answers. His years of agnosticism were a valuable preparatory time, enabling him to offer the wisdom of his research and his conclusions.

I did not view Lee's earlier doubts as a positive thing. I could not possibly know how God would choose to use those doubts for His own good. My vision was limited. Perhaps your spouse is in the process of growing toward God for a specific purpose that only God presently understands.

We must continue to pray with persistence for those who are nonbelievers, even if our vision is too limited to see God's ultimate plan. When we pray with persistence, we are acting in obedience. We are learning to love prayer, to pray unceasingly, and to establish prayer as the cornerstone of our relationship with God.

Mother Teresa said, "Love prayer. Feel often the need to pray, and take the trouble to pray. It is by praying often that you will pray better. Prayer enlarges the heart until it is capable of containing the gift that God makes of Himself. Ask and seek. Your heart will grow capable of receiving Him and holding on to Him."

What a wonderful thing, to know that the more we pray, the more our hearts will grow capable of receiving and holding God! Praying with perseverance is for our own benefit as well as our partner's. It reveals a certain unwillingness to give up; a certain optimism born of undying hope and faith.

Chapter Summary

Praying with **perseverance,** unceasingly and without giving up, means hanging tough through the doubting times, persisting in the face of what appears to be God's silence, and realizing that it is always too soon to quit.

Through persistent prayer, we learn to bring all things, not just our latest wish list, before God. We learn to cling to faith, even in those dark days when our prayers appear to go unheard and unanswered. We exhibit our faith that God will act, in His own time and in accordance with His own will.

When we persist in prayer, we are exhibiting the faith and obedience essential to the Christian faith.

The more we pray, the more our hearts will grow capable of receiving and holding God. Praying with perseverance is for our own benefit as well as our partner's. It reveals a certain unwillingness to give up; a certain optimism born of undying hope and faith.

CHAPTER THIRTEEN

Praying With Faith

"I tell you the truth, if you have faith and do not doubt, not only can you do what was done to the fig tree, but also you can say to this mountain, 'Go, throw yourself into the sea,' and it will be done. If you believe, you will receive whatever you ask for in prayer."
Matthew 21:21

If you found out you had won a million dollars, with the only requirement for collection being that you dial a certain toll-free number, chances are you wouldn't hesitate long. You would make a beeline for the nearest telephone, claiming your prize. There would be no tarrying around, no insistence on actually holding and counting that million dollars before you agreed to accept it. You wouldn't say, "This toll free number might be a wrong number, so I'm not going to dial."

We have something available to us that is far more valuable than a million dollars, yet we hesitate to claim it. We have at our disposal the miraculous, life-changing power of prayer. Prayer is capable of connecting us with God and transforming our lives, but we reject it under the misguided notion that we must see before we believe. We have the power to lift our unbelieving spouse up before God, yet we conclude too soon that our prayers aren't working.

The effectiveness of prayer is demonstrated over and over again in the Bible. Many of us have seen prayer work in the lives of people who were at their wit's end; people who appeared to have no hope. These people turned to God in prayer, received Him into their lives and experienced the miraculous power of God.

But like the phone call needed to collect that million dollars, there is a necessary prerequisite for tapping into prayer's amazing potential. *We must have faith.* Do we truly believe, in the depths of our heart, that God hears our prayer? Do we truly believe He will help us? Do we really think He will change our spouse? If we don't get the answer we want right away, do we hold fast, with unswaying conviction, to the belief that God who does everything for our own good will eventually answer our prayer?

Sometimes, even if we have already witnessed the power of prayer, we reject faith the next time around because we secretly believe, as Mark Twain did, that faith is "believing in something you know really isn't true." How different this is from the definition of faith in Hebrews 11:1: "Now faith is being sure of what we hope for and certain of what we do not see."

Often we wonder why faith must be in the unseen. Our thinking goes something like this: "If I could witness one little miracle with my own eyes, then I'd be able to believe." But God must know this isn't the way human beings work. For one thing, we tend to discount the miracles God *does* show us. We pray for something and that prayer is answered.

We feel elated. Time goes by, and we begin to harbor a secret little seed of doubt. Maybe there was no response to prayer, after all. Maybe things would have happened the way they did, anyway. With this kind of thinking, what's to stop us from discounting any future miracles God might choose to perform?

Seeing Is Not Believing

Even those who were direct witnesses to God's power entertained doubts. The Pharisees and Saducees were privy to a number of miracles, yet they refused to believe. Jesus berated his disciples for not having the faith to heal a boy suffering from seizures. When the disciples asked Jesus later why they weren't able to heal the boy, he told them it was because they had so little faith.

Jesus did not perform many miracles in his hometown, because of the amount of disbelief. "He could not do any miracles there, except lay his hands on a few sick people and heal them. And he was amazed at their lack of faith" (Mark 6:5,6).

The Bible points out starkly and eloquently that seeing is not believing. From the Israelites who experienced God's presence in a pillar of cloud by day and a pillar of fire by night, then turned from their faith to worship a golden calf, to the skeptics who witnessed Jesus' miracles firsthand and refused to believe, people have proven that signs and wonders do not produce the quality of faith God calls us to have.

What we think we see changes every day with our changing circumstances and perspectives. We might believe in a miracle one day, and chalk it up to magic or accident or coincidence the next. *But faith in what is not seen, faith that springs from within, when our very souls are touched and guided by the Holy Spirit, is the stronger and more enduring faith because it cannot be banished by today's doubts in yesterday's miracles.* We can be sure that this kind of faith, without demands for signs and wonders, is richly rewarded. As Jesus told Thomas, who would not believe Jesus had risen from the dead until he saw the nail marks in Jesus' hands, "Because you have seen me, you have believed; blessed are those who have not seen and yet have believed."

Answered Prayer Or Coincidence?

One spring morning a couple of years ago when I was out for a walk, I started thinking about all the extra time on my hands. I had just completed a part time volunteer assignment. Several other volunteer responsibilities were drawing to a close. My children had reached school age, so the heavy demands of infant and toddler care were behind me. (Regardless of what anyone else says about the difficulties of raising teenagers, I firmly believe it is more time-consuming and exhausting to take care of pre-schoolers, who require a mother's undivided and nonstop attention 100 percent of the time!)

With the easing of so many prior responsibilities, it was time to seek a new involvement. But doing what? There were many areas of service crying out for volunteers. I decided to seek God's guidance then and there, in the middle of my walk. "Lord, show me what you want me to do next. Lead and guide me toward the sort of service that is your will for me right now," I prayed.

When I arrived home, the phone rang immediately. A neighborhood acquaintance wanted to know if I would serve as chairman of a service project that would require more time, effort, and commitment than any of the volunteer projects I had undertaken so far. I accepted, and for the next year successfully spearheaded this project.

When my tenure as chairman ended, I once again sought God's guidance. "Lord, show me what to do next." A few minutes after I had prayed this prayer, the phone rang. The caller was a fellow church member, asking that I commit to a chairmanship in our upcoming church building fund campaign.

I was never surprised that God answered my prayers so quickly. I expected it, because I had prayed in complete faith that an answer would be forthcoming. Skeptics might call these incidences coincidence, but too many meaningful coincidences contradict the nature of coincidence.

C.S. Lewis did not believe it was coincidence which led him to the barber shop in response to a barber's prayers. He got up one morning intending to have his hair cut for a visit to London. When the trip to London was postponed, Lewis decided to postpone the haircut, too. But a nagging, inner voice urged him to get his hair cut. Unable to ignore this inner urging, Lewis headed for the barber shop. He was met by a jubilant barber who said, "I prayed that you would come in here today for a haircut!"

Lewis pointed out the impossibility of proving that answers to prayer wouldn't have occurred anyway. God grants some requests and not others. Empirical evidence is therefore unobtainable in a real, scientific sense. According to Lewis, our assurance that God always hears and sometimes grants our prayers comes from our personal relationship with God. Those who know God best would know whether He sent Lewis to the barber's shop because the barber prayed.

His Faith Sustained Him

Belief in the power of prayer is part of this faith we have in the unseen. Eddie Rickenbacker could have told you about that kind of faith. Early in his life, his mother had taught him to pray, and he continued to pray through many crises and difficulties. It was his faith in prayer that sustained him and those with him in one of the most difficult crises he ever had to face.

Rickenbacker's plane was on a war mission when it was shot down in the Pacific. After eight days of drifting in rubber life rafts, Rickenbacker's men were growing desperate. There had been no sign of a boat or plane. Some of the men were sick or delirious. They were scorched by the tropical sun, without food or water, their feet blistered and faces burned.

One of the men had a small Bible, and they took turns reading aloud from it every day. On the eighth day, when they were close to the breaking point, someone suggested reading this passage from Matthew: "So do not worry, saying, 'What shall we eat?' or 'What shall we drink?' or 'What shall we wear?' For the pagans run after all these things, and your heavenly Father knows that you need them. But seek first his kingdom and his righteousness, and all these things will be given to you as well."

What happened next must have seemed like a miracle. A gull flew in out of nowhere and landed on Rickenbacker's head. He reached up and caught it easily. The men were able to eat. There was a rainstorm, and they had their first water. Their prayers were answered!

You can bet there were no longer any unbelievers in those life rafts. The men began to pray with new confidence and faith. They believed, as Eddie Rickenbacker had, that God was with them and they would be saved. They drifted for nearly two more weeks, remaining steadfast in their belief. On the 21st day of their ordeal, they were located by planes and rescued. Following the rescue, what moved people most was Eddie Rickenbacker's explanation, in two words, of the reason for their survival: "We prayed."

How Do We Increase Our Faith?

We can attribute answered prayers to coincidence, or we can elect to have faith, but *faith is always a choice.* Eddie Rickenbacker chose to believe God had answered his prayers and kept him alive. C.S. Lewis chose to believe his visit to the barber shop was in response to a faithful barber's prayer. I choose to believe God guides and directs my life.

Having made the choice to believe in one instance does not mean we will make that choice every time. Our faith could falter the very next day. If you are married to an unbelieving spouse who is very resistant, your faith in the efficacy of your prayers might plummet. But there are certain steps we can take to strengthen and increase our faith, making it more resistant to vacillation and doubt.

Study God's Word

One of the most important things we can do to strengthen our faith is to read the Bible. Greater knowledge of God leads to greater faith, and greater knowledge of God is obtained from a study of His Word. We study His Word by reading the Bible, which acquaints us with the nature of God, with the veracity of His universal truths, and with how we are supposed to act as children of God.

When I read Scripture, I am stirred to a profound excitement that such justice and love and mercy can exist in a world so overrun by evil. God has allowed us a glimpse of Himself, which can only increase our faith.

In order to pray in faith for the unbeliever, we must have faith. To possess faith, we should read God's Word. Through the Bible, God speaks to our Spirit, to each one of us uniquely and individually, filling us with awe and wonder.

Dr. Robert Jeffress writes in *Heaven Can't Wait* that we should approach Bible reading as explorers rather than just tourists, taking time to explore the rich truths of God's Word. We should mark those passages that pique our curiosity for further study, delving ever deeper into the meaning of Scripture and its relevance to our lives.

When Lee accepted Christ, he decided to read the Bible from cover to cover. He wanted to learn everything there was to know about the faith he had recently embraced. How many of us "longtime" Christians are determined to read the Bible from cover to cover, discovering all we can about what we believe? If we were to do this, we might find that our faith did not waver quite so much.

Associate With Believers

Another way of increasing our faith is to associate with believers. In his letter to the people of the church of Rome, Paul said, "I long to see you so that I may impart to you some spiritual gift to make you strong—that is, that you and I may be mutually encouraged by each other's faith."

When Christians get together through church, prayer groups, at work or in social situations, they are mutually encouraged by each other's faith. It is especially important that a believer married to a nonbeliever associate with other believers, since the believer will not have the spiritual support of a like-minded spouse.

Act In Faith

One important faith-builder is to act in faith, even if faith is lacking. We learn to love by loving, learn to be generous by giving, learn to be cheerful by acting cheerfully and learn to be faithful by acting in faith. Mother Teresa said that if you lack faith, you can help others by doing works of love, and the fruit of these works are the extra graces that come into your soul. Then you will begin to open up and want the joy of loving God.

Visualize a Positive Outcome

To increase our faith, we need to expect and visualize a positive outcome. The things our minds dwell on tend to become reality, so it is a good idea to tap into the positive channels of that amazing psychic energy by imagining and expecting the best.

A young woman I know decided to do just that. She was in love with a man who showed no inclination toward marriage. He enjoyed this woman's company, but made no bones about the fact that she wasn't the one for him. He wasn't ready for a commitment.

At first, she was miserable whenever they were together. "I care about him so much," she thought. "What am I going to do when he dumps me?"

These negative thoughts were so persistent that they were almost making her ill. Then that young woman read a book called *The Magic of Believing*. This book talked about the importance of believing that something you wanted to happen was going to happen. The woman decided to implement the suggestions for positive imaging that she read about in this book. When she and the young man were together, she looked him in the eyes and thought to herself, "You are going to marry me!"

Her attitude improved dramatically. She found herself laughing and enjoying the time she spent with her friend. Instead of becoming embroiled in unhappy discussions about why they weren't right for each other, she smiled sweetly and changed the subject when her friend mentioned his reservations about the relationship. She was able to do this because she was thinking, "You are going to marry me, regardless of what you think right now."

Her boyfriend remarked on the change. "You always seem so happy," he said one evening.

"Oh, I am," she replied, smiling mysteriously and thinking to herself, "I'm happy because we are going to be husband and wife."

The end result of all this positive thinking and believing was that the couple *did* become husband and wife. About three months after she had read that book and put its positive principles into action, the woman's friend asked her to marry him.

You need to visualize a positive outcome when you pray for your spouse. Imagine your spouse accepting your faith. Do not allow negative thoughts, such as, "He's never going to change," to undermine your faith. Believe that change is going to happen, expect the best, and open those floodgates of psychic energy that respond to the magic of believing.

What Jesus Said About Faith

Jesus told us to put this principle of believing into action when he said in Mark 11:24: "Therefore, I tell you, whatever you ask in prayer, believe that you have received it, and it will be yours."

His many miracles were a testimony to the vital role of faith. When two blind men followed Jesus, crying out, "Have mercy on us, Son of David," Jesus healed them. But first, he asked them a question: "Do you believe that I am able to do this?"

"Yes Lord," was their unequivocal reply.

Jesus responded by touching their eyes and saying, "according to your faith it will be done to you."

If anyone doubts that faith is the essential ingredient in Jesus' miracles and healings, a reading of Matthew 8:5-13 will dispel those doubts. In this passage, a centurion, or Roman military officer, approached Jesus with a request. "My servant lies at home paralyzed and in terrible suffering," the centurion explained.

Jesus agreed to go and heal the man, but the centurion's reaction was unexpected. Instead of exclaiming for joy that he had managed to extract a promise from Jesus to help, he said, "Lord, I do not deserve to have you come under my roof. Just say the word, and my servant will be healed." The centurion understood the meaning of authority. When he commanded his soldiers to do something, they obeyed. There was no question in his mind that Jesus had the authority to heal.

Upon hearing this, Jesus said to his followers, "I tell you the truth, I have not found anyone in Israel with such great faith...." To the centurion, he said, "Go! It will be done just as you believed it would." The servant was healed.

How Much Faith Do We Need?

How much faith do we need to tap into this amazing power of prayer? What if our faith has highs and lows, leading us to great peaks of confidence one day, certain that we "can do all things through Christ, who gives us strength," only to plunge us into a valley of doubt the next?

Fortunately for us, Jesus tells us we don't need a great mountain of faith. "I tell you the truth, if you have faith as small as a mustard seed, you can say to this mountain, 'Move from here to there,' and it will move. Nothing will be impossible for you" (Matthew 17:20).

It is not the quantity of faith we have, but the quality of our faith which determines the efficacy of our prayers. Even if our faith is pierced by doubts and plagued by those highs and lows that send us hurtling from mountain to valley, we can tap into the power of prayer when we possess the faith to pray and to act on our beliefs.

When the church I belong to was in the midst of a building fund campaign, the pastor, Dr. Joe Bowen, asked me to give my testimony at a celebration banquet which was to be the culmination of the campaign. Outwardly calm, I agreed to speak. Inwardly, I panicked. Having always suffered from an overwhelming fear of public speaking, I quaked at the thought of addressing several hundred people from the stage of a hotel banquet hall. Talking to a handful of listeners made me nervous. How could I possibly speak to hundreds?

In addition to planning and practicing my talk, I began to pray in earnest. Still, as the night of the banquet drew closer, my terror increased. Lee's reassurances, my prayers and Scripture readings, and my own internal admonitions to "get a grip and exhibit some confidence" did little good. Panic washed over me anew each time I thought of the banquet night. Why had I ever agreed to give my testimony? I would never be able to get through that dreaded evening!

Prior to the celebration banquet, several church members hosted fellowship desserts for the purpose of discussing and praying about the building fund campaign. It was customary at these get-togethers for someone to present a brief testimony. Following one of these fellowship desserts, my panic soared to new heights. I was driving home when I realized how difficult it would have been for me to give my testimony before even this small group of people. How on earth, then, was I going to speak at a banquet?

It was at this point that I prayed a very specific prayer: "Lord, I need to hear something right now that is going to give me confidence and ease my fears about public speaking." I clicked on the radio, which had been tuned to a Christian station. Since the station was an a.m. one and I was outside the city limits, the first noise to fill my car was static. But before I could turn off the radio, the static cleared. One sentence of a minister's sermon boomed with the impact and resonance of thunder: *Where there is fear, there is no faith, and where there is faith, there is no fear.*

This was the only sentence I was able to hear. Once again, static blotted out the station. But that one sentence was enough. I experienced the elation and confidence I had been longing for; the assurance that faith would cast out fear. That sentence came back to me over and over again in the ensuing week. *Where there is fear there is no faith, and where there is faith, there is no fear.* I was able to give my testimony at that crowded celebration banquet, without notes and without faltering, not because I have ability as a public speaker, but because God was with me.

I tell this story because it reveals that, even though I fell far short of the faith I should have had, I possessed enough faith to say "yes" to giving my testimony. When we take a step of faith, God reaches across the chasm of our doubts and fears, helping us to new heights of accomplishment and faith. But we must have a mustard seed of faith—enough to say "yes" to God's call.

Faith-size Requests

How can we acquire even a mustard seed's worth of faith? What must we do to take that first step of faith, if doubt seems to dominate? In *Prayer: Conversing With God,* Rosalind Rinker wrote about making faith-size requests, or asking for those things we can really believe God will do. She pointed out that although this does not limit what God can do, it honestly recognizes the size of our faith.

Rinker related the story of Karen, who prayed for the conversion of her boyfriend, Chuck. Karen was unable to believe he would be saved the first week, but she was able to believe that on their next date, she would be able to tell Chuck about Christ. After this, she prayed that Chuck would accept her gift of a New Testament; then that he would be willing to read it. Finally, after many preliminary steps, Chuck made an open acknowledgment of faith.

Rinker recommended that instead of trying to take the giant leap from the bottom of the stairs to the top, we take the conversion of a loved one a step at a time, as Karen did. Then we will be able to exercise the faith that God wants us to have.

Remember—we only need a mustard seed of faith, and God will do the rest. We can make faith-size requests, as Karen did. Or we can pray with complete faith and assurance that God hears all our requests, as Eddie Rickenbacker did. But wherever our faith lies along the wide spectrum from little to much, we can be sure that praying in faith allows us to tap into the awesome, life-changing power of prayer. God will not fail to hear us as we lift up our spouse and our marriage to Him.

Chapter Summary

Seeing is not believing. Faith in what is not seen, faith that springs from within when our very souls are touched and guided by the Holy Spirit, is the stronger and more enduring faith because it cannot be banished by today's doubts in yesterday's miracles.

Faith is a choice. To increase our faith, we need to:
*Act in faith.
*Read the Bible.
*Visualize a positive outcome.
* Associate with believers.

Jesus said, "According to your faith, it will be done to you."
It is not the quantity of faith we have, but the quality of our faith which determines the efficacy of our prayers. When doubts seem to dominate, we can acquire more faith by asking for those things which we can really believe God will do. Although this does not limit what God can do, it honestly recognizes the size of our faith.

Wherever our faith lies along the wide spectrum from little to much, we can be sure that praying in faith allows us to tap into the awesome, life-changing power of prayer.

CHAPTER FOURTEEN

Praying With Praise

"Give thanks to the Lord, call on His name; make known among the nations what He has done. Sing to Him, sing praise to Him; tell of all His wonderful acts." 1 Chronicles 16:8,9

Most of us have heard the expression, *attitude of gratitude*, and most of us have experienced it's opposite: the sullen face of ingratitude. Think of how you felt when the driver you let in front of you sped off without a wave of his hand or any other sign of appreciation. What about the meal you delivered, hot and homemade, to a recipient who grabbed it without a gracious word?

Once I allowed a man behind me at a checkout counter to go first, since he had fewer purchases. Instead of a thank you, or even a nod of acknowledgment, he shoved to the front, heaved his items on the counter and proceeded to carry on a long conversation with the sales clerk as if I didn't exist.

What ingratitude! What rudeness! We fume and stew, wishing we had not done the good deed. If we weren't making a concerted effort to act Christ-like, we might be tempted to snatch back that meal or reclaim our place in line. The smallest display of gratitude makes our efforts seem worthwhile, whereas ungraciousness fans the flames of resentment.

Jesus experienced the attitude of *ingratitude* when he healed ten lepers. "Have pity on us," the men cried as Jesus passed them on his way into a village. Jesus instructed them to show themselves to the priests, the men followed his command, and they were healed. Only one man returned, praising God. This man, a Samaritan, threw himself at Jesus' feet and thanked him.

Jesus reacted by asking, "Were not all ten cleansed? Where are the other nine? Was no one found to return and give praise to God except this foreigner?"

It is important to avoid the attitude of the nine lepers who never returned to thank Jesus. Acknowledge and be thankful for your spouse's move toward faith, no matter how small the steps. Do not brush aside or relegate to insignificance the halting progress of another's spiritual journey. Do not indulge in your own attitude of ingratitude when a spouse does not live up to your preconceived notions or lofty aims.

Say "Thank You"

I try to instill in my children a sense of gratitude. "Say thank you," I've told them since they were toddlers. "Write thank-you notes," I've prodded since they were old enough to write. Sometimes it's a battle. To sit inside during Christmas vacation and work on thank you notes is a tedious endeavor when the rest of the world is careening past on new roller blades and bicycles. I remind my disgruntled offspring of the gift givers and the trouble they took to find desirable gifts, because it is important that my children learn the value of thanks and the virtues of sincere appreciation. Maybe, if they start when they are young, they will cultivate an "attitude of gratitude" that will last them all their lives.

Just as we want our generosity acknowledged with a simple thank you, God wants us to acknowledge Him with praise. This is evident throughout both Old and New Testaments. When King David brought the Ark of God to the City of David, he "danced before the Lord with all his might."

The Psalms emphasize over and over again the importance of praising God. Paul said, "By prayer and supplication with *thanksgiving* let your requests be made known to God." Yet many of us, even while we fume and fret at the lack of gratitude expressed toward us, forget to thank God for answered prayers. When our teenage driver pulls into the driveway, is our thanks for his safe arrival as heartfelt and emotional as the initial petition that he return home safely? Do we even remember all those little prayers that are answered in the course of a day? Most of us can relate to Kahlil Gibran's words in *The Prophet:* "You pray in your distress and in your need; would that you might pray also in the fullness of your joy and in the days of abundance."

The person who cultivates a grateful attitude is the person who is most likely to live a full, abundant life. Benjamin Franklin exemplified the virtues of a positive, thankful attitude. His mother and father were the parents of ten children, so finances were always strained. At ten years old, Franklin was forced to quit school and become an apprentice in his father's candle making shop. He continued to study and read in his free time, striving to secure the education he was unable to obtain formally.

Franklin endured poverty and setbacks, dealings with unscrupulous business acquaintances, illness, the death of a son, and numerous other obstacles that might have soured the most optimistic of people. He was a hard worker, spending long hours at his printing press when other young men his age were socializing in local taverns. Yet Franklin considered himself fortunate. He wrote in his autobiography that he wished in all humility to thank God, to whom he owed his happiness and success.

Benjamin Franklin did not dwell on the negative. He embraced the positive, praised God and lived a life of abundance, productivity, and accomplishment that has seldom been equaled.

An Expression Of Joy

We should always praise God for answered prayer, because praise expresses joy, and "the joy of the Lord is our strength" (Nehemiah 8:10). Our praise is an expression of joy which leads to even greater gladness in all God's blessings. Dancing before the Lord in an abandonment to joy as David did, singing hymns of praise, our voices rising in a wonderful crescendo of hallelujahs that reverberate from the very walls of the church, and flinging our arms wide to embrace the awesome beauty of a winter snowstorm are expressions of sheer gladness that fill us with an even greater, deeper joy.

God must be pleased when such uncontained happiness bubbles from the very essence of our beings, spilling over into exuberant expression. *Praise is good for us, because an acknowledgment of God's gifts makes us ever more aware of blessings piled upon blessings.* When we are making mental notes of things we have, it is harder to lament the absence of things we don't have.

When I was a child, I remember turning over and over again to a favorite page in a volume of children's poetry. The picture of a child with a king's crown on his head, surrounded by a wonderful variety of animals, always captured my imagination. Beneath the picture were these words: *The world is so full of a number of things, that I'm sure we should all be as happy as kings.* When I read those words and pored over that marvelous picture, I never failed to feel as happy as a king, with an exuberant joy that was silent praise to God just for *being*.

The more we practice praise, the more we develop a joy in living that transcends the suffering and difficulties encountered in life. Dr. Norman Vincent Peale said that thanksgiving is one of the most important, most creative capacities of the human mind. Practice praying with praise, develop an attitude of gratitude, and a spirit of thanksgiving will begin to permeate everything you do.

How Can I Be Thankful?

What about the person who feels he has nothing to be thankful for? Maybe you are married to an unbeliever who is not supportive of your spiritual life. As a result, you are experiencing friction at home. Maybe finances are a struggle, or a personality clash with your adolescent daughter seems destined to reach an unpleasant climax. Maybe you have lost a job, a loved one, or are having to leave your friends and church and move to a different state. "How can I be thankful when there is nothing to be thankful for?" You might ask yourself. "Why can't things be different? Why can't I be married to a person who shares my faith? Why can't I get along better with the kids? Why did a less deserving person end up with the promotion?"

It is at these times, when joy does not spring spontaneously and abundantly from the inner recesses of our being, that we need to remember Paul's words in 1 Thessalonians 5:16: "Be joyful always; pray continually; give thanks in all circumstances, for this is God's will for you in Christ Jesus." Paul did not say be thankful some of the time, or even most of the time, especially when things are looking good. He said to give thanks in *all* circumstances, for this is God's will.

Once on a car trip I was listening to a tape by inspirational speaker and writer, Zig Ziglar. Ziglar was discussing a particular woman's thorough dislike of and dissatisfaction with her job. There was nothing at all she enjoyed about her occupation. Ziglar began asking the woman questions, such as "Do you receive a paycheck? Is the place you are working air conditioned? Do you receive health benefits?" The questions went on and on, with the result being that this woman soon realized there were a number of good things about her job. With a changed attitude, she became a productive and happy employee.

We have much to be thankful for that we take for granted. We tend to criticize a lot about our country—its leaders, the news media, the school systems, our welfare system, our high taxes. But would we rather have been born one of the starving masses in India, or under the iron rule of a totalitarian regime? Would we have preferred to live at a time when penicillin was unheard of and smallpox decimated entire populations? When we get up in the morning, do we revel in the blessings of a warm house, a hot cup of coffee, and a refrigerator full of food? Even when joy and praise do not flow spontaneously, we need to cultivate the habit of thankfulness. We need to praise God for the small gifts that bestow an unexpected grace, a moment of comfort, or a touch of beauty.

And Just When Things Were Going So Good

It is an ironic characteristic of human nature that when things are going well, we tend to make life worse. Newspapers printed the story of a husband and wife who won $27.4 million in the lottery. They had been a happy couple before this windfall, but now they were divorcing and could not sleep at night for fear of losing their fortune. The woman said there were times she wished she had not won that money.

History shows us that when countries grow wealthy and hardships decrease, people turn from religion. A moral and social decay sets in, leading to a proliferation of lawlessness, a devaluation of human life, and the ultimate loss of freedom.

This loss of freedom is followed by a time of persecution and suffering, which kindles a revival of faith.

People forget to pray during the good times as well as the bad. They neglect to thank God for blessings, with the result being that faith is lost.

We should all heed the words of one vacation bible school teacher who said, "I pray all the time, because if I don't, I might lose connection with God. Then, when I really need something, He won't hear me."

When we can't find anything we like about a situation, we might need to look a little harder for the blessing God means us to derive. If we still can't find anything to praise, we need to praise God anyway. Otherwise, we might "lose the connection."

Amazing Things Happen

Amazing things happen when people praise God through all circumstances. Paul and Silas were stripped, severely beaten and thrown into prison, their feet fastened in stocks, after casting an evil spirit out of a slave girl. They were in dire straits, assigned to an inner cell of the jail with the jailor commanded to guard them carefully. Yet at midnight, instead of moaning about their plight or crying out to God to right this injustice, they were praising God with hymns. The other prisoners who were listening to Paul and Silas must have been astonished at this display of faith and joy in the middle of a jail cell. Those prisoners must have been even more astonished when a violent earthquake shook the very foundations of the prison. All at once the prison doors flew open and everybody's chains came loose. Yes, amazing things happen when people praise God. Try it! Fill your prayers with praise as well as petitions. And don't forget to thank God for His answers.

Thanking God for Fleas

Corrie Ten Boom, the unmarried, middle-aged daughter of a Dutch watchmaker, never dreamed that her ordinary life would undergo a drastic change. Content with the prospects of taking over her aging father's business, happy with the quiet, uneventful days that seemed to be her lot, Corrie never anticipated becoming a leader in the Dutch Underground. But God frequently chooses those who appear to be least likely for the fulfillment of his purposes. When Corrie, her father, and her older sister Betsie received a knock on their door one evening, they ushered in a frightened Jewish woman, and the transformation began.

The Nazis had invaded Holland, and Jews were disappearing. A business or an apartment would be abandoned overnight, whole families vanishing as if its members had never existed. Corrie did not know if these Jews, many of them longtime friends and acquaintances, had been whisked off to concentration camps, murdered, or if they had escaped into hiding. She only knew that a terrible evil had invaded her beautiful country. The peace she loved had vanished as suddenly and completely as her Jewish neighbors.

Corrie and her family were Christians who found comfort and sustenance in prayer. But there came a time when they were called to do more than pray. The frightened woman at their door was only a beginning. More and more refugees showed up. Corrie, her father, and her sister could not turn their fellow human beings away. They began hiding Jews in a specially built room of their house, aiding their escape from the Nazis.

Eventually, the Ten Booms were captured. Sentenced to concentration camps, they experienced firsthand the brutal horrors of war and evil. Forced to sleep on roach-infested mattresses crowded with ragged, filthy prisoners, to labor long hours on meager rations and to watch the bodies of dead prisoners discarded like so much garbage, they realized death was always imminent. Yet in the midst of their misery, they found joy and hope through their faith in God.

At one point, when Corrie and Betsie were transferred to a particularly notorious extermination camp, they almost despaired. Assigned to an overcrowded, filthy barracks swarming with fleas, Corrie wailed to her sister, "Betsie, how can we live in such a place!"

"Lord, show us how," Corrie heard her sister praying. Suddenly Betsie turned excitedly to Corrie. He's given us the answer," Betsie exclaimed, imploring her sister to look up First Thessalonians in the Bible they had managed to smuggle into the barracks.

Corrie read these words: "Rejoice always, pray constantly, give thanks in all circumstances, for this is the will of God in Christ Jesus..."

How could they possibly give thanks in these circumstances? Corrie was skeptical. She stared around her at the dark, foul-smelling barracks. Her sister began by thanking God that they had been assigned to a barracks together. Next, they thanked God for the fact that there had been no inspection when they entered, which would have revealed their Bible. But Corrie was aghast when Betsie thanked God for the fleas. How could God ever make a person grateful for fleas?

Give thanks in *all* circumstances, Betsie reminded her. Corrie felt sure her sister must be wrong as they stood between the rows of bunks and gave thanks for fleas. Corrie was to find out later how much of a blessing the fleas actually were. She and Betsie began holding Bible readings in the filthy barracks. Beneath the pale, yellow light cast by a small light bulb, they read the Bible to an ever larger group of women hungry for a ray of hope. The crowd swelled as these "services" began. Corrie and Betsie were able to translate the Dutch text into German, since their father had long ago insisted that they learn the language. Then a marvelous thing happened. Corrie heard the life-giving words passed back along the aisles in French, Polish, Russian, Czech, and back into Dutch. God's truth found a way through the darkness and misery, shedding light where no one had expected light!

What did the fleas have to do with all this? At first, Betsie and Corrie called these meetings cautiously. The guards were just outside, patrolling the area. As night after night passed with no guard showing up, they grew bolder. Why was there no supervision, or interruption of these services? It was only later that Corrie realized why they were left alone to read their Bible. It was the fleas! None of the guards wanted to come near such a flea-infested barracks!

When All Else Fails

Don Gossett, author of *There's Dynamite in Praise*, said when all else fails, praise prevails. A number of years ago, I experienced the truth of this statement. I began to suffer from a depression that seemed to descend from nowhere like a great, gray curtain, bringing with it a nameless anxiety. Sometimes the curtain lifted slightly, allowing a glimmer of sunlight to shine through. But most of the time it pressed heavily, a leaden weight robbing me of joy.

I turned to prayer, petitioning God to release me from the throes of this depression. Over and over again I made my request, despairing when it was not answered. I employed all my powers of determination, vowing to beat this thing. But nothing happened. The mysterious darkness continued to nibble away at my happiness. I became physically ill, which lowered my mental reserves even more. When our bodies are struggling to overcome sickness, it is hard to maintain mental and emotional health. It is as though all of our reserve strength is going into making the body well.

I became convinced my prayers were not going to be answered and I was destined to suffer this depression for the rest of my life. It was at this point that I took a different approach to prayer. I relinquished my fervent requests for happiness. Instead, I began praising God. "Thank you for my depression and anxiety and anything else you want to send my way," I prayed as I gazed through my bedroom window at the green world outside. "Maybe this present unhappiness will help to make me a more compassionate person, better understanding the despair other people might feel."

In the days that followed, as I continued to praise God, an amazing thing happened. I grew physically stronger. The curtain of depression lifted. Like a butterfly emerging from its cocoon, my spirits took wing and soared to new heights of joy, leaving behind that mysterious dark curtain of depression.

Whatever anxieties we suffer from, whatever illnesses rack our bodies or our minds, whatever problems we face, we can be sure that by praising God we are exhibiting the faith that will help us overcome them.

As a believer praying for your unbelieving partner, you need to fill your prayers with praise as well as petitions, thanking God for every good thing about the person you love. Thank God for whatever characteristics attracted you to that person initially. Praise God that you have an opportunity to bring the message of faith and salvation to an unbeliever. Thank God ahead of time for opening your partner's mind and heart to God's message.

Do as we are exhorted to do in Psalm 100. "Shout for joy to the Lord, all the earth, Worship the Lord with gladness; come before Him with joyful songs. Know that the Lord is God. It is He who made us and we are His; we are His people and the sheep of His pasture. Enter His gates with thanksgiving and His courts with praise. Give thanks to Him and praise His name. For the Lord is good, and His love endures forever; His faithfulness continues through all generations."

Chapter Summary

The Bible emphasizes over and over again the importance of praising God. Just as we want our generosity acknowledged with a simple thank you, God wants us to acknowledge Him with praise.

The person who cultivates a grateful attitude is the person who is most likely to live a full, abundant life. Our praise is an expression of joy which leads to even greater gladness in all God's blessings.

Praise is good for us, because an acknowledgement of God's gifts makes us ever more aware of blessings piled upon blessings.

Amazing things happen when people praise God through all circumstances. Whatever problems we face, we can be sure that by praising God, we are exhibiting the faith that will help us overcome those problems.

As a believer praying for your nonbelieving partner, you need to fill your prayers with praise as well as petitions, thanking God for every good thing about the person you love.

CHAPTER FIFTEEN

Hindrances To Prayer

"Hear my prayer, O Lord; listen to my cry for mercy. In the day of my trouble I will call to you, for you will answer me." Psalm 86: 6

I pray and pray," one woman complained. "But my prayers aren't answered. What am I supposed to do now?"

Like this woman, most of us struggle with the problem of unanswered prayer. An entire church congregation prayed for the safe return of a missing girl. One week later, the murdered girl's body was discovered. A devout Christian wife prayed daily for her husband, who seemed distant and preoccupied, and for their marital relationship, which had been strained. One day she received the horrifying news that her husband was a serial rapist.

How do we reconcile these apparently unanswered prayers with Jesus' words in Matthew 7: "Ask and it will be given to you; seek and you will find; knock and the door will be opened to you. For everyone who asks receives; he who seeks finds; and to him who knocks, the door will be opened"?

Claiming the promise we read here, we pray for something and expect to get it. When we don't, we are bitter and resentful, occasionally even losing faith. Does God hear some prayers, but not others? Are the Bible's words false? Does it mean that we aren't as good as somebody else, or that we lack faith, if we pray for healing and healing doesn't come? Does it mean that God doesn't really involve himself in the affairs of men if He hasn't answered my prayer that my spouse become a believer?

Christians have always contended with the problem of unanswered prayer. We try to reconcile the failure to obtain the things we ask for with the promise that we have only to ask, and we will receive. What many people fail to understand is that several conditions for answered prayer are mentioned in the Bible. Hindrances to prayer must be acknowledged and dealt with if we are to build our faith into a fortress that is undiminished by the reality that we might not get everything we want. Overcoming the hindrances to prayer will enable us to pray more effectively for the unbeliever.

Lack of Forgiveness

A shrill siren startled me from the calm, after-school chat I was having with my son. Flashing blue lights greeted my glance in the rearview mirror. Carefully, I eased to the shoulder of the road. I knew I had been driving under the 45 mile per hour speed limit. Maybe the policeman was trying to follow someone further ahead and my car was in the way.

That hope vanished when the police car, its lights still flashing, swerved to the shoulder behind me. Genuinely puzzled, I stared at the officer striding toward my car. "What did I do?" I stammered.

"Let me see your license and proof of insurance," he answered gruffly.

Fishing the requested information from my purse, I handed it over and waited for his explanation.

"You know you've got an expired tag?"

"No," I gulped weakly.

"You didn't stop until I turned on my siren, even though I followed you for about a mile," he accused.

"I didn't notice you until you turned on the siren."

He wrote out a ticket, adding in large block letters, "MUST NOT DRIVE."

"I'm going to keep your driver's license. You can pick it up on your court date. You'd better get that tag taken care of right away. Another officer could stop you five minutes down the road," he added before stalking off.

On the way home, memories flooded back. I knew I had paid for a new tag! In fact, the memory was particularly vivid because of the exorbitant cost of that tiny sticker. Back at home, I called the license tag office. No, they didn't have a record of my having bought a tag, the woman replied politely. Riffling through the file drawer marked "automobiles," I failed to turn up any evidence of the purchased tag. Next, I pored through our canceled checks. Although I didn't find a canceled check, I did manage to locate a carbon of the check I had written several months earlier. Evidently, the check had gotten lost in the mail. I had been driving around with an expired tag, after all.

I headed straight for the license tag bureau and purchased a new tag. The manager of that office added over forty dollars in penalties to my cost, in spite of the fact that I showed him the check carbon as proof that I had mailed in a check. For the next several days, I seethed over the injustice of it all. Here I was, a law-abiding, taxpaying citizen, yet the policeman had chosen to confiscate my driver's license and write "must not drive" on my ticket. Criminals got off scot free, yet I was harassed because some officer had been insulted that I didn't stop until he turned on his siren. Why would I have stopped before he turned on his siren? That's what sirens were for, weren't they...to alert someone to a policeman's presence? The thoughts I directed at that police officer were not kindly ones.

As my court date drew near, I noticed something. My prayers did not seem to be as sincere and effective. It was as if a barrier had been erected to block those open communication channels I had come to take for granted. Resentment spilled into everyday life, coloring everything I did. My boiling anger did not allow me to approach God with a humble and contrite heart. Although I could acknowledge my carelessness in not paying proper attention to my affairs, I could not forgive the police officer's surly manner, or his confiscation of my driver's license for such a minor offense.

I held onto my unreasonable resentment for a couple of weeks. But harboring anger and resentment leads to a spiritual separation from God. A hardened heart characterized by lack of forgiveness diminishes the joy derived from the spirit-filled life. One condition for receiving God's forgiveness is that we forgive others. "For if you forgive men when they sin against you, your heavenly Father will also forgive you. But if you do not forgive men their sins, your Father will not forgive your sins" (Matthew 6:14). God's closeness eludes us when we fail in that most emphatic command to forgive.

Knowing what I had to do to "make things right" in my spiritual life, I decided to discard anger and resentment. It was difficult, at first, to relinquish a grudge I had nursed so assiduously. But finally, I was able to admit my own culpability. The policeman had, after all, only been doing his job. I thought of the many hard-working, professional police officers who put their lives on the line every day to protect average citizens like me. In the end, I paid my fine cheerfully and reclaimed my driver's license.

Turn To God When Forgiveness Is Difficult

It was easy to forgive the police officer when I admitted that I had been at fault. Sometimes it is harder to forgive. When we are unjustly accused, or when someone hurts us and exhibits no remorse, forgiveness is foreign to our most basic instincts. Yet, we are called on to forgive, anyway. At these times it is imperative that we turn to God, asking him to pour into our hearts the forgiveness we are unable to produce on our own. Only then will bitterness give way to a reintroduction of the Holy Spirit into our lives.

There is a legend that Leonardo da Vinci painted the head of his enemy on the shoulders of Judas when he was working on *The Last Supper.* That night he couldn't sleep. The following day, he had planned on painting the head of Christ, but every time he tried to see the face, it blurred. Following another sleepless night, he got up, went to his studio and erased the head of his enemy from the shoulders of Judas. Immediately, he was able to see the head of Christ clearly, and to finish his famous painting.

Like the painter who couldn't see Christ until he had erased the evidence of his grievance, we need to erase the evidence of our grievance by forgiving others. The husband who still holds a grudge against his wife for some long-ago grievance, the wife who can't overcome a simmering resentment toward her husband, are dramatically decreasing the effectiveness of their prayers. Forgiveness is a prerequisite for answered prayer. The lack of it will throw an unnecessary stumbling block in our path.

Unrighteousness

A man I will call Bob prayed almost daily for an upstanding Christian woman to come into his life. He felt sure he could be happy if God would send him a beautiful, kind, loving wife. Bob went to church, openly professing his faith. He joined all the singles groups. He felt he was doing everything he was supposed to do to meet the right woman, but his prayers went unanswered. Fifteen years after he began praying for a Christian wife, Bob was still single.

There was another side to Bob's life that I need to mention here. Sexually promiscuous, he indulged in premarital sexual relationships with many of the women he dated. He justified this, saying, "Sex is a normal human function given to us by God. If God isn't going to send me the right woman, am I supposed to lead a celibate life?"

Bob blamed God for not responding to his prayer. He never thought to ask himself if unrighteous living might be the real reason his prayer was unanswered after fifteen years. Psalm 34:15 tells us that "the eyes of the Lord are on the righteous and His ears are attentive to their cry." James 5:16 promises that "the prayer of a righteous man is powerful and effective." Proverbs 28:9 warns, "If anyone turns a deaf ear to the law, even his prayers are detestable."

The church deacon who has a secret passion for pornography, the Christian woman who engages in an adulterous relationship, the Christian businessman who cheats on his income taxes or is dishonest with customers; all these people, if they remain unrepentant and continue in their sin, are throwing up hindrances to effective prayer.

There are those who would disagree here, pointing out that salvation is not by works but by faith. Some religious leaders go so far as to indicate that as long as we profess belief in Jesus Christ as Lord and Savior, our actions are of little or no consequence. If this were the case, Bob's righteousness or unrighteousness would have little if anything to do with whether or not his prayers were answered.

Advocates of this viewpoint are right in one sense. Salvation is a gift from God, by grace through faith in Jesus, and not something we can accomplish by our good works. Thank goodness we don't have to earn our way to salvation! Jesus' death on the cross took care of that. Paul speaks in

Romans 3:21 about the futility of trying to earn our way into God's grace by clinging to a meticulous adherence to man-made laws.

The Fruit Of The Spirit

To believe that righteousness is irrelevant because we are saved by faith and not by deeds is to misinterpret the meaning of faith. At the time Paul wrote his letter to Romans, there were many who believed that following a rigid set of religious laws and regulations was more important than the state of a person's heart. These followers of the law revealed an astounding coldness of heart when they condemned the healing of a man on the Sabbath because it interfered with their stringent regulations. Jesus, with his message of faith and love, criticized this coldness of heart. It was wrong for a set of religious rules to replace the love and compassion people should have for one another.

If a profession of faith comes without a corresponding change of heart, then that profession of faith is as hollow and meaningless as the obsession with laws had become in Paul's time. Jesus said, "Not everyone who says to me, Lord, Lord, will enter the kingdom of heaven, but only he who does the will of my Father who is in heaven" (Matthew 7:21). This statement would certainly indicate that the way we lead our lives is important.

The apostle James went to great lengths to dispel the idea that true faith can be something apart from our actions. "What good is it, my brothers, if a man claims to have faith but has no deeds. Can such a faith save him?......Show me your faith without deeds and I will show you my faith by what I do. You believe that there is one God. Good! Even the demons believe that and shudder....As the body without the spirit is dead, so faith without deeds is dead" (James 2:14).

Does all this mean that we have to be perfect and righteous to win salvation. No! We can come to God over and over again, confessing our sins and repenting, and He will forgive us. We all fall short, because we are human, but faith leads to repentance and the desire for a changed lifestyle.

Psalm 66:18 tells us, "If I had cherished sin in my heart, the Lord would not have listened." The person who knowingly and willfully pursues a sinful lifestyle without repentance or an attempt to change is running the very real risk that God will not listen to his prayer.

Lack of Faith

Lack of faith is a hindrance to prayer. Scripture not only lets us know that faith is important. It lets us know that without faith, there is no way on earth, no matter what we do, that we are going to please God. "And without faith, it is impossible to please God, because anyone who comes to Him must believe that He exists and that He rewards those who earnestly seek Him" (Hebrews 11:6).

We are even warned not to think we will receive any answers to our prayers if we lack faith. "But when he asks, he must believe and not doubt, because he who doubts is like a wave of the sea, blown and tossed by the wind. That man should not think he will receive anything from the Lord; he is a double-minded man, unstable in all he does" (James 1:6-7).

Sometimes we *do* receive what we pray for, even though we doubt. Sarah bore a child in her old age, just as God had promised, although she had laughed at the idea of becoming pregnant at such an advanced age. She even lied about laughing when confronted with the evidence of her doubts.

Knowing that God in his goodness would listen to us in spite of our doubts should serve to build up our faith. When we pray, we need to picture the answer we want instead of dwelling on the negative possibilities of unanswered prayer. Visualizing a positive answer to our prayers, acting on a "mustard seed's" worth of faith, and remembering past times when God has been faithful will all serve to shore up and bolster a wavering faith.

Our Prayer is a Conflict of Interests

Following a disappointing loss in a tennis match, my son said, "I prayed beforehand that I would win."

"What if your opponent prayed the same thing?" I asked. "Which one of you is God going to listen to?"

My son didn't have an answer for this, but his look clearly said, "What am I supposed to pray for, then?"

"Next time, pray that you will play your best and accept the outcome with good sportsmanship," I advised.

My daughter said once, "I should stick with small prayers, because too many people interfere with the answers to larger ones."

"What do you mean?" I wondered, not sure I understood exactly what she was talking about.

"If I pray for something simple, it happens," she responded. "But sometimes when I pray for big things, such as my friend's parents not getting divorced, they get divorced anyway. I feel like those parents were so determined to fight and argue that they blocked my prayers."

Occasionally, our prayers seem to interfere with the prayers or desires of another person. If this is the case, we need to make sure we are praying for our or their spiritual well-being instead of for our own selfish purposes, as in the case of the tennis match. And we need to continue to lift people up in prayer in spite of their apparent intransigence, as in the case of the divorcing parents.

Ultimately, the person being prayed for has to make a decision to accept Christ. This is consistent with the free will God has granted us. If someone persistently and vehemently renounces faith, we should, of course, continue to pray. But that person's stubborn will could be a tremendous stumbling block to the efficacy of prayer.

The Christian woman who married a rapist did not prevent his capitulation to evil with her fervent prayers. One night before she discovered the truth, she experienced such a real and frightening sense of evil that she was only able to overcome it with repeated prayers in Jesus' name. This woman lived through a nightmare which her prayers did not eliminate. But God helped her to rebuild her life. Her husband was apprehended and convicted before committing murder or harming his family, and she eventually married a fine, Christian man.

A Christian woman grieved that her son was an atheist. "You are going to hell," she told him just before she died. Maybe the son will become a believer, and maybe he will remain an atheist. His ultimate response to God will be the result of God's working in his heart, and of this man's willingness to believe. Prayers are vital to the Christian life, but they do not nullify the effects of our free will.

Our Prayer is Outside of God's Will

Sometimes we pray without getting what we want because our request is outside of God's will. This is the most difficult kind of unanswered prayer to deal with, because our limited perspective does not allow us to see God's overall plan. You have probably heard that common saying: "Be careful what you pray for. You might get it."

I'm reminded of the joke about the Christian in ancient Rome who was being pursued by a lion. He ran down the city streets, then into the woods, running and running until it became obvious that continued flight was hopeless. The lion was going to catch up. Turning to face the beast, the Christian dropped to his knees and prayed desperately, "Lord, make this lion a Christian!" Immediately, the lion dropped to his knees and prayed, "Thank you Lord for this meal of which I am about to partake."

We don't always know what is good for us. I am relieved and thankful that some of my prayers were never answered in the way I wanted them to be answered at the time. Like the Christian pursued by the lion, I would have ended up regretting that particular answer to prayer. God, in His wisdom, knew what was best.

To say that some prayers are outside of God's will for us is not a cop out meant to encompass and excuse all unanswered prayer. God hears our prayers, and He will answer them in His own time, according to His will. God's concern is for our spiritual lives, and His kingdom is "not of this world." If a particular prayer interferes with His overall plan or is detrimental to our spiritual growth, He might not grant our request. At these times we need to relinquish control to Him, as Jesus did in Gethsemane. Knowing his arrest and crucifixion were imminent, Jesus prayed, "My Father, if it is possible, may this cup be taken from me. Yet not as I will, but as you will."

When we pray the Lord's prayer that Jesus taught us to pray, we say, "Thy will be done, on earth as it is in heaven." This is relinquishing ultimate control to God, asking that His will, which is for our spiritual good, be accomplished in this life and in the life to come.

One thing we can be sure of is that it is within God's will for all of us to come to Him in faith. "Do not be afraid, little flock, for your Father has been pleased to give you the kingdom" (Luke 12:32).

The believer praying for the unbeliever can take heart, persevering in prayer with the assurance that this prayer will not go unheard. The believer must relinquish his own hindrances to prayer, forgiving others, praying with faithfulness and perseverance, repenting of any unrighteousness that is a stumbling block to prayer, and realizing that God's time frame is different from ours. When we overcome hindrances to prayer, we can pray for the unbeliever, knowing that prayers offered up in faith and hope, with acknowledgment of God's sovereignty, are always heard.

Chapter Summary

Hindrances to prayer must be acknowledged and dealt with if we are to build our faith into a fortress that is undiminished by the reality that we might not get everything we want.

Some hindrances to prayer are:
*Lack of forgiveness
*Unrighteousness
*Lack of faith
*Prayers that interfere with the desires or prayers of another person
*Prayers that are outside of God's will

The believer must relinquish his own hindrances to prayer, forgiving others, praying with faithfulness and perseverance, repenting of any unrighteousness that is a stumbling block to prayer, and realizing that God's time frame is different from ours.

When we overcome hindrances to prayer, we can pray for the unbeliever, knowing that prayers offered up in faith and hope, with acknowledgment of God's sovereignty, are always heard.

"But now, Lord, what do I look for? My hope is in you."
Psalm 39:7

Part Four

Overcoming The Barriers To Belief

CHAPTER SIXTEEN

Faith Plus Proof

"I do believe; help me overcome my unbelief!" Mark 9:24

You are setting a joyful Christian example, living your faith with integrity and enthusiasm. Your marriage is improving as you nurture it with your time, love and commitment. You are continuing to pray for your spouse. Yet he says, "I just can't believe without some sort of proof." *What do you do next?*

Many intelligent, thoughtful people pose legitimate questions that need to be addressed before they can topple the barriers to belief. They are willing in spirit. They have seen faith in action through the joyful Christian example set by their spouse. They may have experienced the power of prayer, only to rationalize away the results once prayers were answered. They probably have discounted the many miracles of life we all experience. The barriers are real and seemingly insurmountable. Belief in God, to them, seems irrational.

This is where *apologetics* comes in. Making a reasonable case for the existence of God and the resurrection of Jesus Christ based on available evidence proves that sound judgment does not have to be cast aside for the sake of faith. The purpose of this last section is to help you overcome your partner's barriers to belief. The fertile soil prepared with your joyful Christian witness and planted with the seeds of prayer is ready for the illuminating sunshine of truth.

The Case For Proof

Some Christians frown on the idea of defending their faith. One Christian acquaintance voiced the opinion that basing our beliefs on anything factual was a repudiation of faith. He felt that examining the foundations for his faith was somehow a violation of God's will.

Nothing could be further from the truth! Scripture encourages us to be prepared to give the reason for the hope that we have. God sent us His son, Jesus Christ, and Jesus performed hundreds of miracles that people might see and believe. In Matthew 15:10, Jesus exhorted the crowd he was addressing to listen and understand. It was not enough that they listen. They needed to use their reasoning abilities to comprehend what he was talking about. Jesus felt it was important for people to grasp his message. They must be more than sponges, soaking up his words. People must also use their minds so that, understanding his words, they could apply his message to real life and resist being swayed by those who would question their beliefs.

The benefits of wisdom and knowledge are emphasized over and over again in the Book of Proverbs:

> "Blessed is the man who finds wisdom, the man who gains understanding, for she is more profitable than silver and yields better returns than gold" (Proverbs 3:13,14).

"Wisdom is supreme; therefore get wisdom.
Though it cost all you have, get understanding"
(Proverbs 4:7).
    "The heart of the discerning acquires knowledge;
the ears of the wise seek it out" (Proverbs 18:15).

We do not have to renounce reason to embrace faith. We
do not need to suspend knowledge to accept Jesus Christ as
Lord and Savior. God did not endow us with intelligence in
order to encourage our belief in something illogical or unreasonable. He provided us with a blueprint for life that is immi-
nently reasonable and logical. He blessed us with intelligence
and provided us with the resources to learn about Him.

In our present era, when belief in God is no longer taken
for granted, it is more important than ever for believers to be
able to present an intellectually defensible position for their
beliefs. Christians who cannot articulately and intelligently
defend their faith will find themselves losing the verbal
argument to atheists and agnostics who are well read and
prepared to drive home their own point of view.

*If I cannot give a reason for my hope when my partner
expresses an honest desire to understand, I am losing a vital
opportunity to witness.*

Richard L. Strauss wrote in his book, *Win The Battle For
Your Mind,* that God made human beings with minds, so that
we could get to know Him, enter into a mutually satisfying
relationship with Him, enjoy His fellowship, and glorify Him.
If our spouse is a nonbeliever who says, "I don't believe
because the existence of God cannot be proved," we are
challenged to employ our God-given minds and intellectual
faculties to expose the fallacies of this claim. *By pointing out
the historical accuracy of the Bible, the veracity of its universal
truths, the significance of our own experience of faith, and
the evidence in favor of a godly life, we can reveal to our
partner the logic of believing.*

What The Believer Should Do

It is vitally important that *all discussions of faith with the unbelieving spouse take place within a context of love and respect.* When Peter said we should be prepared to give an answer for our hope, he also stated that we should do this with gentleness and respect. We are not to launch into a discussion of apologetics with the intention of undermining or getting the best of our spouse. Our questions should be asked gently, our answers given humbly in response to the search for understanding.

Recognize Barriers

The second thing a believer married to a nonbeliever should do is recognize that there are several commonly cited barriers to faith. These include a lack of evidence for the existence of God, the presence of misery and unhappiness in a world created by a good, omnipotent God, a perceived conflict of biblical truth with science and logic, the atrocities some people have committed in the name of religion, and the idea that a strong faith in Jesus Christ must necessarily conflict with worldly goals such as success and happiness.

The unbelieving spouse might present some or all of these arguments as a basis for disbelief. You need to understand your spouse's personal barriers to faith, with your response designed to bridge the gap between skepticism and belief. The believer who recognizes an unbelieving partner's particular barriers to faith can more readily address those barriers.

Prepare Your Defense

The third task of the believer is to acquire sufficient knowledge to answer common objections. Reading and studying what other Christians have written in defense of the Christian faith can go far toward helping us understand and verbalize our beliefs. There are a number of excellent Christian writers, some of whom I have mentioned in this book. They can offer insight into our most troubling and difficult questions, but our primary source should always be Scripture. Familiarity with God's Word is the best possible defense of faith, enabling us to counter erroneous statements about what Scripture does and does not say. The Bible contains the divine answer for all our deepest needs, providing us with God's infallible word as guidance.

You should not feel compelled to provide an answer to every question or challenge. Let your spouse provide some of the answers, and always be ready to admit that there are some questions you cannot answer.

Maximize Understanding

When I was in college, my philosophy professor instructed class members to write a research paper proving one of two things: either that God existed, or that He didn't exist. My class performance up until then had been mediocre, but the professor's assignment inspired me to new levels of enthusiasm and diligence. I decided I was going to write such a good paper proving the existence of God that my instructor, who had already announced his atheism, would be unable to refute it.

I don't remember now what I said in that paper. I only remember that I made an A, and that my professor wrote in the margins, "You make some good points, but I still disagree."

The professor will always disagree, unless he can acquire a mustard seed's worth of faith. No matter what we are able to prove or disprove, belief in God ultimately boils down to at least some faith to go along with the mountains of "proof" that God has provided for us. This is not unusual, since all aspects of a successful, happy life involve a certain level of faith.

Our proof will take us only so far. Faith must do the rest. This is part of the mystery which keeps us forever searching and forever striving to know God. Perhaps without the search, an intimate and loving relationship with our Creator would be impossible. It is the ultimate mystery which draws us through successive stages of spiritual development, causing us to leap with joy at each new revelation. If all were known, would we thrill with wonder when a ray of light, brilliant and sudden as a lightning flash, pierced the unfathomable dark of our ignorance? Would we experience the ecstasy of illumination in that moment when God chose to speak to our very soul? Perhaps God, in His wisdom, knew we needed the mystery. He has given us insight into the mystery through His divine guidance, revealed to us in the Bible.

A fourth task of the believer is to maximize a spouse's understanding of God's Word. Both believers and nonbelievers sometimes complain about the difficulty of understanding Scripture. But with the advent of readable Bibles, written in plain English with study guides and explanatory notes, Scripture need not be difficult. When Lee was ready to read and study God's word, it was important for him to have a Bible that maximized his understanding and enjoyment of Scripture. The believer who can steer a receptive partner toward a Bible that optimizes that person's understanding will be helping the nonbeliever gain insight into God's divine guidance. The ecstasy of illumination is within our grasp. God will speak to our soul through His divinely revealed Word!

Do Not Be Impatient

Paul said, in his letter to Romans, "Accept him whose faith is weak, without passing judgment on disputable matters." Believers must avoid passing judgment or expressing impatience if a loved one's spiritual growth appears to be slow. It is tempting to feel spiritually superior to someone who is just beginning his walk with Christ. But remember Paul's warning: "You, then, why do you judge your brother? Or why do you look down on your brother? For we will all stand before God's judgment seat" (Romans 14:10).

As you move toward overcoming the barriers to belief, recognize that barriers can serve the legitimate purpose of strengthening our faith. Dr. Norman Vincent Peale said, "When you struggle through doubt, you toughen your faith." As a student at the theological seminary, Dr. Peale encountered one particular professor who claimed he was going to knock the faith of his students to pieces and put it together for them again. "If I don't, then when you get out into the world, the world will knock it to pieces," this wise professor warned.

The person who has overcome the barriers to believing is the person who is prepared to answer a world that would knock his faith to pieces. He has tackled the obstacles to believing and emerged with a stronger faith that can withstand additional onslaughts. He has faced his doubts and overcome them with a truth so deeply embedded that it will not be shaken. So do not be impatient if your partner's spiritual growth appears to be slow. A fifth task of the believer is to exercise patience in the face of a partner's skepticism and doubts.

Improved communication as a result of building the marriage relationship has set the stage for a discussion of faith. With our witness, our love, and our prayers, we have paved the way for sharing God's message of eternal salvation. Now we are ready to tackle the barriers to belief. We are ready to move toward spiritual oneness, becoming soul mates because we have agreed to place Christ first in our lives.

Chapter Summary

Many intelligent, thoughtful, people pose legitimate questions that need to be addressed before they can topple the barriers to belief. Making a reasonable case based on available evidence for the existence of God and the resurrection of Jesus Christ proves that sound judgment does not have to be cast aside for the sake of faith. **If I cannot give a reason for my hope when my partner expresses an honest desire to understand, I am losing a vital opportunity to witness.**

By pointing out the historical accuracy of the Bible, the veracity of its universal truths, the significance of our own experience of faith, and the evidence in favor of a godly life, we can reveal to our partner the logic of believing. **Surmounting barriers to belief can result in a stronger faith.**

It is vitally important that all discussions of faith with the unbelieving spouse take place within a context of love and respect. In addition, when the unbeliever is beginning to discuss and think about reasons for faith, the believer should be prepared to recognize several of the commonly-cited barriers, acquire sufficient knowledge to answer common objections, help maximize a spouses' understanding of God's word, and exercise patience in the face of a partner's doubts.

CHAPTER SEVENTEEN

"You Don't Have Any Proof"

"Do not believe me unless I do what the Father does. But if I do it, even though you do not believe me, believe the miracles, that you may know and understand that the Father is in me and I in the Father." John 10:37,38

Josh McDowell set out to disprove Christianity. In his book, *A Ready Defense,* he writes about how, as a college student, he used to wait for a Christian to speak up in the classroom. Once the Christian had expressed his beliefs, McDowell could have the pleasure of exposing the fallacy of those beliefs. But one day, some Christian students challenged him to examine their claims that Jesus was God's son who took on human flesh, walked the earth among real men and women, died on the cross for the sins of mankind, and arose three days later. Could McDowell prove otherwise?

Unable to resist the challenge, McDowell began examining the evidence. This is when he made his amazing discovery: Jesus Christ must have been who he claimed to be! The evidence was overwhelming! Instead of disproving Christianity, McDowell became a Christian who spent the next fifteen years documenting why he believed faith in Jesus Christ to be intellectually feasible. The facts associated with Jesus as our Savior, combined with even the smallest amount of faith, are compelling.

The Physical Evidence

When a nonbeliever requests proof, he is generally asking for physical evidence to verify the existence of God. To satisfy that need, the Christian can point to archeological discoveries supporting many of the Bible's claims. No amount of historical evidence on any subject is capable of providing perfect proof that a given historical event occurred. But we can prove "beyond a reasonable doubt" to a person who is willing to have a "mustard seed's" worth of faith that the Christian faith is built upon good, solid evidence.

The Bible: Fact Or Fiction?

A 1995 *Time* cover story, *Is The Bible Fact or Fiction?* mentioned recent archaeological discoveries in the Holy Land that have effectively disposed of previous claims that certain biblical characters were the stuff of myth and legends. Skeptics had long maintained that King David was a mythical figure because his name had not been found outside the Bible. Then a team of archaeologists uncovered a 9th century B.C. inscription in the north of Israel with the words "House of David " and "King of Israel" carved into a chunk of basalt.

In 1990, Harvard researchers unearthed a silver-plated bronze calf figurine resembling the golden calf mentioned in the Book of Exodus. Clay tablets bearing the seals of Jeremiah's scribe which were made around the time the prophet was supposed to have lived confirmed that Jeremiah existed.

Israeli archaeologist Gabriel Barkay found two tiny silver scrolls inside a Jerusalem tomb. When scientists at the Israel Museum unrolled these scrolls, they discovered a benediction from the Book of Numbers etched into their surface, making it clear that parts of the Old Testament were being copied long before some skeptics had believed they were written.

The times, places and people referred to in both the Old and New Testaments are real. Archeological discoveries are constantly confirming the historical accuracy of Scripture. There are hundreds of other factual arguments to be made in favor of the accuracy of the Bible. One is the fulfillment of specific biblical prophecies, with about 2,000 prophecies having already been fulfilled. Another is the Bible's survival through criticism, persecution, and skepticism. It is ironic, in light of Voltaire's boast that the Bible and Christianity would be extinct in 100 years, that within fifty years of his death, Voltaire's press and house were used to produce stacks of Bibles!

A Confirmed Atheist

Sir William Ramsay, a confirmed atheist with a Ph.D. from Oxford, devoted his life to archeology in an effort to disprove the Bible. After more than two decades, he was so impressed with the accuracy of Luke's writings and with the hundreds of things he had uncovered confirming the historicity of the Book of Acts that he surprised the world by declaring himself a Christian.

The list of discoveries goes on and on, leading even the most ardent nonbelievers to concede that all biblical characters and events are not fictitious. Christians who take time to study the growing body of evidence confirming biblical statements will be sufficiently armed to counter one of the primary arguments of atheism: the Bible is fiction. Information should not be presented in an argumentative or dogmatic way to an unbelieving spouse; rather, interesting facts based on thorough research can be the basis for thought-provoking and intelligent conversations.

The Evidence For Jesus

An atheist, denying belief in any God, of course denies that Jesus is Lord. Some skeptics try to deny that Jesus even existed, but these denials are merely spurious, totally unsubstantiated objections. Other people, though admitting to a belief in God, refuse to believe that God sent His son to die on the cross for our sins. I have heard people say, "Jesus was a very good man, but I don't think he was the son of God." They fail to realize that it is impossible to view Jesus as a very good man, while at the same time denying his divinity. Jesus claimed to be God, and that claim must be either true or false. If someone accepts Jesus as an honest, sane man of integrity, his statements regarding his divinity must be accepted as true.

Josh McDowell points out in *Evidence That Demands A Verdict* that if Jesus' claim is false, he was either a liar or a lunatic. If Jesus was a liar, he was also the consummate hypocrite for telling others to be honest. If he was a lunatic, operating under the sincerely mistaken notion that he was God, we would have to conclude that his remarkable intellect, calmness in the face of persecution and death, sympathy for others and extraordinary knowledge of human nature were also the characteristics of a lunatic.

Those who profess disbelief in Jesus' divinity must also conclude that his disciples were deluded to the point of dying martyr's deaths in defense of their beliefs. Yet these same disciples wrote some of the most beautiful literature in all the world, in spite of the fact that they were common, ordinary men. They exposed their own faults and failings when it is standard practice for people to gloss over or hide personal weaknesses. They presented to the world a message undiminished and undiluted by the passage of time.

The nonbeliever would have to believe that all eyewitness accounts were lies, even though Peter did not lie about his own denial of Jesus and Paul did not lie about his earlier unbelief and persecution of Christians. The supposition that these men, after refusing to glorify or promote themselves by lying or downplaying their own faults, would lie about someone who had already died, is inconsistent with human nature.

A Small Leap Of Faith

Archeological discoveries cannot prove that miracles occurred, that God made a covenant with Abraham, or that Jesus is the son of God. Christians who can prove the Bible's uniqueness, relevance and reliability will still not be able to convince adamant skeptics that it is the inspired Word of God. But archeological evidence supports biblical historical claims and dispels any contention that the Bible is all myth. A study of the gospels reveals the profound and unequaled hope of men who did not fully believe until they had seen the risen Christ. By citing these facts, we can lend intellectual credence to our arguments for the existence of God and for the resurrection of His son.

Jesus was either who he claimed to be or he was not! Historically verifiable facts and a logical analysis of them clearly indicate that Jesus existed and was, indeed, our Savior and the Son of God. Even if your spouse doubts, he should be able to see the logic of taking a very small leap of faith to receive the benefits of life with Christ. The spouse who has worked to build the marriage relationship into a loving partnership will be able to judge a partner's readiness for a conversation about this most crucial aspect of the Christian faith.

The Evidence For Faith

While biblical facts are confirmed by archeological discoveries and tests of historicity, factual evidence also confirms the benefits of faith. This may come as a surprise to those who believe the value of faith is subjective and cannot be measured. A look at the evidence shows otherwise. Statistics reveal that communities are more likely to thrive, people are happier and health is better when religious commitment is strong.

The Community Is Better Off

In his autobiography, Benjamin Franklin wrote about the positive effect religious faith had on the inhabitants of his town. Acting on this observation, he contributed financially to a number of different churches, although he was not a member of any particular denomination.

Had he been living today, Benjamin Franklin could have offered some advice to the founders of Seaside, a planned community on the Florida Coast. Touted as the ideal community, Seaside includes a nearby town center designed to encourage a sense of community. Each Victorian-style house in Seaside is required by law to have a front porch, since the town's planners decided front porches would encourage porch sitting and socializing with neighbors.

But according to an article in the *Wall Street Journal,* community life never rose to meet the high expectations envisioned by its architects. Those who had so meticulously planned its town center and its homes made no provisions for a church. Benjamin Franklin could have warned them.

One of the most profound testimonies for the truthfulness of the Bible and its applicability to daily life is our observation of the world around us. When humans conclude there is no God, all ethical standards are subject to the moral authority of the moment. This renders values vulnerable to rationalization and change, which in turn leads to a moral breakdown in society. We are witnessing just such a breakdown, with widespread and devastating repercussions. We have taken God out of the community, and the community has suffered. Benjamin Franklin recognized the truth that communities are more likely to thrive when religious commitment is strong. There are measurable benefits to an active faith!

The Faithful Are Happier

Religious faith doesn't just enhance community life. Objective studies have also shown what Christians already know: the religiously committed are happier. A study conducted by the University of California at Berkeley in 1971 found that religiously committed people suffered much less psychological distress than the uncommitted. The higher the level of religious attendance, the more equipped people were to handle diversity, anxiety and pressure.

The *Washington Times* reported results of a study released by the Heritage Foundation showing the power of religion in daily life. According to the study, social science and clinical surveys provide evidence that:

> Churchgoers are more likely to be married, less likely to be divorced or single, and more likely to manifest high levels of satisfaction.
>
> Church attendance is the most important predictor of marital stability and happiness.
>
> The practice of religion moves people out of poverty.
>
> Religious belief and practice contribute substantially to the formation of personal moral criteria and sound moral judgment.
>
> Regular religious practice can inoculate people against social problems such as suicide, drug abuse, out-of-wedlock births, crime and divorce.

Practice of religion encourages mental health, including less depression, more self-esteem and greater family and marital happiness.

In repairing damage caused by alcoholism, drug addiction and marital breakdown, religion is a major source of strength and recovery.

In the face of all this evidence, the positive effects of faith on lifestyle and happiness are undeniable. We might not be able to prove to an adamant skeptic that God exists, but we can certainly prove that believing in Him leads to a statistically greater chance of being happy!

The Faithful Are Healthier

Psychology Today published some interesting statistics compiled by David Larson, a psychiatrist and president of the National Institute for Health Care Research. Warned by school advisers against incorporating religion into his psychiatry practice, Dr. Larson decided to prove them wrong. For two decades, he researched the healing effects of religion, utilizing both his own and other people's observations. Among his findings were the following:

A report on 232 people who underwent elective open-heart surgery showed that those who received no comfort from religion were more likely to die within six months of the operation.

A decade-long study of 2,700 people revealed that, after accounting for risk factors, increased church attendance was the only social attribute that lowered mortality rates.

Among women recovering from hip fractures, those who held stronger religious beliefs were less depressed and could walk further after being discharged from the hospital.

In *Shattering The Myths About Aging and Health Care,* author Donald J. Murphy, MD, writes that the healthiest seniors have developed and nurtured their spirits as well as their bodies. Dr. Murphy, a geriatrician and the medical director of the Senior Citizens Health Center at Presbyterian/ St. Luke's Medical Center in Denver, cites examples of seniors whose faith has made them unique in their ability to face crises.

It is hard for anyone to deny that the Bible advocates a healthy lifestyle. "Do not join those who drink too much wine or gorge themselves on meat, for drunkards and gluttons become poor, and drowsiness clothes them in rags," we are advised in Proverbs 23:21. Objective, scientific data reveals that the faithful are healthier. Modern psychiatrists and doctors attest to the healing effects of religion. The Bible has attested to the positive effects of prayer and faith on health for several centuries!

The Personal Testimony

Archeological evidence, statistics bearing out the positive effects of faith on health and happiness, and the relevance of the Bible to everyday life support the believer's contention that God exists. But nothing is as likely to persuade the nonbeliever as powerfully as the witness of a changed life. *The example you set by the life you lead is your own personal testimony, profound and indisputable.*

"How do you know God is real?" Lee asked when he and I were dating.

My answer surprised him. "From my own experience," I replied. "God has answered too many of my prayers for the answers to be coincidental."

At that time, I had not delved into apologetics or analyzed my reasons for believing. I had not studied archeological revelations or seen statistics on the correlation between religion and health. But I had an answer for faith that is difficult to refute: the validity of personal experience.

The nonbeliever can argue that personal experience is too subjective to be legitimate, but most nonbelievers accept that certain subjective emotions are real and valid. Few people would say that love, hate, anger, and compassion don't exist simply because they are subjective. Few believers or nonbelievers would reject the notion that a positive attitude characterized by faith, hope, and love has great power. *Just as love manifests itself in the caring and commitment exhibited between two people, faith manifests itself in the changed life of the believer.*

He Lives!

We know God exists because we have a personal relationship with Him. This is our own personal testimony. One of my favorite hymns, *He Lives!* written in 1933 by Alfred H. Ackley, beautifully and eloquently expresses the Christian's basis for faith:

> *I serve a risen Savior, he's in the word today;*
> *I know that he is living, whatever foes may say.*
> *I see his hand of mercy, I hear his voice of cheer,*
> *And just the time I need him, he's always near.*
>
> *In all the world around me I see his loving care,*
> *none other is so loving, so good and kind.*
>
> *He lives, he lives, Christ Jesus lives today!*
> *He walks with me and talks with me along life's narrow way.*
> *He lives, he lives, salvation to impart!*
> *You ask me how I know he lives? He lives within my heart.*

What a wonderful thing, to know that Christ Jesus lives today, in the hearts of those who believe! He has changed my life, bringing immeasurable joy and hope, and this is more real to me than all the other evidence in the world.

Your spouse will be unable to refute the evidence of a changed life as you exhibit the joy and conviction of a person totally committed to faith in Jesus Christ. When the love of Christ flows freely in your life, you are able to express a greater love for your partner. This, as much as anything else, is your proof. Believe the miracle of your own experience. Share the miracle with your spouse!

Chapter Summary

The believer can point to archeological discoveries supporting many of the Bible's claims. Christians who take time to study the growing body of evidence confirming biblical statements will be sufficiently armed to counter one of the primary arguments of atheism: that the Bible is fiction. **Historical records and logical examination of the facts lead an open-minded individual to conclude that Jesus is the Son of God.**

While biblical facts are confirmed by archeological discoveries and tests of historicity, factual evidence also confirms the benefits of faith. **Statistics reveal that communities are more likely to thrive, people are happier and health is better when religious commitment is strong.**

Nothing is as likely to persuade the nonbeliever as powerfully as the witness of a changed life. Some of the most dramatic conversions occur when people are moved by the sincerity of a person whose life has been changed by faith. This is why it is so vital that Christians live their faith with joy.

Your spouse will be unable to refute the evidence of a changed life, the joy and conviction of a person totally committed to faith in Jesus Christ. **When the love of Christ flows freely in your life, you will be able to express a greater love for your partner.**

CHAPTER EIGHTEEN

"Why Do Good People Suffer?"

"In this world you will have trouble. But take heart! I have overcome the world."
John 16:33

Attendance was high at the Palm Sunday worship service. As children sang part of an Easter cantata the electricity died, leaving them without lights or organ accompaniment. Suddenly, in the darkened sanctuary, disaster struck. A tornado ripped through the church, toppling walls and hurtling the church roof toward a terrified congregation. At least six children, including the four-year-old pastor's daughter, were killed.
Why, Lord? Why?

Another set of parents asked this same question. Their little girl struggled to breathe, each breath more difficult than the last. Thick mucus clogged her lungs and blocked important ducts in her pancreas. She had been born with cystic fibrosis, an incurable hereditary disease. At first, there had been good days when she went to school and played outside with friends. But gradually her condition deteriorated. There came a time when she was confined to bed, too weak to sit up for long. She was a sweet-tempered child, uncomplaining even when disease racked her frail body. Her parents watched helplessly, their hearts ripped apart by an agony of sorrow, as their little girl, the love and light of their lives, breathed her last tortured breath.

Why, Lord? Why?

A church bus returning from a youth retreat careens around a curve, crashes through a guardrail and plunges off a cliff.

A father and daughter paddling their inflatable raft at the ocean's edge drift too far. A massive search is called off when hurricane winds churn placid waters into raging seas. The family's church prays for the safe return of father and daughter, but hope ebbs when the deflated raft washes ashore.

An African man has listened to missionaries, accepted Jesus into his heart, and had his wife and seven children baptized. A few months later, the Ebola virus, a ruthless killer without a cure, strikes this man's household. Within weeks, the whole family is dead.

Why, Lord? Why?

If God is good and God is all-powerful, why does He allow so much pain and suffering? Why does He not intervene to rescue those who believe in Him? Christians, enduring and witnessing the tragedies that are an inherent part of life on this planet, ask these eternal questions over and over again.

The reality of suffering is one of the biggest single obstacles to faith, leading nonbelievers to reject God and Christians to see their faith shaken to its core.

We see the unfaithful, the unscrupulous, and the unethical reaping monetary windfalls. We watch those who openly and arrogantly flout God's laws soar rapidly to the heights of worldly success. We experience the heavy hand of injustice and the apparent triumph of evil. We grapple with these things until we either turn away from, or further toward, our faith.

What can the believer say to the nonbeliever in the face of misery and injustice? How do we, as Christians, respond when the nonbeliever says, "If God is good, why did He allow this to happen?" How can we convince our spouse to accept our faith if we are so stymied by the problem of suffering that we have nothing to offer except our own feeble and wavering acknowledgment that there is no answer?

God's Kingdom Is Not Of This World

When the problem of suffering is a stumbling block to faith, we would do well to remember Jesus' words in John 18:36: "My kingdom is not of this world." Christians and unbelievers alike experience the trials and tribulations marking our sojourn from birth to death. God does indeed cause "his sun to rise on the evil and the good, and sends rain on the righteous and the unrighteous" (Matthew 5:45). We must accept the fact that God's kingdom does not focus on the materialism, success, and physical health we so often focus on. His kingdom is of the spirit and soul, for all eternity.

Christians are promised an eventual end to suffering. The tribulation which is part of life on this planet will pass away following physical death, when we are heirs to God's kingdom forever. But the kingdom of God can also be found within each of us right now, accessible in spite of, or maybe because of, our suffering. It is a peace which transcends suffering because it is born from the knowledge that God's spirit has a permanent dwelling place in our hearts.

Joni Eareckson Tada wrote in her book, *Secret Strength*, that God and the things He is creating for us will never shake or shatter. Our confidence and hope must always rest in the One who never changes. When our focus becomes spiritual, the changing nature of our world will not overwhelm us because God lives within us, changeless and eternal.

It is difficult for us to break free of our worldly focus. We are spiritual beings confined to an earthly body, subject to every temptation and weakness of the flesh. But break away we must, if we are to achieve the peace which passes understanding. We can find joy in the Holy Spirit. We experience a small taste of the joy that is to come when we realize that our earthly existence is not the grand finale. Life is like a regular season game compared to the Super Bowl. It is important. It serves as a training field. There are ups and downs, triumphs and disappointments. But the biggest game, the culmination of all our efforts, is yet to come.

Jesus said, "The kingdom of heaven is like a treasure hidden in a field. When a man found it, he hid it again, and then in his joy went and sold all he had and bought that field" (Matthew 13:44). We are promised a joy so profound that it will be of inestimable value, worth more than all we have. This might not comfort those caught in the relentless throes of suffering. Our present agony is very real. But Christians, knowing this life is not all there is, take comfort in God's presence during suffering, and the promise of eternal life to come.

Our Knowledge Is Limited

Through studying Scripture, we learn that we cannot know the answer to all of life's wrenching questions while we are still confined to our earthly and very finite existence. Paul expressed this inability to fully know God's purposes in 1 Corinthians 13:12: "Now we see but a poor reflection as in a mirror; then we shall see face to face. Now I know in part; then I shall know fully, even as I am fully known." Although we are fully known by Christ now, we will not have full understanding until the Lord returns.

Isaiah 55: 8 points out that we cannot hope to comprehend all God's ways, because they are beyond the range of our limited understanding: "For my thoughts are not your thoughts, neither are your ways my ways, declares the Lord."

Our incomprehension compared with God's knowledge is expressed again in Romans 11:33: "Oh, the depth of the riches of the wisdom and knowledge of God! How unsearchable His judgments, and His paths beyond tracing out!"

The Bible is filled with examples of righteous people whose suffering must have seemed inexplicable at the time. Naomi saw no hope for her future when she lost her husband and two sons. All she had left was a daughter-in-law who stubbornly refused to desert her. "Where you go I will go, and where you stay I will stay. Your people will be my people and your God my God," this stubborn daughter-in-law, Ruth, declared in one of the most poignant expressions of love and loyalty ever recorded.

Naomi and Ruth, both suffering tragic losses, made their way back to Naomi's homeland. There Ruth married Boaz, a relative of Naomi's on her husband's side. In keeping with Levirate law, Boaz stood by his obligation to make sure their firstborn son inherited the name and property of Ruth's dead husband. Thus, as a result of Ruth's unselfishness, Naomi was blessed with a grandchild to carry on her family name. Even more significantly, this grandchild became the grandfather of King David, a genealogy that led ultimately to Jesus Christ. Our knowledge is limited, but just as God worked through the tragedies experienced by Naomi and Ruth, He works through our experiences to bring about His ultimate will.

A Test Of Faith

Jacob was heartbroken when told that his favorite son, Joseph, had been killed by a wild animal. All his other sons and daughters rallied around, trying to comfort him, but Jacob refused to be comforted. He had already lost Rachel, the wife he dearly loved. Now he had lost their son. Imagine the agony he endured in the years that followed, before he discovered that Joseph lived. How he must have questioned a God who would allow his beloved son to be so cruelly wrenched away!

At the same time, Joseph's faith was undergoing a tremendous test. First, he was sold into slavery by his jealous brothers. Then, just when he was prospering as the slave to one of Pharoah's officials, his master's wife noticed Joseph's physical appeal. She invited him to bed and Joseph refused. His reward for doing the right thing was that his master's wife decided to seek revenge. She falsely accused him of trying to seduce her, with the result being that Joseph was imprisoned.

Joseph's faith must have been amazing. We are never told that he despaired and cursed the God who was supposed to be his source of comfort. Instead, we are told that the Lord remained with him through his trials. God gave him the power to interpret dreams, which eventually brought Joseph to Pharoah's attention. Even then, Joseph remained humble.

"I can't interpret your dreams," he told Pharoah. "But God will give Pharoah the answer he desires" (Genesis 41:16).

The climax of this story occurred when Joseph, who eventually became a man of great influence and prestige, was reunited with his family after his brothers traveled to Egypt seeking relief from a worldwide famine. What began as an act of deplorable jealousy among brothers who sold their own brother into slavery was used by God for the good of the Israelites facing starvation.

Trust God!

We can examine history from the perspective of stories that are completed and results that are obvious. Reading about these suffering men and women, we see the ultimate triumph of God's will. Yet Joseph, spending tortured nights in prison, had to trust in God's goodness when all discernible evidence pointed to the contrary. Naomi stared into the vast void of God's apparent silence and clung to her faith. Jacob plumbed the depths of grief before his son was restored to him.

When we ask, *Why, Lord, Why?* we can guess that Joseph and Jacob and Naomi, Daniel, Mary, Peter, and all those other men and women of God marching through the pages of biblical history asked that same question. The answer became evident to them, just as our answers will become evident to us. But in the meantime, we must live in the trenches of life, trusting God as we do battle without benefit of the long view. *Now we see but a poor reflection as in a mirror; then we shall see face to face.*

The Suffering Of Job

The subject of suffering almost always includes a discussion of Job, a man whose godliness and righteousness did not spare him from bitter travail. Job was moral and upright, described in the Old Testament as blameless and shunning evil. We are even told that God delighted in Job. Yet when Satan accused Job's righteousness of being self-serving, God allowed Satan, within certain limits, to have his way with this righteous man. The result was a series of tragedies that would have left any normal person questioning the goodness and love of God. Job's servants were murdered by bandits, fire burned his sheep, and his camels were stolen. A mighty wind swept in from the desert, causing Job's oldest son's house to collapse, killing all Job's children, who were having dinner together at the time. As if that weren't enough, Job was afflicted with painful sores. Yet when his wife urged him to curse God, Job's reply was, "You're talking like a foolish woman. Shall we accept good from God, and not trouble?"

Job's friends were not any more comforting than his wife during his ordeals. With obnoxious self-righteousness, they blamed Job for some undisclosed sin and spouted pious platitudes about God's will.

In the end, Job was vindicated before his friends. They were chastised for blaming his misfortunes on sin and for their own spiritual arrogance. Job's fortune was restored, with the latter part of his life being blessed more than the first. But a logical reason is never given for Job's suffering. He was not being punished, nor did he lose favor with God. The message seems to be that God wanted Job to choose to love Him, regardless of the blessings God bestowed. Job's faithfulness through adversity proved that his love for God was not based on his prosperity.

Suffering Results From Freedom

Rather than creating us as puppets or robots incapable of choosing to have a relationship with God, God allowed us freedom. This freedom lends meaning and relevance to our love for God because it is a chosen response, but it also allows for the other choice: rejection of God. *Your spouse has the ability to embrace or reject faith, because this is the only option that could possibly lead to a meaningful relationship with Jesus.*

Freedom introduced sin into the world, first through Adam and Eve, and subsequently through every human being who has ever lived. Since sin cannot exist in a perfect world, its very existence rendering the world imperfect, God's creation became flawed. We no longer had heaven on earth. Suffering and death became an inevitable part of the life cycle. But God, because of His compassion and love, allowed humans a second chance. He gave us an opportunity to experience eternal life, not because of our own merit, but through His grace. He sent His son to die for our sins, if we choose to accept that gift through faith.

"I Still Don't Understand"

What if your spouse says, "I still don't understand how a good God could allow nice people who believe in Him to suffer so much. Did the little girl with cystic fibrosis sin more than some other little girl?"

Of course the answer is no. The little girl was not being punished as a result of some individual sin any more than Naomi was. Her suffering was the sad result of living in a world in which suffering and death exist.

Sometimes it is easy to see the direct consequences of sin and evil. Hitler's slaughter of millions, the mass graveyard that is Rwanda, atrocities in the Bosnian war, the brutal slayings of a serial killer, the blowing up of a federal building; all bear horrible witness to the evil which can spring from the hearts of men. Innocent lives are lost when caught in the path of such destructive forces.

It is not as easy to relate a situation to the consequences of our own sins. Single mothers struggling to raise children in drug-infested slums, violence proliferating among our teenagers, a federal government spending without accountability, and the murder of innocent babies are not directly our fault. But we have the freedom to elect the officials who make our public policy decisions, to patronize or not patronize the movies that offer a steady diet of sex and violence, to exercise the self-discipline necessary to serve as an example to our children, and to tolerate or refuse to tolerate the devaluation and destruction of life.

Many of us are able to live in luxury and relative isolation from the violence, the social ills, and the poverty percolating slowly through our nation. But we cannot remain isolated for long. Just as the teenage pregnancy problem now threatens our middle class, so will the increase in violence, drug use, antibiotic-resistant diseases and other ills soon plague the entire nation. We pay for our sins, individually and as a whole. No one is immune.

It is even more difficult to reconcile diseases and disasters wrought by the apparently random forces of nature with the existence of a just and loving God. This may be where your spouse faces his biggest obstacle to faith. We cannot see how the volcano that buries a city or the earthquake that kills thousands is in any way related to sin. We have a hard time fathoming how a loving God would allow a family that has just accepted Jesus to be wiped out by the Ebola virus.

We need to remember two things: The first is that we don't have the long view. Only God knows what would have happened to that stricken African family had they been allowed to live. Would they have retained their faith throughout their lives? Maybe, or maybe not. The only thing we can know is that they were fortunate enough to accept Christ before their deaths. Their eternal life is secured.

The second thing we need to remember is that when sin was introduced, death became an inevitable part of the life cycle. Life on earth is transitory, but the Christian view is a view of the eternal as opposed to the temporal.

Isaiah 57: 1-2 defines the stark contrast between a worldly view and a heavenly view of death: "The righteous perish, and no one ponders it in his heart; devout men are taken away, and no one understands that the righteous are taken away to be spared from evil. Those who walk uprightly enter into peace; they find rest as they lie in death."

Our focus should be on the life of the soul, not the life of the body. We need to constantly remind our spouse, and ourselves, too, for that matter, that *it is our spiritual growth and development which are important.*

A Different Kind Of World

With the life of the soul as our focus, let's examine the probability of spiritual growth in a different kind of world. What if God intervened directly each time someone called out to Him in prayer? It sounds wonderful on the surface, but would this be jeopardizing the very freedom which God has given us? Suppose that whenever Christians prayed for healing or some other form of divine intervention, that intervention was granted. Christians would never suffer pain or death. Nonbelievers would see the miraculous results of Christian prayers and become believers as soon as they were faced with a problem. Their belief would not be based on love for God or any sort of relationship with God that resulted from the gradual spiritual growth common to the Christian experience. It would be a belief based purely and simply on "what God can do for me."

There would be little need for accountability, faith, justice, mercy or compassion. These things would never have an opportunity to take root and grow, because all our desires would be granted immediately. There would be no faith, no relationship with God, to distinguish the believer from the nonbeliever. Each time a problem arose, a hasty prayer could be depended on to bring God swooping in for the rescue.

If the world is viewed as a spiritual training ground designed for our spiritual growth and a personal relationship with God, then the kind of world I just described would have the opposite effect. It would be similar to shutting a child away in a room and handing her everything she asked for. She could have whatever she wanted to eat or play with or read. Her whole life would be spent in this room, freeing her from the need to work, from the emotional ups and downs of personal relationships, and from outside dangers and illness.

What a terrible existence, to have all her needs met, while never being allowed to experience the outside world in all its glories, and, yes, dangers. She would never experience the growth and development, sometimes painful, that is part of the life process. She would remain forever a child, isolated from the world, with no possibility of attaining true adulthood.

Suffering Leads To Spiritual Growth

From this perspective, suffering takes on a new dimension. It can be seen as having the potential to foster spiritual and personal growth through the development of fortitude, compassion, humility, and perseverance. Suffering can create renewed faith in God by breaking down our self-sufficiency and leading us to depend on Him.

It is an ironic fact of human nature that spiritual qualities often spring from hardship and persecution rather than ease and abundance.

Two hundred years after Christ, the pagan population tortured and murdered hundreds of Christians. Believers who denounced their beliefs were allowed to go free, but those who refused to recant were burned alive or thrown into public arenas to be gored by bulls or killed by gladiators.

One leader in the Christian community was forced to sit on a chair of red hot iron and roast to death. A slave girl who refused to renounce her faith was tortured all day, bound in a bag and thrown into the arena of an amphitheater to be gored to death by a bull. Observing her courage, some people came to believe that Christ made his martyrs insensitive to pain.

During this time of persecution, the church began to grow. Many nonbelievers, seeing the heroic refusal of hundreds of Christians to denounce their faith under torture, became believers. Those same pagans who had urged the destruction of Christians began risking death to hide Christians in their homes. Tertullian wrote, "The blood of martyrs is seed to the church."

I am humbled and amazed by these stories of men and women who refused to cry out, "Why, Lord?" As I sit in the comfortable pews of my church, surrounded by friends, anticipating a nice lunch or an afternoon nap, I can only marvel at the sufferings endured and the faith exhibited by these people of God. In the face of such faith, the question could well be, "Why not me, Lord?"

Christians confronted cruelty and persecution with hope and faith, until at last they were victorious over the empire that would have destroyed them. A hundred years later, the Church had grown strong, becoming one of the richest religious organizations in the empire. The terrible persecutions had ceased. The emperor Constantine embraced Christianity as his own religion.

We would expect to see Christianity flourishing during this time of ease and acceptance, but within a year of Constantine's conversion, the Church was torn by an internal schism that led to chaos and violence among the believers themselves.

Over and over again through history, we see persecution and suffering leading to a renewal of faith, with luxury and abundance leading to its demise. Look at our own country. We live in the wealthiest nation in the world, yet we are plagued by crime and poverty. Our citizens are more willing to embrace a godless secularism than to follow the God who is the source of our blessings. Most people take air conditioning, cars and television for granted. Grocery stores offer a mind-boggling smorgasbord of selections. We can worship as we please in a church of our choice, we can say whatever we want about the government without fear of reprisal, we can choose our vocation without being relegated to a particular caste, and we can travel freely all over the country. Yet studies show that a majority of high school and college students think it is okay to cheat. Teenagers are killing other teenagers. Drug use is increasing dramatically.

People turn from God during times of abundance and toward Him during times of tribulation. This is nothing new. It was articulated 2,000 years ago in James 1:2-4: "Consider it pure joy, my brothers, whenever you face trials of many kinds, because you know that the testing of your faith develops perseverance. Perseverance must finish its work so that you may be mature and complete, not lacking anything."

Our Response To Suffering Is What Counts

If the earth is a training ground for our souls rather than a playground for our pleasures, then blessings begin to be viewed in a different light. We have to ask ourselves which one of these is blessed: the beautiful actress endowed with looks, talent, and fortune who leads a life of self-indulgence and promiscuity, or the handicapped child who has been forced through hardship and need to develop a strong spiritual life dependent on God? *When we approach suffering from this perspective, we see that it is the Christian's response to suffering, not the existence of suffering itself, which becomes the relevant issue.*

In a follow-up article one year after the Palm Sunday tornado tragedy in Alabama, a newspaper reporter interviewed several survivors. Some had lost family members. Others were coping with the loss of friends or with the horrors they had witnessed. But as I read the article, I began to observe a toughness of spirit and resilience of faith emerging through the words and actions of these people. A community, determined to rebuild its church, had drawn together in love and support. While people still grieved, they experienced God's presence in the midst of their sorrow.

Agreeing with James, Paul pointed out in Romans 5 that suffering can produce the sort of character God wants His children to have: "And we rejoice in the hope of the glory of God. Not only so, but we also rejoice in our sufferings, because we know that suffering produces perseverance; perseverance, character; and character, hope."

This theme, repeated in the Bible many times, is an important principle. Christians can take heart from the knowledge that our trials are not meaningless, since "in all things God works for the good of those who love Him, who have been called according to His purpose" (Romans 8:28).

We Choose Our Responses

A *Wall Street Journal* article stated that stressful elder-care situations are notorious for driving a wedge between adult siblings. Rapport disintegrates as siblings disagree over how to divide parents' assets and what type of care to pursue. The article described how one brother and sister resolved to avoid this pitfall by putting their parents' interests first. Instead of separating into opposing battle zones, they drew closer together as they sought the best care for their mother.

Dismayed by what they saw in long-term care facilities, the siblings decided on in-home care for a while. Sister and brother talked by phone as often as five times a day in order to share the multitude of day-to-day decisions. They were forced to make sacrifices in their own lives in order to meet the demands posed by two parents with rapidly-declining health. During this process, brother and sister gained new respect for each other. When their mother died, the brother became a long-term care activist. The sister, describing her new awareness of mortality, found herself reaching out to aid other families with ailing elders.

A newspaper published the very different story of a woman who abandoned her aging, mentally incompetent father by dropping him off in another state. For several weeks, officials could not discover this man's identity. No one knew where he had come from or whether he had any family.

Will we respond to life's trials with compassion and fortitude, rising to meet its challenges? Or will we refuse the opportunity to embrace that broadening of our spirit which is the antithesis of selfishness and despair? Facing adversity isn't easy. I have seen great potential wasted in a graveyard of despair, and magnificent triumph exhibited by those who have refused to succumb to rage and bitterness.

Joni's Struggle

Joni Eareckson Tada met tremendous adversity with faith and courage that stand as testimony to God's power through suffering. When she was a teenager, Joni broke her neck in a diving accident. Left a quadriplegic, unable to dress herself, brush her teeth or comb her hair, this active girl who loved horseback riding and swimming was devastated. At one point, she even wanted someone to help her take her own life. She had difficulty reconciling her faith in a loving God with the apparent hopelessness of her condition.

But gradually, her bitterness gave way to trust in God. Through years of rehabilitation, she was able to maneuver a motorized wheel chair. She has learned to paint beautiful scenes of the world she loves so ardently with the process of mouth-artistry. Now an inspirational speaker, writer and artist, married and living a full life, Joni captivates audiences with her vigor and enthusiasm. Few people have so moved and inspired people to triumphant faith.

We cannot always choose our circumstances, but we can choose our response. We can allow the care of an aging parent to rip apart our family life, alienating us from siblings and spouse, or we can accept the responsibility with grace, love, and a determination to act in another's best interests.

Few will have to suffer as Joni Earickson Tada has suffered, but we can draw inspiration from her life and courage from her faith. Suffering can drag us into a state of perpetual victimhood, causing us to bemoan an unjust fate, or it can force us to develop the perseverance and hope that Paul promises can be ours. When we cling to bitterness, we block the channels to recovery and ultimate triumph. When we respond in love and faith, we open the channels through which God's love flows, enabling us to exhibit the best, most noble attributes of the human spirit.

God Is Present During Times Of Suffering

Although we cannot eliminate adversity from our lives, our Christian faith assures us that God is with us during our suffering. This fact was brought dramatically home to me in the story of the little girl with cystic fibrosis. Before she breathed her last breath, she sat up in bed, stretching her arms toward something no one else in the room could see. "I see Jesus!" she exclaimed, a joyous expression on her face.

Though all of us may not have such a dramatic encounter with Jesus while on this earth, we can experience the very real comfort of God's presence. With the Bible as our handbook, we can turn to words such as those in the 23rd Psalm that have comforted and sustained God's people through the ages: "Even though I walk through the valley of the shadow of death, I will fear no evil, for you are with me; your rod and your staff, they comfort me."

To the unbelieving spouse who says, "I can't reconcile an omniscient and loving God with the existence of suffering," we can respond by saying, *Christianity is the greatest hope ever offered in the history of mankind to deal with the fact of suffering on this earth.*

The Christian faith offers compassion and dignity to the miserable and afflicted, equality before God regardless of race, personal attributes or social class, forgiveness of sins, and the promise of spiritual strength. Christ preached peace, love, and the glorious hope of eternal life. Unjustly accused and nailed to the cross, he was the ultimate righteous sufferer. Just as his suffering was short-lived, a prelude to the triumphant victory of life over death, so our suffering is but a drop in the bucket of eternity.

"In this world you will have trouble," Jesus told us. "But take heart! I have overcome the world!"

Chapter Summary

The reality of suffering is one of the biggest single obstacles to faith, leading nonbelievers to reject God and Christians to see their faith shaken to its core.

Suffering and death became an inevitable part of the life cycle when sin was introduced into the world. But God gave us an opportunity to experience eternal life through his grace, by faith in Jesus Christ.

Suffering can create renewed faith in God by breaking down our self-sufficiency and leading us to depend on Him. Spiritual qualities often spring from hardship and persecution rather than ease and abundance.

Although we cannot eliminate adversity from our lives, our Christian faith assures us that God is with us during our suffering. We must accept the fact that God's kingdom is not of this world. His kingdom does not focus on the materialism, success, and physical health we so often focus on. His kingdom is of the spirit and soul, for all eternity.

To the unbelieving spouse who says, "I can't reconcile an omniscient and loving God with the existence of suffering," we can respond by saying, **Christianity is the greatest hope ever offered in the history of mankind to deal with the fact of suffering on this earth. It is, in fact, the hope we have for transcending death itself and living eternally with God in Heaven!**

CHAPTER NINETEEN

"Christians Have To Give Up Pleasure And Success"

"I have come that they may have life, and have it to the full." John 10:10

In his book, *Free To Succeed,* Steve Diggs writes about a meeting that took place in 1923, when the world's most successful financiers got together at a Chicago hotel. Among the high-powered businessmen and political leaders attending were presidents of a leading steel manufacturer, the largest utility company, the New York Stock Exchange, the Bank of International Settlements, and a member of the President's cabinet. These men controlled more wealth than the amount of money contained in the United States Treasury. Magazines and newspapers had printed their success stories, encouraging young people to follow their example.

Diggs describes what happened to these men 25 years later: "Charles Schwab, the great steel magnate, spent the last five years of his life living on borrowed money and died penniless. Richard Whitney, president of the New York Stock Exchange, had recently been released from prison. Albert Fall, the member of the President's cabinet, was pardoned from prison so he could die at home. Leon Fraser, president of the Bank of International Settlement, committed suicide. Ivar Kreuger, head of the world's greatest monopoly, also killed himself."

These men reached the pinnacle of worldly success. They were wealthy and influential, their names an inspiration to young business entrepreneurs. Yet, not one of them achieved happiness. Ultimately, their lives reflected a spiritual poverty that could not be overcome by money and power.

Laboring under the misconception that fame, fortune, acceptance by our peers, success at meeting a predetermined goal, or indulgence in a hedonistic lifestyle can produce happiness, we pursue these things relentlessly. At the end of our labors, we are too often rewarded with the bitter dregs of disappointment. Without faith, we can achieve the trappings of success, whatever we have determined success to be. But like the men at that Chicago meeting in 1923, we will have achieved a hollow victory. We will not have tapped into the true source of joy and life in abundance.

Maybe your spouse has concluded that pleasure and success are incompatible with faith. If he rejects a relationship with Jesus Christ because he feels that Christians "don't have any fun," that believers must forego worldly success, or that acceptance by his peers and society at large will vanish when he embraces a faith often criticized as intolerant and narrow-minded, then he is laboring under a false assumption about what Christianity is all about. Using the Bible as a guidebook, the believer can show the nonbeliever that faith does not preclude success. On the contrary, faith makes success more likely, and is indispensable to the enjoyment of success.

Does Being A Christian Mean I Have To Be Poor?

Before Lee became a Christian, he concluded that Christianity advocated socialism and frowned on success. This was directly at odds with his belief in free enterprise. Unable to reconcile a desire to do his best and derive the most out of life with a belief that Christianity called for the sacrifice of all worldly ambitions and rewards, he rejected faith in Jesus.

What does the Bible really say about worldly success and the accumulation of wealth? What did Jesus mean when he said, "It is easier for a camel to go through the eye of a needle than for a rich man to enter the kingdom of God" (Matthew 19:24)? Jesus told a wealthy young man to sell his possessions and give everything to the poor. Must we give away everything we own to be followers of Jesus? Must our spouse relinquish all ambition to become a believer? Does the Christian faith conflict with being a successful executive, lawyer, mechanic, salesman, provider?

Scripture shows us that worldly success is not synonymous with sin. There is nothing wrong with attaining success and reaping a monetary reward. Sin stems from our *attitude* toward wealth, rather than the acquisition of wealth. This is made clear in 1 Timothy 6:10: "For the love of money is a root of all kinds of evil. Some people, eager for money, have wandered from the faith and pierced themselves with many griefs."

Too often, the accumulation of wealth comes at the expense of a person's spiritual life. Greed and the love of money lead to dishonest business practices or to the abandonment of principled, godly behavior. When we place materialistic pursuits first, we cannot place God first. We are violating Jesus' command to seek first the things of God's kingdom and His righteousness, and other things will be given to us as well.

Scripture reveals that many people of God possessed great wealth. Abraham had "become very wealthy in livestock, and in silver and gold." There was no one as wealthy as King

Solomon, with 1 Kings describing in great detail the splendor of his possessions. The exemplary woman depicted in the final chapter of Proverbs was a shrewd businesswoman, wealthy enough to employ servants, buy land, give to the poor, and wear the finest clothes.

Why, then, would Jesus instruct a wealthy man to sell all his possessions? If it was okay for other men and women in the Bible to own property and fine clothes, why should one man be singled out to give away everything he owned? The answer lies in this man's attitude. He placed wealth above a relationship with God. He wanted to earn eternal life through his good works, as long as he was not required to give anything up. Material comfort and possessions came first.

Jesus was not a socialist or a capitalist. He was an advocate for the downtrodden, the poor, the wretched and the homeless. Jesus also visited a wealthy, dishonest tax collector named Zacchaeus. He wanted all, rich and poor alike, to experience the hope and joy that come through faith. He knew that wealth could be a stumbling block to total commitment, as it was with the young rich man who asked him, "What can I do to gain eternal life?"

Christians do not have to be poor, but they *do* have to keep material things in perspective. Jesus knew how difficult it would be to place God first when other pursuits become a primary objective. He was aware that riches and lavish living are not conducive to the development of a humble and contrite heart. Spiritual hunger is not always so urgent when fulfillment of the flesh is paramount. For these reasons, some people might be called on to relinquish their possessions. Others will be called on to be good stewards, supporting the church and the poor with a portion of their income. But whatever God calls us to do will be for our spiritual benefit, encouraging us to place God first in our lives.

The Church Just Wants My Money

Maybe your spouse objects to the Christian emphasis on giving. He might feel that financial success will forever elude him if he is required to give part of his money away. Many Christians also balk when it comes to surrendering a significant portion of their income. I have heard people say, "The church just wants my money. Money is all the minister talks about." This is an understandable sentiment, given the proliferation of televangelists with a "name it and claim it" message.

"Give wealth to God and God will give wealth to you," these preachers intone, going on to cite evidence for their contention that all you have to do to be rich is to send them money. Your reward, of course, will be God's financial blessing. This is a false message. It fosters a selfish motive for giving, with little thought to the spiritual benefits of generosity.

Giving Is For Our Spiritual Well-Being

Giving financially, or being good stewards of the gifts God has entrusted to us, helps us focus on God instead of money. It opens our heart to caring for others. It removes us from the rat race of materialism by leading us to place material things in perspective. There is one hard and fast rule about money: when we give it away, it becomes less important. As Steve Diggs says in *Free To Succeed,* "One of the greatest blessings of learning to give is the way it frees us from being slaves to our money. One can't be ruled by something he or she has given away."

Financial Blessings Are Possible

To be sure, giving generously can result in financial blessings. "Whoever sows sparingly will also reap sparingly, and whoever sows generously will also reap generously. Each man should give what he has decided in his heart to give, not reluctantly or under compulsion, for God loves a cheerful giver. And God is able to make all grace abound to you, so that in all things at all times, having all that you need, you will abound in every good work" (2 Corinthians 9:6-9). This passage does not say God will make us rich if we give. It says God will give us what we need so we can "abound in every good work."

Some Christians will be blessed with wealth and others won't. But we can be sure of one thing. When we give generously, God will provide us with the things we need most for our own spiritual growth.

Giving From The Heart

Giving is meaningless if it is done reluctantly or under duress. This is why Christianity is not synonymous with socialism. Giving should flow naturally from our love of God and our desire to please Him. Giving should be coupled with complete faith that God will take care of our financial needs.

The believer should not insist that an unbelieving or recently-saved spouse contribute financially to the church. In addition to breeding dissension and conflict, a begrudged offering defeats the spiritual benefits of giving. A desire to be generous grows as our relationship with Jesus Christ grows.

A new Christian who objects to church tithing might be willing to contribute to a cause that is dearer to his heart. When Lee became a Christian, his first step in giving was to sponsor children through the Children's Christian Fund. A desire to contribute to the church came later, when he had established a habit of giving and developed confidence in the church as an important ministry.

As Lee discovered, we are sometimes in a better position to perform the work God would have us do if we are financially blessed. Being a Christian does not mean we have to be poor. What being a Christian *does* mean is that we will never place wealth first. It is never to become a stumbling block to total commitment. Christians need never succumb to the despair exhibited by those wealthy financiers who possessed everything, yet ended up with nothing.

Does Being A Christian Mean I Can't Have Fun?

Franklin Graham, son of world famous evangelist Billy Graham, was the proverbial prodigal son. Rebelling against his legacy, Franklin indulged in hard liquor, tobacco, fast motorcycles, high-speed car chases and rock music. Piloting small airplanes took precedence over studying in college. On one occasion, he drove a Land Rover from London to a religious hospital in Jordan, steering wheel in one hand, bottle of Scotch in the other. In his autobiography, *Rebel Without A Cause,* Franklin describes how he found the things of this world pleasurable and fun. He didn't like being around Christian people. He was afraid of being "spiritually handcuffed" if he surrendered himself to God.

Eventually, Franklin reached a point of spiritual crisis. Something was missing. In spite of his pursuit of pleasure, he wasn't finding joy and fulfillment. The result was that he turned his life over to Christ. A month after he was born again, a friend who ran an international aid mission invited Franklin on a two-month tour of the Far East. When the friend died of leukemia three years later, Franklin took over the organization, called Samaritan's Purse. This ministry seemed ideally suited to his proclivity for excitement. Under his leadership, it grew into a $32 million-a-year operation providing food, medicine and other aid in global crisis zones. Along with the material supplies, Franklin delivered a spiritual message through preaching the gospel. With Franklin frequently in the cockpit, Samaritan's Purse parachuted into places like Bosnia, Haiti, and Ethiopia.

Franklin once told *GQ* magazine, "When I die, I'll go immediately to the presence of God, and yet in life I had a blast."

An article in *Time* magazine said the Lord had not clobbered Franklin for being what he was; God had not handcuffed him. Instead, faith in God had set Franklin free. God had taken the very daredevil traits that Franklin thought he had developed to spite God and had turned them to His own purposes.

Dr. Ben Carson, pediatric neurosurgeon and bestselling author, writes in his book, *Think Big,* "God does not want to punish us, but rather to fulfill our lives. God created us, loves us, and wants to help us to realize our potential so that we can be useful to others."

Pleasure In God's Service

God created us to find pleasure in His service. He wants us to use our talents and abilities, at the same time discovering the joy and fulfillment that come only through spiritual development. Franklin Graham discovered that serving God did not mean surrendering his yen for adventure. Psalm 37 makes it clear that becoming a believer does not necessitate abandoning our desires and ambitions: "Delight yourself in the Lord and he will give you the desires of your heart."

This is not to say that sinful desires and behavior can be indulged. The Christian may be required to abandon something he has considered "fun." Transient pleasures are often life destroying. Alcohol and drugs lure us with the promise of a temporary high, yet can lead to addiction and destruction. Sex, created for pleasure and procreation within the framework of marriage, leads to ruined families and disease when indulged in promiscuously.

Sin has devastating consequences, even when it is disguised as "innocent fun." A woman asked her doctor if her nine-year-old son's severe learning disabilities could be the result of her drinking and drug use during pregnancy.

"It's possible," the doctor replied, "but there is nothing we can do about that now."

Too often, we find that we "can't do anything about it now." The person seeking immediate gratification might discover that his pursuit of pleasure has led to the loss of a job, marriage and children. What started as an office flirtation or a few drinks after work is no longer a source of enjoyment when it destroys homes and wrecks lives.

Yes, being a Christian might mean relinquishing destructive behavior. No, being a Christian does not mean surrendering joy to a God who would "spiritually handcuff" us.

Psalm 84 should put to rest any assumption that faith in God would strip us of an ability to enjoy life: "Better is one day in your courts than a thousand elsewhere; I would rather be a doorkeeper in the house of my God than dwell in the tents of the wicked. For the Lord God is a sun and shield; the Lord bestows favor and honor; no good thing does he withhold from those whose walk is blameless."

Our Search For Meaning

Our pursuit of pleasure is a search for meaning, purpose and acceptance. We experience these things temporarily by suppressing the spiritual part of our being; by deadening that restless inner voice which forever seeks the reason for our existence. But because our ultimate purpose is not to pursue the transient, fleeting pleasures of the moment, we find upon obtaining these pleasures that our restlessness has only been momentarily appeased. This is as it should be. God planted within us the desire for a relationship with Him. It is for our good and our growth that we must seek before we find. There is enough mystery about the search to kindle in us a glorious sense of wonder. There is enough concreteness in God's response to surprise and thrill and delight us. How wrong to think that becoming a Christian could spiritually handcuff us when, in truth, it sets us free.

Does Being A Christian Mean I Won't Be Accepted?

When I was in elementary school, a particular substitute teacher evoked exclamations of dismay every time she showed up to teach. A stern disciplinarian, she began each class with these words: "I'm not here to win a popularity contest."

Christians in this post Christian era, when it is often "politically incorrect" to express biblically-based viewpoints, bring to mind that teacher's words. We aren't likely to win a popularity contest. We might even be criticized and vilified for our beliefs if we are open about expressing them.

Politically Correct And Tolerant

The possibility of criticism and disapproval could be a big stumbling block to the spouse who yearns for political correctness, acceptance, and approval. It is natural to want the approbation of our peers. The unbeliever who thinks embracing Christianity will lead to charges of intolerance and narrow-mindedness might reject Christianity on that basis. If he has come to accept the popular but erroneous notion that religion propagates hatred and intolerance, a look at Jesus' words should prove otherwise:

"Do not resist an evil person. If someone strikes you on the right cheek, turn to him the other also. And if someone wants to sue you and take your tunic, let him have your cloak as well" (Matthew 5:38-40).

"You have heard that it was said, 'Love your neighbor and hate your enemy. But I tell you: Love your enemies and pray for those who persecute you, that you may be sons of your Father in heaven" (Matthew 5:43-45).

"Do not judge, or you too will be judged. For in the same way you judge others, you will be judged, and with the measure you use, it will be measured to you" (Matthew 7:1,2).

Do these sound like the words of intolerance and hatred? Humans, being fallible and imperfect, will forever fall short of the example set by Christ. But no other religion or lifestyle so clearly demonstrates the importance of loving others regardless of race, social class, or personal characteristics. Since we are all made in the image of God and are loved by Him, we are instructed to love one another.

Once again, this is where a spouse's example of faith in action is crucial. The believer has created an environment in which an unbelieving spouse is already loved and accepted, making it easier for him to risk repudiation by others. A marriage relationship strengthened by commitment, mutual respect and shared pleasures is strong enough to withstand outside disapproval or rejection. Couples who nurture and encourage each other are less vulnerable to a lack of encouragement elsewhere.

Becoming a believer could mean relinquishing acceptance by certain groups. But acceptance by these groups always hinges on whatever response is politically correct at a given time. Rejection is probable for the member who expresses an opinion at odds with the group's consensus on what beliefs are appropriate.

Acceptance by Jesus Christ, on the other hand, is total and complete. It will not be revoked when we backtrack into sin or express an unpopular opinion. It is eternal acceptance into God's kingdom.

Does Being A Christian Conflict With Success?

"Does being a Christian mean I have to give up any hopes of ever being successful?" the young man wondered. He held a lucrative job with a well-known company. What exactly would following Jesus Christ mean to his career? He had seen some executives rise to top positions through intimidation and hard-nosed business decisions. How could he embrace his wife's religious beliefs if it meant he would never win another promotion? Was it possible to practice biblical principles in the workplace, when cutthroat competition seemed to be the norm? This man could benefit from considering people who have risen to the top of their fields, not after denouncing biblical principles, but after embracing them.

Joyce Hall, the founder of Hallmark Cards, finished only three grades of a country school. He grew up in a poor but religious family. Yet, he managed to build a billion-dollar greeting card industry by implementing his "Amazing Prosperity Plan." His plan involved the simple principle of giving. "Give yourself, your mind, your love, your interest, and your affection. Give to people and to God, and you will obtain success, prosperity, and happiness."

Dave Johnson won the bronze medal at the Barcelona Olympics in 1992, and is America's top decathlete. In his book, *Aim High,* he tells how he overcame injury and heartbreak and grueling competition by holding onto a faith that gave him the focus to aim high in life.

Eric Liddell, the celebrated British track star, became a gold medalist in the 1924 Olympic Games despite numerous obstacles. Expressing faith as a focal point of his life, he said, "When I am running, I feel the pleasure of God."

Pat Boone, accomplished singer, actor, author, and television performer, has sold more than 45 million records. He is also a dedicated Christian who wrote *The Miracle of Prayer.* He has served as national chairman and host of the

Easter Seal Society telethon, and he has worked as cochairman of the National Day of Prayer.

A positive faith has the power to overcome the fears and conflicts that would prevent us from drawing upon a great reservoir of untapped potential. God has endowed us all with the seeds of greatness! He wants us to rise to the challenge of nurturing them to fruition!

Success At All Costs?

The Wall Street Journal reported that theft of minor items such as note pads and light bulbs is costing American business about $120 billion a year. One reason employees gave for filching small items was that they wanted to even the score with their employers. Employee theft had serious repercussions several years ago when a major company went bankrupt as a result of one employee's embezzlement of millions of dollars. The employee was convicted, and hundreds of people were left without jobs. More recently, a prominent dentist and his family were accused of hiring a convicted criminal to steal luxury items such as Armani suits and fine crystal for the family's own use.

More and more, a "success at all costs" mentality seems to be permeating our culture. Unbridled ambition appears to take precedence over fair business practices and integrity. Embezzlement might seem like a long step from the occasional theft of minor items, but most things begin gradually, with small steps leading to larger ones until the line of distinction grows blurred. God's commandments are not blurred. "Thou shalt not steal" is clear and unequivocal, with no room for varying degrees of theft, justification, or rationalization. Those who are never apprehended experience spiritual repercussions. "Ill-gotten treasures are of no value, but righteousness delivers from death" (Proverbs 10:2).

Even for the unbeliever who doesn't worry about the spiritual ramifications of disobeying God's commandments, biblical advice is sound business practice. A "success at all costs" mentality can have devastating repercussions. A lawbreaker runs the very real risk of exposure. Dishonest business practices can lead to the loss of job, reputation and, in some cases, liberty. One of Lee's manager's once wisely said, "Never do anything you wouldn't want to read about the next day on the front page of the paper."

There are other practices that, while not illegal, do not embody biblical principles. Shoddy workmanship, reneging on a promised raise, or demanding that employees sacrifice family time for the company without just compensation are not likely to send people to jail. They might seem, at first glance, to help the bottom line profit margin of a business. But in the long run, they lead to low morale, high turnover and unhappy customers. The proliferation of sexual harassment lawsuits exemplifies one pitfall of failing to employ an attitude of integrity and respect when dealing with others.

Blueprint For Success

Earlier in this chapter, I wrote that faith makes success more likely. Biblical principles also provide a blueprint for success. The Bible is not only an account of how God has revealed himself to humankind over the course of several thousand years. It is a detailed guide for effective, successful living. In the Bible, we find guidelines for attaining mental, emotional, and physical health that have withstood the test of time and the advent of modern treatments. We discover practical advice regarding everything from taking care of the poor to running a criminal justice system. We have access to a wealth of wisdom for the aspiring entrepreneur. Believers and nonbelievers alike will discover, upon reading the Bible, that being a Christian does not conflict with success. Biblical principles make success more likely.

In his bestselling book, *Over The Top,* Zig Ziglar shows how applying these values makes perfect sense in the business world. According to Ziglar, "people and companies who build their lives and business on an ethical base, and operate on the belief that their purpose in life is to serve others, are the ones who enjoy the greatest success." This is the Golden Rule in action!

Integrity

The book, *Profiles of Leadership,* states that when America's top business and government leaders were asked what quality they thought most important to their success as leaders, they gave a unanimous answer: *integrity.* Honesty and integrity make sense in the business world. Dishonest or unlawful practices not only lead to exposure and punishment; they shatter business relationships and trust among co-workers and customers.

In sales, building a long-term relationship with a customer is actually the most proven technique for sales success. This relationship, constructed on a foundation of trust, respect and dependable service, can weather many competitive challenges. Sales professionals are constantly looking for "win/win" relationships with their customers and the company they represent. These relationships are far superior to the "lose/win," "win/lose" or "lose/lose" relationships frequently portrayed in sitcoms or comics.

In an *Atlantic Monthly* article adapted from his book, *Integrity,* author Stephen L. Carter laments the loss of integrity characterized by discernment, or the ability to tell right from wrong. Where discernment is lacking, incorrect moral judgments may result. Carter cites the example of a business manager who gives the women who work for him less challenging assignments because he believes women to be inherently inferior. The manager has betrayed his obligation to the company he works for and his duty to objectively evaluate his employees because he has refused to examine preconceived notions.

According to Carter, integrity requires three steps: discerning what is right and what is wrong; acting on what you have discerned, even at personal cost; and saying openly that you are acting on your understanding of right and wrong.

Dealing fairly with others, treating them as we would have them treat us, is the solution to mistrust, mismanagement, and misunderstanding in the business community. Proverbs 10:9 tells us that "The man of integrity walks securely, but he who takes crooked paths will be found out." Once again, we see that biblical principles are sound business practice!

Hard Work

Another biblical principle indispensable to business success is the principle of hard work. The nonbeliever concerned with surrendering worldly success might be surprised to learn that the Bible is such a strong proponent of hard work. A reading of proverbs confirms the virtues of diligence:

> "Lazy hands make a man poor, but diligent hands bring wealth" (Proverbs 10:4).
> "Diligent hands will rule, but laziness ends in slave labor" (Proverbs 12:24).
> "The sluggard craves and gets nothing, but the desires of the diligent are fully satisfied" (Proverbs 13:4).

The Apostle Paul urged church members to work with their hands, so that their daily life may win the respect of outsiders. In an even sterner admonition, he warned against idleness: "For even when we were with you we gave you this rule: 'If a man will not work, he shall not eat'"(2 Th:3:10). Christians need to set the standard for hard work in the marketplace. Ruth gleaned the fields of her future husband,

Boaz, gathering the leftover grain for herself and her mother-in-law. Working hard, she was richly blessed. The converse of hard work is found in Jesus' parable of the rich man who produced a good crop, then decided to "eat, drink and be merry." That very night, his life was demanded of him.

A Willingness To Serve

Hard work needs to be coupled with a willingness to serve, expressed by Zig Ziglar as "helping enough other people get what they want." Any business which hopes to be successful must place a premium on good service.

Lao-tse, the sixth century Chinese philosopher, said, "A leader is one who serves."

Jesus said, "Whoever wants to become great among you must be your servant."

A desire to serve can be impeded by pride, or by the disgruntled feeling that others aren't doing their fair share. Since serving others frequently means going above and beyond the call of duty, a service mentality based on anything other than the desire to please God can backfire. When we are intent on pleasing people, our attitude can deteriorate into "He's not doing his share, so why should I do mine," or "It's not appreciated, so why should I keep working so hard?"

A servant's attitude, based on pleasing God, transcends what people think and lends a certain immunity to the letdown we experience when others don't appreciate our efforts. The business person who continually strives to serve customers and company to the best of his or her ability because it is the *right thing to do* will meet with *real success* unachieved by those who abandon service in the name of expediency.

A Daring Adventure

While exhibiting integrity, treating people well, and working hard are key elements to success, a willingness to take risks allows us to soar above mediocrity, attaining new levels of achievement. A strong faith underscored by the knowledge that God is in control can provide us with the self-confidence necessary to pursue many goals that we would feel inadequately suited to pursue on our own.

In his book, *Heaven Can't Wait,* Robert Jeffress says, "Living as citizens of heaven while still residents of earth should give all of us the same liberation and motivation; liberation from the stress of this life, since time here is so limited, and motivation to develop the attitude and character that we will carry into eternity."

When we are liberated and motivated by the knowledge that God is in charge, we should be freed from a paralyzing fear of failure. This is not to say that we should be totally fearless, or that we should refuse to weigh reasonable risk factors. Exercising caution and common sense is the prudent course, as Proverbs 22:3 points out: "A prudent man sees danger and takes refuge, but the simple keep going and suffer for it."

But a willingness to take worthwhile risks is crucial if we are to seize certain opportunities that could be killed by indecisiveness and procrastination. Helen Keller wrote that "Life is either a daring adventure, or it is nothing." Life can be a daring adventure when we follow Christ wherever he leads, deriving confidence and peace from our positions as children of God.

The believing spouse can set an example of faith by supporting a partner's decision to change careers or take reasonable risks. As Christians, we can proclaim our belief that God is in control by exhibiting a calm faith and strength when our partner is laid off or demoted in a company downsizing. The believer's faith transcends concerns over material comforts. By setting an example of faith in action, we encourage our spouse to realize the freedom inherent in knowing that we are in God's hands.

Christians do not have to give up happiness and success. The Bible offers a blueprint for success that surpasses anything else ever written. Faith is also critical to the enjoyment of success. As Jesus said, "What good is it for a man to gain the whole world, yet forfeit his soul?" Who is really happy without peace of mind and love? No amount of material success, health or fame can substitute. You cannot take those things with you, and you cannot even enjoy them here on earth if you have "forfeited your soul."

Instead of attaining a meaningless success, like those entrepreneurs who met in a Chicago hotel, we can hold fast to the promise that "those who hope in the Lord will renew their strength. They will soar on wings like eagles; they will run and not grow weary, they will walk and not be faint" (Isaiah 40:31).

Chapter Summary

Faith makes success more likely, and it is indispensable to the enjoyment of success. Being a Christian does not mean we have to be poor. Sometimes we are in a better position to perform the work God would have us do if we are financially blessed. What being a Christian *does* mean is that we will never place wealth first. It is never to become a stumbling block to total commitment.

God created us to find pleasure in His service. He wants us to use our talents and abilities, at the same time discovering the joy and fulfillment that come only through spiritual development.

Becoming a believer could mean relinquishing acceptance by certain groups. But acceptance by these groups always hinges on whatever response is politically correct at a given time. **Acceptance by Jesus Christ, on the other hand, is total and complete.** It will not be revoked when we backtrack into sin, or express an unpopular opinion. It is eternal acceptance into God's kingdom.

Biblical principles provide a blueprint for success. The Bible is not only an account of how God has revealed himself to humankind over the course of several thousand years. It is a detailed guide for effective, successful living.

CHAPTER TWENTY

Other Barriers To Believing

"For God so loved the world that He gave His one and only Son, that whoever believes in Him shall not perish but have eternal life." John 3:16

The preceding chapters of this section dealt with some of the most commonly cited barriers to belief. In this chapter, I will touch briefly on several other frequently mentioned stumbling blocks. While one chapter cannot present an in-depth look at each objection, it can serve as a starting point for the believer confronting one or more of these arguments. The unbelieving spouse who is genuinely searching for truth will benefit from his partner's ability to logically and coherently address these issues.

Martin Luther said, "The Bible is alive, it speaks to me; it has feet, it runs after me; it has hands, it lays hold on me."

It is my prayer that God's Word will "lay hold" of the nonbeliever, convicting him of God's truth. It is my hope that an examination of the remaining barriers to belief will dispel the notion that faith in Jesus Christ is unreasonable, illogical, insignificant, or in conflict with things we know.

"The Bible Conflicts With Science"

Many unbelievers maintain that the Bible conflicts with science. Citing evolution, they claim that the biblical account of creation is at odds with scientific knowledge. How do Christians respond if a spouse's major stumbling block to faith is an inability to reconcile science and religion? What do we say when our partner discounts creation science in favor of evolutionary theory? Frequently the believer cannot respond to a spouse's skepticism because the believer also has difficulty accommodating both science and religion. Some Christians, accepting certain scientific theories as fact, try to reconcile the inconsistency of these theories with a biblical account of creation. They arrive at an uneasy truce between science and religion, concluding that one or the other must be wrong. But believers would do well to remember that scientific theories come and go as new discoveries cast doubt on older ones. Our view of the world is ever-changing, with old hypotheses dashed against the shore of more recent theories.

Professor Louis T. More, a vocal evolutionist, said, "The more one studies paleontology, the more certain one becomes that evolution is based on faith alone."

Dr. D. James Kennedy wrote in his book, *Why I Believe,* "Every peg upon which evolution has stood is collapsing and crumbling about it today, and more and more scientists are in rebellion."

British astronomer Sir Fred Hoyle referred to the idea of the random origin of life "as ridiculous and improbable as the proposition that a tornado blowing through a junkyard may assemble a Boeing 747."

We have relied too much on pseudoscientific doctrine, even when it has meant jettisoning common sense and observable laws of nature. Evolution contradicts the second law of thermodynamics, which implies that things become less ordered rather than more complex as time passes. Things die or decay, whereas evolution states that life becomes gradually more complex. Nature shows that most mutations are harmful, although evolution holds that mutations are beneficial.

In his *BreakPoint* radio commentary, Chuck Colson described a set of calculations performed by Yale University physicist Harold Morowitz and mentioned in Robert Shapiro's book, *Origins*. Morowitz calculated the probability of generating a single bacterium by chance as 1 chance in 10 to the 100 billionth power. Shapiro concluded that the "improbability involved in generating even one bacterium is so large that it reduces all considerations of time and space to nothingness."

Scientific truths are truths until they are shattered under the microscope of additional evidence. Biblical truths are eternal, withstanding the rise and fall of civilizations, the continual rebellion of humankind and the numerous theories and postulates trotted out by our experts of the moment.

We have been given a remarkable book, written over a 1,500 year span, which has never been disproved. The Bible's universal truths have endured, its prophecies have come to pass, and its relevance remains undiminished by the passage of time. The Bible tells us that "In the beginning God created the heaven and the earth" (Genesis 1:1).

If your spouse has concluded that the Bible conflicts with science, you can point out that no scientific discovery has ever disproved one word of the Bible. Our theories fall into disarray as we continue to explore the wonderful mysteries of our universe, but God's word is never-changing and constant.

"The Church Is Full Of Hypocrites"

What if your spouse argues against attending church because "the church is full of hypocrites?" Most Christians have heard this argument and are familiar with its comeback, "There's always room for one more."

We can find hypocrites in church just like we can find them anywhere else, since the church is made up of fallible human beings. But many people levying the hypocrisy charge are operating under the misconception that church people claim to be free of sin. If this were true, it would indeed constitute hypocrisy. But in reality, Christians admit to being sinners. We are not in church professing perfection. We are there seeking forgiveness as we strengthen our relationship with Christ and other believers.

How Christians are perceived is important. "If we claim to have fellowship with Him yet walk in the darkness, we lie and do not live by the truth" (1 John 1:6). Chapter Four states that exhibiting faith in action means we refuse to be hypocrites, professing to believe in Christ's love but failing to reflect that love in our own lives. When we have exhibited our faith through the lives we lead, when we have exercised unconditional love and commitment toward our spouse, we have effectively refuted the charge that all Christians are hypocrites. Our spouse has seen at least one Christian who is trying hard to avoid hypocrisy.

"Most Wars Are Fought Because Of Religion"

When given as a reason for spurning Christianity, the contention that most wars are fought because of religion is similar to the hypocrite charge. It rests on the assumption that Christianity's validity is based on the way people act rather than on the person of Jesus Christ. People who point to the Crusades, the Spanish Inquisition, or the various Holy Wars as a reason for renouncing religion have erroneously concluded that travesties perpetrated in the name of religion represent the essence of religion.

Yet most critics of religion do not attack the character of Christ. How could they? There is nothing in Christ's character to attack. But it is Christ's character which must be condemned if one is condemning Christianity. Christ is the essence of Christianity. He teaches love, forgiveness, and compassion. Our faith is in Jesus, not in mankind's activites done under the guise of religion.

The flip side of the argument that wars have been perpetrated in the name of religion is that much progress has been made and much beauty created in the name of religion. The great cathedrals are a magnificent testament to faith. The Sistine Chapel has on its walls and ceilings some of the greatest art ever produced in the Western World. Books and learning which might have been obliterated in the bloodbath of war were preserved in monasteries and churches. One of the first books printed was a Bible, written in Latin. Historian and author Will Durant referred to great art as a child of a triumphant faith.

In addition to inspiring great art and preserving great literature, faith has played a major part in civilizing the barbaric aspects of human nature. Following the Christian conquest of Europe, Monks were responsible for cultivating the wilderness, draining swamps, cutting roads, erecting schools and industrial centers, and organizing charities.

When we consider the evils committed in the name of religion, we must also consider art and literature, the cultivation of land, and the civilization of humankind as a triumphant product of faith. We need to recognize the role of religion in steadfastly pointing out the horrible immorality of many of the atrocities committed in wars throughout the ages. *Most importantly, we must remember that the essence of Christianity is found in Christ, not in human activity.*

"It Doesn't Matter What You Believe"

"It doesn't matter what you believe, as long as you believe something," one Christian man's wife announced blithely. "What's right for me might not be right for somebody else."

There are others who sound a little more sophisticated when making this argument. They mention such things as situational ethics or an absence of moral absolutes. But the premise, that we create our own truth because there is no supreme moral authority, is the same whether we couch it in sophisticated terms or simply state that it doesn't matter what we believe.

This used to be the argument of choice among atheists and agnostics. Christians turned to Scripture as their basis for believing that God's laws are supreme. But more and more, Christians are embracing the humanistic argument that man is his own moral authority. They are beginning to conclude that right and wrong are a matter of circumstance and personal opinion.

An unbelieving spouse might accept popular thinking regarding situational ethics without examining all the ramifications of such a belief system. Even a believer can have trouble arguing against the prevailing wisdom if he has not carefully examined his beliefs in light of Scripture. God could have left us here on earth to work out all our relationships with our fellow man without a guide book. It would be similar to playing a basketball game with each player making up his own rules as the game progressed. Instead, God revealed to us through the Bible and the evidence in our own lives that there are, indeed, rules. Unless our faith is firmly grounded in God's Word, we are ill-equipped to swim against the tide of secular humanism. *If we do not understand the reasons for our beliefs, we will be subject to the rationalizations and false logic of those who conclude that humankind can know no absolute truth.*

"We're Not Hurting Anyone"

An article in the June, 1996 issue of *Reader's Digest* reported that retailers lose between $10 billion and $12 billion annually to shoplifters, with offenses more than doubling in the past 20 years. In researching the article, *Reader's Digest* interviewed more than 100 shoplifters, asking how and why they committed their crimes.

One of the surprising results was the way many shoplifters rationalized their actions. A devout Catholic who had not skipped mass in 27 years felt no compunction about shoplifting because she didn't consider it stealing. Her reasoning was that the stores wouldn't miss the item. Other shoplifters agreed. One woman compared her actions to stealing from the rich and giving to the poor. Another man said merchants could afford this, and he wasn't hurting anyone. Some shoplifters had the approval of their families, who didn't view shoplifting as a problem. When an adolescent girl was caught shoplifting, her father laughingly told her not to get caught next time.

If God is disregarded as the supreme moral authority, His commandments not to steal and not to covet can be rationalized away. Anything can be justified, because "my truth might not be your truth." By claiming that it doesn't matter what we believe, we lay the groundwork for a humanistic approach to life that soon leaves us able to condone any action.

"But Everybody Agrees On Some Things"

"We can replace God with certain moral absolutes that everybody agrees on. After all, most societies agree that hatred and murder are wrong." This is a popular argument used in defense of mankind's ability to make correct moral judgments without God. Does this argument work? Who decided murder was wrong, and how was this conclusion reached?

If we answer that murder is wrong because it is for the good of society that people not kill each other, someone else might offer this argument: "the world is overpopulated, so it is for the good of society that we reduce the number of people competing for natural resources." Or maybe someone could argue that homeless people are not contributing to the good of society, therefore they should be killed. You see why "the good of society" is not a valid argument in defense of moral decisions.

Beliefs do not make something a fact. Even if everyone reached the consensus that the sun revolved around the earth, the belief would not make it so. There is no validity to the argument that just because everybody agrees on something, it is true.

Marxism refers to morality and religion as phantoms of the human brain. Nietzsche called morality the herd instinct of the individual. Different beliefs are embraced at different times in history, with devastating consequences. We should not be surprised by this, since the Bible emphasizes that what we believe is extremely important. Jesus said, "If you do not believe that I am the one I claim to be, you will indeed die in your sins (John 8:24)." So much for thinking it doesn't matter what we believe!

Some Final Arguments

When Lee became a believer, his decision followed years of questioning, searching, and study. As the teacher of a senior high Sunday school class, one of his goals has been to help students deal with the challenges to faith posed by a secular world. His own period of skepticism and doubt equipped him for this goal. He asked the questions, presented the challenges, and, finally, overcame the barriers to belief. Reprinted below is a summation of the arguments used in his Sunday School class:

"There are several things to remember when your faith is challenged:

1. As believers, we all too often find ourselves on the defensive when asked to prove or explain our beliefs. We should feel free to ask just as many questions of the unbeliever. We take many things on faith, such as the fact that the sun will rise tomorrow; that people are living in other countries, even though we can't see them; that our airplane pilot knows what he is doing. Even nonbelievers must acknowledge that they already have faith in many areas.

2. There is overwhelming evidence in nature, our daily lives (the effects of love, results of prayer and miracles), and history (the Bible and world events) that there is a divine creator, that Jesus was here, and that Jesus is the Son of God. God's way has consistently proven to be the best way to live on this earth in our present lives.

3. We choose to believe based on faith and proof. The burden of proof is on the person who insists that everything be proven.

4. The nonbeliever may try to make it seem more intellectual or sophisticated not to believe based on faith. But we base many of our beliefs on faith. If we waited until we knew everything on this earth, we would never take any action.

The potential down side of not believing in God is so great that no rational person would renounce God if given any evidence whatsoever. No doctor, researcher, or business person in his or her right mind would turn down the promise of eternal life after weighing all the evidence. The odds are high that Christians are right. The down side is unthinkable. The upside is great! The return on our investment in a "mustard seed" of faith is astronomical and eternal. *Believe and live!*"

Chapter Summary

Some other commonly-cited barriers to belief are:
The Bible conflicts with science.
The Church is full of hypocrites.
Most wars are fought because of religion.
It doesn't matter what you believe, as long as you believe something.

An examination of these statements dispels the notion that faith in Jesus Christ is unreasonable, illogical, insignificant, or in conflict with things we know.

Scientific truths are frequently shattered under the microscope of additional evidence. **Biblical truths are eternal, withstanding the rise and fall of civilizations, the continual rebellion of humankind, and the numerous theories and postulates trotted out by our experts of the moment.**

Many people who call churchgoers hypocrites are operating under the misconception that church people claim to be free of sin. In reality, **Christians admit to being sinners. We are not in church professing perfection, but rather, seeking forgiveness as we strengthen our relationship with Christ and other believers.**

The contention that most wars are fought because of religion rests on the assumption that Christianity's validity is based on the way people act rather than on the person of Jesus Christ. **We must remember that the essence of Christianity is found in Christ, not in human activity.**

The premise that we create our own truth because there is no supreme morality is in direct conflict with Scripture. **What we believe is extremely important.**

CHAPTER TWENTY ONE

In Closing

*"My command is this: Love each other as I
have loved you." John 15:12*

Our lives have changed since that long-ago time
when Lee said, "I just can't believe in God without some sort of proof." Your life can change,
too. That is why I have written this book. You and your partner
can grow together in faith as you embark on an exciting
spiritual journey. You can live joyfully in the fullness of God's
love, drawing on a source of power that is both awesome and
inexhaustible. If you have read this far, incorporating the
biblical principles outlined here, you are probably well on
your way toward reaping the rewards of a renewed marriage
and a renewed life.

God created us to be lovers. The more we love God, the more open our hearts are to loving each other. He gave us the ability to realize the fullest expression of human love through marriage, when we love physically, mentally, emotionally, and spiritually. The power to achieve this love relationship is within our grasp. The strength of our love for our partner can draw him toward Christ and bring glory to God. Change is possible, because God pursues people relentlessly.

Keep in mind these guidelines as you set out to become soul mates with your partner:

If your spouse is resistant to a love relationship based on placing God first, be patient. God is patient, "not wanting anyone to perish, but everyone to come to repentance."

Remember to live your faith joyfully, with enthusiasm, revealing that you possess something wonderful and vital. Exhibit the power of faith in action through your willingness to forgive, your service, and your faith.

Life is a fine adventure. Relish the beauty and opportunity that abound in every day.

Build the marriage relationship through commitment and unconditional love. Create an arena conducive to spiritual change by nurturing your relationship with the gifts of shared laughter, praise, physical expressions of love and time spent together.

Do not neglect to pray with faith and perseverance, unceasingly, until life itself becomes a prayer. Pray for your spouse and your marriage, remembering to thank God for His answers and His blessings.

Refuse to grow discouraged. Read the Bible daily, and God will speak to your heart. You will be encouraged by His answers and His presence.

When you have kindled in your spouse a desire to know more about your faith, be ready to answer his questions. Even if you do not have all the answers, you can show that the Bible provides excellent advice for achieving success, prosperity and happiness, and that Christianity offers the greatest hope ever offered in the history of humankind.

Remember that most worthwhile achievements are accomplished over formidable obstacles, when we are called upon to exercise great fortitude, perseverance, and faith. A wonderful marriage, with faith in Jesus Christ as its foundation, is an achievement worthy of the greatest endeavor. It is a gift to us. It is God's perfect plan, fulfilling that inner longing in the depths of our being for a soul mate to travel beside us on this always challenging, sometimes daunting, and frequently glorious pilgrimage.

Believe and Love and Live! And "may the grace of the Lord Jesus Christ, and the love of God, and the fellowship of the Holy Spirit be with you all" (2 Corinthians 13:14).

AFTERWARD

Thank you for reading my wife's book and considering its message. Bebe and I have prayed that it will be of assistance to you, your spouse, your relationship, your family, and all of God's kingdom. This afterward is just one more attempt to prayerfully focus and gently coach you in the use of this book, so the ideas presented here can be as helpful as they have been in affecting my own life.

First of all, please pray that all things you do and say are done with the deepest love and caring for your partner. The change you want cannot be separate from the sincere interest in and love of your spouse. With love as your primary motivation, you will exhibit more steadfast confidence in your actions, and your spouse will be much more open to the journey ahead.

Please believe strongly in the good you are doing! Your spouse will be saved, of course. He or she will benefit greatly from a spiritual relationship with God. Your spouse will also be happier, feel more successful, be better able to handle pressures and problems, have greater peace of mind, and become more open to accepting love.

Learning to believe, trust, love, and hope can take a long time for someone who has fallen away from believing in God and Jesus. Please have the patience and faith to stick with your spouse and your beliefs long enough for this change to take place. Please don't, though, expect too much too soon. Have perseverance and patience. God will see you through.

It might take a certain event to trigger the motivation for change. In my case, it may have been the awareness that one of the most important jobs any of us has is to raise our children so they will have bright and meaningful lives. Your spouse may start to realize that his or her "philosophy" or doubts won't make the grade in this regard, and that only Christianity offers this hope to your cherished little ones in both their present lives and their eternal future. What a grave responsibility it is to lead your children down the right path— especially in areas where the consequences are eternal! You aren't just playing with your own life anymore. The results are multiplied and directly affect those who innocently look to your spouse as one of their two primary heroes and/or best friends. Have the patience to prepare and wait for similarly significant kinds of thoughts and considerations to enter the center of your spouse's consciousness.

Even when your spouse begins his or her journey back to God and Jesus, don't expect full and immediate acceptance and participation in every and all aspects of Christianity too soon and too fast. We're talking about a massive change here. You've had the patience to get this far, so there is no need to push too far and fast. Continue to show faith, love, and patience as your spouse grows in understanding, commitment, and strength of belief. Just as Christians who have never really strayed from the church might nevertheless have doubts, the new believer may still entertain doubts and misunderstandings for some time. We are all in a learning and growing process. Accept the fact that we all grow in this life with our own speed of acceptance, openness to advice, and number and angles of exposures necessary before something finally sinks in.

Not all Christians have unquestioning faith and only a few Christians see exactly eye to eye on the interpretation of every aspect of our religion. Your spouse probably did a lot of hard thinking and questioning—or at least went through a considerable amount of disillusionment—to reach the point where he or she strayed from God. Don't expect that part of your spouse's personality or character to disappear overnight.

I would also like to reemphasize, as follows, certain key points made in this book:

1. Again, make sure everything is done in love. Use the Golden Rule liberally to shape your words and actions. Use all available help that can have a positive influence. Constantly ask Jesus for guidance.

****

2. I can't possibly say enough about the importance and impact of setting a joyous example. This can be a huge challenge, but your daily joy as a Christian speaks volumes to the non-Christian spouse. He or she is, deep down, seeking a purpose for and a happiness from life. You know the answer, but your example will speak louder than any words.

****

3. The power of prayer is one the things that is hardest for the nonbeliever to come to grips with, but that doesn't keep you from using prayer for your (God's—in this case) purposes! Use it!

Regular and sincere prayer, no doubt about it, can be one of the most effective tools in shaping a positive, thankful attitude. You may want to encourage your spouse to start his or her prayer experience with simple prayers of attitude shaping (becoming more optimistic, hopeful, patient, forgiving, and confident, for example) and focusing on one's blessings. Intimacy with God through prayer and accepting the miraculous power of prayer will come later.

****

4. You will probably want to let your spouse read the "Overcoming Barriers to Belief" section as food for thought. Your job is only to expose these ideas, love, and pray—not to prove your beliefs through a debate. The ideas are valid. The reward/risk ratio is infinitely weighted in the direction of faith—whether those who depend on faith every single day of their lives will admit it or not. God offers us a tremendous "deal" for just a mustard seed of faith. Sometimes the smallest glimmer of acceptance is all that is needed as a first step toward a very strong faith.

What should you, the believing spouse, do when you spouse decides to accept Jesus Christ into his life? Althoug there is no "right" course of action for you to take at thi point, you might want to pray together. You could encourag your partner to affirm his commitment publicly by asking ho he feels about joining a church. A celebration would certainl be appropriate, since this is an exciting and joyous occasior You should continue to lead by example, nurturing th marriage with your love, your commitment, and your prayer Since God's salvation is a gift, and He has worked in you partner's life to bring him or her to this point, you do not hav to worry about not doing the right thing. You have done what you were called to do. Salvation is in God's hands. Now you and your spouse can start on an exciting spiritual adventure as you grow together in love and joy.

My deepest and eternal thanks to all you brave spouses out there (and specifically to you, Bebe) who are embarking on the very challenging journey involving my fellow (in my case "past") nonbelievers! You are truly Jesus' beloved and valued disciples. May God be with you, dear reader, (and your spouse, of course) in love and hope and joy. I sincerely wish you and your spouse all of the success in the world as you work in love together to build a marriage and family firmly centered on and benefiting from a belief in Christ.

Remember, though, first and always, to love.

May God, Jesus, and the Holy Spirit be with you and yours in faith, hope and love now and forever!

                              In Christ's Love,
                              Lee Nicholson

BIBLIOGRAPHY

Grateful acknowledgment is made to the following authors, publishers, and other copyright holders for the use of material quoted in this book. I have made every effort to locate the copyright holders. If material has been used without proper permission, please notify the editor so corrections can be made in future editions. There are other authors who, while not quoted directly, helped me with their thoughts and insights. I acknowledge with gratitude their contributions to the learning process which is part of every writer's cumulative experience.

BreakPoint © 1996, Prison Fellowship, for material by Chuck Colson. Used by permission.

Broadman and Holman Publishers for material from page 140 of *Experiencing God* by Henry T. Blackaby and Claude V. King. Copyright © 1994. All rights reserved. Used by permission.

Broadman and Holman Publishers for material from page 15 of *Heaven Can't Wait* by Robert Jeffress. Copyright © 1995.

Doubleday Dell Publishing Group, Inc., *A Special Kind of Hero,* by Chris Burke and Jo Beth McDaniel, copyright 1991.

Fleming H. Revell Company for material from *Free To Succeed* by Steve Diggs. Copyright 1992.

Fleming H. Revell Company, *The Hiding Place* by Corrie ten Boom with John and Elizabeth Sherrill. Copyright 1971.

Harper Collins Publishers for material from *Thinking Big* by Ben Carson. Copyright 1992. Used by permission.

Harper Collins Publishers, *Loving God* by Charles Colson, copyright 1987.

Houghton Mifflin Company, *The Good Marriage* by Judith S. Wallerstein and Sandra Blakeslee, copyright 1995.

Thomas Nelson Publishers, *The Positive Power of Praising People* by Jerry D. Twentier, copyright 1994.

Thomas Nelson Publishers for material from *Evidence That Demands A Verdict* by Josh McDowell.

Thomas Nelson Publishers, *If Christ Were Your Counselor* by Christ Thurman, copyright 1993.

Thomas Nelson Publishers, *The Life God Blesses* by Gordon MacDonald, copyright 1994.

Thomas Nelson Publishers for material from *Over The Top* by Zig Ziglar. Used by permission.

Time, Inc., for material from *How True Are The Stories In The Bible?* December 18, 1995.

Time, Inc. for material from *The Return and Rise of the Prodigal Son,* May 13, 1991.

Tyndale House Publishers, Inc., for material from *When God Doesn't Make Sense,* by James Dobson. Copyright © 1993. Used by permission. All rights reserved.

Victor Books, *What Happens When Women Pray* by Evelyn Christenson, copyright 1975.

Victor Books, for material from *Win The Battle For Your Mind,* by Richard L. Strauss.

Whitaker House, *There's Dynamite In Praise* by Don Gossett, copyright 1974.

Word, Inc., Dallas, Texas, for material from page 53 of *Why I Believe* by D. James Kennedy. Copyright 1980. All rights reserved. Used by permission.

Word, Inc., Dallas, Texas for material from *Can Man Live Without God* by Ravi Zacharias, copyright 1994. All rights reserved. Used by permission.

Your Health, for material from August 8, 1995 issue, *Super Senior Healing Secret* by Donald J. Murphy.

Zondervan Publishing House, *Becoming A Contagious Christian* by Bill Hybels and Mark Mittelberg, copyright 1994.

Zondervan Publishing House, for material taken from *The Marriage Builder* by Dr. Larry Crabb. Copyright © 1991 by

The following newspapers and magazines were helpful sources of information and/or inspiration:

The Atlanta Journal/Constitution
The Atlantic Monthly
Focus On The Family Magazine
Plus, The Magazine of Positive Thinking
Reader's Digest
The Wall Street Journal

NOTES

ABOUT THE AUTHOR

Bebe Nicholson, a former newspaper editor, is a graduate of Louisburg Junior College and the University of North Carolina at Chapel Hill, where she earned degrees in Journalism and English Literature. As a freelance writer, she has written both fiction and nonfiction for religious and inspirational markets. It has long been her goal to share with others the route her own marriage took from religious conflict to spiritual oneness, in the hope that many more couples can learn to develop loving, lasting relationships. Bebe and her husband Lee live in Georgia with their three children.